Voices of Zimbabwe

The Pain • The Courage • The Hope

Glyn Hunter, Larry Farren, Althea Farren

Published by Alfa (Pvt) Ltd
Distributed by Covos Day Books, 2001
Oak Tree House, Tamarisk Avenue
P O Box 6996, Weltevredenpark 1715, South Africa
E-mail: covos@global.co.za

First edition

ISBN 0-7974-2322-2

COVOS DAY
Johannesburg & London

CONTENTS

✦•✧•✦•✉•✦•✧•✦

INTRODUCTION

This book was conceived in January 2001. We were relaxing at a beautiful lodge on the edge of the Matobo Hills near Bulawayo. Each day we awakened to tranquillity and to birdsong with a sense of regeneration. The year 2000 had been filled with trauma, stress and anxiety, as we watched the economy of our country, Zimbabwe, steadily crumble. As the days passed gently and peacefully in this nurturing environment, we were overwhelmed by a desire to do something constructive that might, in some small way, make a difference.

The "something constructive" is this book. We have tried to present a balanced picture of what is happening in Zimbabwe as the government-instigated violence tears our country apart. Even the views of those with whom the authors adamantly disagree are presented frankly. We want you to hear the voices of our people speak of their pain, anger, despair, frustration and hope. We also want you to be aware of the arrogance, the brutality, the futility, the courage, the endurance and the goodwill. We want you to appreciate, as most of us who live here do, the loving warmth and kindness that is an integral part of the culture of this country.

So many people in our beautiful Zimbabwe feel confused, afraid and alone. We hope that, when they read this book, they will realise that they are not isolated. Zimbabwe is worth standing up for. We must work together to elect a truly representative, honest, competent and caring government, and to build a nation worthy of our people.

We hope that many who live in other parts of the world will also read "Voices of Zimbabwe". We wish to draw attention to our situation, as we need your support. It will be easier to enlist your help if you understand us.

There are a number of friends who have helped us compile the stories and illustrations. Their support has been invaluable. We would also like to thank those whose acknowledged contributions are featured. Many wish to remain anonymous for security reasons. They have all enriched "Voices of Zimbabwe".

We pray for a country where our people will no longer have to live in fear.

Glyn Hunter, Larry Farren, Althea Farren.   July 2001

ZIMBABWE

The Republic of Zimbabwe was formerly known as Southern Rhodesia (1911 - 1964); Rhodesia (1964 - 1979) and then Rhodesia or Zimbabwe Rhodesia (1979 - 1980).

Zimbabwe achieved majority rule and internationally recognised independence in April 1980. The era of British colonial rule was followed by a 15-year period of white-dominated minority rule after the government's Unilateral Declaration of Independence (UDI) in 1965, which was never recognised internationally.

The country shares a 125 mile (200 km) border on the south with the Republic of South Africa and is bounded on the south-west and west by Botswana, on the north by Zambia and on the north-east and east by Mozambique.

Its total area is 150 873 square miles (390 759 square kilometres). The capital is Harare (formerly called Salisbury). The population is estimated to be 12 million (July 2000). Approximately 98% of the population is Black, 1% White and 1% Mixed and Asian.

Nevah Kumalo

"Burn down your cities and leave our farms,
and your cities will spring up again as if by magic;
but destroy our farms and the grass will grow
in the streets of every city in the country."

William Jennings Bryan

Nevah Kumalo

THIS LAND IS MY LAND?

This land is my land, this land is your land...
This land was made for you and me.

Song by The Seekers composed by Guthrie

trong and diametrically opposed views are held on the colonial occupation of Zimbabwe. When you know with absolute certainty that dreadful wrong has been done to you, to those close to you, or to your social or ethnic group as a whole, it is difficult for you to entertain the possibility that the perpetrators have any justification, any argument, any case at all. Unfortunately, there are few absolutely right sides in human conflict. It is necessary for even the most righteously angry of us to attempt to see the overall picture. If we want to be fair, to reach reconciliation, we must try to see the other side's point of view.

In particular, this is required as regards a settlement of the land issue in Zimbabwe. It is vital that a solution to this problem is found very soon as, at the moment, our economy is disintegrating rapidly and irreparable harm is being done.

It is in the interests of all the affected parties to recognise the important truth that they have a considerable amount of common ground, and more to gain by working together than by opposing one another. Here we will attempt to state clearly and separately the arguments for opposing sides. The contradictory views expressed are not necessarily ours, but what we consider to be those of the protagonists.

There will then follow a series of viewpoints, or voices, from different segments of our population, in an attempt to give voice to each. In the end, we will attempt a neutral analysis of the overall situation. You may surprise yourself with some of the conclusions you may be forced to face up to on considering, logically, the opposing arguments. You are likely to find a great deal both to agree with and to disagree with in the scenarios presented, and you may need to stretch your tolerance of opposing points of view to the limit so as to consider, at least, some of the opinions presented. Calm and the exercise of logic will be required of those who have set views, or even strong prejudices, on the issues addressed, but this analysis is a necessary catharsis. Those of us who are Zimbabweans need to exorcise the remnants of an era in which our black and white countrymen fought a civil war - two if you count the Matabeleland and Midlands dissident conflict in the 1980s. We Zimbabweans need to exercise great self-restraint, as we have to contend with entrenched attitudes.

A Black Zimbabwean's View

The view of the black Zimbabwean is that the white settlers under Cecil John Rhodes tricked their way into Zimbabwe. They negotiated with Lobengula, the leader of the Matabele, who was based in the south-west of what later became Zimbabwe, and obtained the right to mine in Mashonaland, in the east of the territory. This right was set out in the Rudd Concession of 30 October 1888. The first wave of white settlers, the Pioneer Column, arrived in Zimbabwe in 1890, and established settlements in and around present-day Harare (which they called Salisbury) and Masvingo (which they named Fort Victoria).

The Matabele did not live in Mashonaland, and were recent immigrants themselves. They had invaded the region in 1838 under the leadership of the South African Zulu chief, Mzilikazi, Lobengula's father, and were fleeing from the more powerful Zulu king, Tshaka. They settled in and entrenched their power in Matabeleland, in the west of Zimbabwe, and frequently sent raiding parties east to Mashonaland to seize cattle and slaves. They considered Mashonaland to be under their dominion or control. The Mashonas at the time might have viewed the Matabele as a curse or a nuisance, or even as de facto leaders in the area because of their military superiority. They certainly would not have accepted their moral or legal authority to allocate permanent and exclusive land rights to foreigners.

Once in, the settlers used the excuse of the Matabele making one of their routine raids on Shona-speaking Karangas in the Fort Victoria (Masvingo) area to fight a war with the Matabele. This, the newcomers won, largely because of their superior weaponry. The Matabele in 1893 were the first to face machine guns in a war, and found them to be horrifyingly effective. The white invaders quelled another uprising a few years later by both the Mashona and the Matabele. After negotiating a treaty with the Matabele leadership, they declared themselves owners of the country, and of many of the cattle previously owned by Lobengula and his subjects. They then settled down to enjoy the fruits of their conquest.

The concept of private ownership of land was not familiar to the indigenous people of the country, which became known as Southern Rhodesia. Land was in plentiful supply, with only a few hundred thousand people living in an area more than one and a half times the size of the United Kingdom. People settled in an area, grazed their cattle and grew their crops, and moved on to fresh land when it was exhausted. They were almost all illiterate, and understood neither the importance of the pieces of paper (title deeds) issued to white settlers, nor that they signified their own exclusion from most of the land they lived in. Had they done so, they might have asked, "By whose authority was this done?" and, "Do the spirits of our ancestors approve of this?"

Ancestor worship was the basis of their religion, and the mediums who were the link between the living and the spirits of their ancestors were a most important factor in the wars of the 1890s and during the liberation struggle some 80 years later. It was a very serious matter to ignore the wishes of one's ancestors, as relayed by a medium. If the mediums relayed a message from the spirits decreeing that a cause should be supported, or that a war should be fought, their directions had to be followed. This occurred twice after the arrival of the Europeans - in the 1890s and during the liberation struggle. Europeans had a habit of dismissing the traditional religion of the African as being superstitious nonsense and of little consequence, forgetting their own adage that one man's religion is another man's superstition. This would be to their cost.

The newcomers settled the black people of what they called Southern Rhodesia in areas that were designated as being "Native" or tribal lands. This was accepted without too much fuss, as there was then plenty of land for everyone, and the Matabele and the Mashona were in no mood to face the Gatling guns of the new arrivals again. The settlers allocated huge tracts of land to themselves. The indigenous people were neither consulted nor compensated. Rhodes' British South Africa Company had a "Charter" from the British queen which, they considered, gave them full authority to do as they wished within the limits of the Roman Dutch legal system they had imported from the Cape. Land grants were recorded and title deeds were handed out to the lucky recipients, who might have had to pay a nominal price for the land bestowed upon them.

The land allocated for blacks, who were always much more numerous than the whites, became inadequate for their requirements as their numbers increased. Land hunger became intense, and became one of the major factors which ignited the liberation struggle, eventually concluded in 1980, with the Zimbabwe African National Union (ZANU) in control of the government of the newly independent state.

The nationalist would say that the title to land in the commercial farming areas in Zimbabwe is fatally flawed. This title's legitimacy originates with the British Government, through the Chartered Company, which granted itself the ownership of land that did not belong to it thousands of miles away. This so-called "right" was that of the thief or the robber, right of conquest, which is not recognised by any society in dealings between its own people, as opposed to its relations with outsiders.

If Zimbabweans had somehow suddenly and magically been incorporated into the British Empire by Her Imperial Majesty in the 1890s, as was claimed by the colonialists, then their status as citizens of the Empire had given them little of the protection subjects might expect from their supposedly benevolent Queen-Emperor. Could it be that the fabulous and revered Empire was merely a cloak, a clumsy camouflage for the aggrandisement of the ethnic white or British masters of this alleged brotherhood of unequal peoples?

The whole basis for the validity of title deeds to land in Zimbabwe is, therefore, based on an invalid claim. In effect, the white settlers awarded themselves a large portion of the best farming land, and all of the mining rights of Zimbabwe, and had the power to take (you could say "steal") them. Was it not a colonial Englishman who said "Let them take who have the power, and let them hold who can?" All very well for the powerful, but is it lawful in relation to the land of Zimbabwe? The settlers took it "without claim of right made in good faith". In terms of the definition of theft in the Roman Dutch law imported by the settlers from the Cape, this action constituted that crime. It was in their interests to ignore their own law when it suited them, but hardly in the interests of their black predecessors in the country. Why should the dispossessed accept this as just or legal?

The nationalist would maintain that, apart from the fact that the invaders stripped his people of the majority of their resources without any logical or legitimate claim to them, the indigenous people deeply resented being degraded and relegated to an inferior status. At best they were treated like children, condescended to or patronised. At worst, they were considered to be inherently inferior or even declared, by some, to be sub-human. They were allowed no control over their own affairs in national issues.

It cannot be denied that black Zimbabweans were the victims of prolonged and marked racial discrimination for nearly a century. They, or many of them, were the sons of the warriors of Tshaka, who had conquered millions. They were a proud and warlike people. Discontent smouldered. It was only a matter of time before it would ignite.

Prior to independence in 1980, it was incredible the way many whites (usually, but not always the less sophisticated) referred to the real or imagined failings of their black countrymen as a group in front of their black domestic workers or their black subordinates at work. It must be emphasised here that the guilty parties referred to were just as likely to be recent immigrants from Europe as second or third generation white Zimbabweans. Their attitudes were, it seemed, formed more by their current surroundings, interests and fears, and their inherent character and disposition, than by their upbringing. Some seemed to be racists within minutes of getting off the plane from overseas, where they might seldom have seen a person of a different complexion, much less felt threatened or offended by one. African-born whites often had a more balanced view.

This first category of whites spoke openly of blacks en mass in a most disparaging way, as though those blacks within hearing were blocks of wood and not human beings with normal human emotions, not least of which was a desire for self-respect and dignity. They may have meant no offence, and often had superficially good relations with their black subordinates, despite their extraordinarily bad manners. They may have told themselves that they were merely speaking the truth, and thought that their black employee or junior did not resent his race being pilloried because he did not complain. They were very wrong. The black did not complain for fear of victimisation. We all, black or white or brown, bleed, hurt, feel, laugh and cry in response to the same stimuli.

These whites were reacting to a defensive/aggressive impulse born of fear, for the writing was already clearly on the wall for them, though they would have thought it treason to admit it. British Prime Minister Harold MacMillan's "winds of change", then sweeping through Africa, were approaching gale force, but they did not want to recognise them for the overwhelming cataclysm that they were. They did very serious harm to inter-race relations, for they were poking their future masters with a stick. By the 1960s the blacks had had four generations of being treated as grossly inferior beings, and were sick to death of this state of affairs. The discontent that had smouldered for nearly a century was ready to burst into flames.

The spark that lit the fire of armed rebellion was the election to government in Southern Rhodesia of the Rhodesian Front (RF). The pre-RF constitution in Southern Rhodesia allowed blacks the vote if they reached certain standards of education or income. The RF in the parliamentary election campaign of 1962 warned that, if nothing were done to prevent the calamity, according to their calculations, the blacks would come to power peacefully by qualifying for a majority of the vote in a mere thirty years' time. That would have been in 1992.

On taking power, the RF succeeded only in bringing that evil hour forward by 12 years - less if one counts the Muzorewa government of 1978-1980, which was, at least nominally, led by a black Zimbabwean. Apart from that blunder, their main achievement was that they made inevitable a war in which thousands died and antagonistic attitudes of the races towards one another were more firmly etched in the souls of both communities. The effect was that they put the continued domicile of whites in Zimbabwe at great risk - would they be welcome there when the blacks eventually secured the political power their numerical superiority guaranteed?

The RF were adamant that they would not allow the country to sink into the morass of black majority rule through the ballot box. The nationalists saw no hope of ever taking control of the country peacefully. With an RF government in charge, they feared that full-scale apartheid was soon to come. Armed rebellion was their only way forward.

A Conservative White Zimbabwean's View

A conservative white Zimbabwean could claim that the pacification of the Matabele by the Pioneers (as the early white settlers were known in Southern Rhodesia), was necessary and long overdue. It was primarily to the benefit of the Mashona majority, and even to that of the bulk of the Matabele themselves, who were freed from the brutal, bloodthirsty and arbitrary dictatorship of kings who ruled with appalling cruelty. For example, there is the story of the Matabele king's cattle herder, some of whose charges died while crossing a flooded river. Lobengula had him tied hand and foot, and thrown into the river to "Look for them" and, of course, to drown. People were likely to be put to death for the most minor or totally imaginary offences. It was felt by Lobengula's people, and, apparently, by the king himself that, if he did not exert his authority in this manner, he would not be respected as a strong ruler.

The settlers saved the local people from the scourge of witchcraft, which, in traditional Zimbabwean society, had caused the death of countless innocents. In the pre-Christian culture of Zimbabwe, any unexpected death or serious misfortune was not believed to be a result of bad luck, ill health, disease or other natural causes. It was often held to be the result of a curse placed upon the unfortunate by a "witch". (These beliefs are still held by many Zimbabweans today.) As in Europe and America only a few hundred years earlier, innocent people were often accused of being witches, and paid for it with their lives. (Women wrongfully accused of witchcraft were being executed in Salem, Massachusetts, as recently as 1692).

Professional witch-hunters in Zimbabwe made a luxurious living by, literally, smelling out witches, and terrorised the whole society. To keep their positions and enhance their credibility, income and influence, they had to expose regular batches of witches. This they managed to do very well. No one knew when he or she might be marked out for death.

The Chartered Company allocated land to the early settlers either as a reward for military service, or sold it to them at a price which may have been very low, but was still the ruling market price at that time. The price was low because it took into account the fact that the buyers were expected to leave the comfort and security of their homes in the far-off Cape, or farther-off Britain, to take possession of the offered property in a strange, wild and dangerous land. This also applies to properties sold after the Second World War to white war veterans at a low price, as an inducement to settle in and to help develop the country. This opportunity was not made available to indigenous Southern Rhodesian servicemen, who, it is said, were each issued with an overcoat on termination of their service.

The Pioneer would have claimed, and would have believed deeply and sincerely, that the British were entitled to invade and occupy African land, and to parcel it out to whites. The natives, he would have maintained, should be grateful that the British had arrived to bring them all the benefits of a superior civilisation and culture, and to develop their country for them. That was the way most Europeans in general, and the British in particular, thought during that era.

Few white people in Zimbabwe at the time of Rhodes would have disputed the moral and legal authority of the British Crown to govern the territory - or anywhere else in the undeveloped world, for that matter.

The land within Zimbabwe was divided among the black and white people in a suitable allocation in relation to their needs and ability to make use of it. The Colonial authority sold land to those who were able to pay for it, and who could best develop it. The resident "natives" were illiterate and did not have sufficient formal education or training in farming, mining, industry or commerce to undertake the development of a modern economy. That was why the country was underdeveloped and ill-defended in the first place, the colonialist would have said.

The indigenous people benefited immeasurably from the Pax Britannica and from modern medicine and the population grew at a phenomenal rate. A hundred years after the settlers' arrival, a mere four generations or so on, there were 40 or 50 times as many indigenous people in the country as there had been in Rhodes' and Lobengula's time. The land designated for the use of the estimated 12 million tribesmen had become grossly insufficient for their requirements. Since the population growth had outstripped the capacity of urban-based industry, commerce and mining to provide employment for the overflow from the rural areas, the asset of farming land became a drastically scarce resource in the communal areas.

It was unfortunate that the fertility of the "natives" had exceeded the capacity of the land available to support them, our white person might have said in early 2000. That, however, was no reason to hand over the highly efficient agricultural industry of the country to people who did not know how it worked, and who could not, therefore, manage it efficiently. The industry developing in the towns and cities still had the potential to provide work for the masses, and offered the best chance of providing a decent life for all. All that was needed was a few more decades of efficient (white) management.

The vast majority of the commercial farming land in February 2000 was owned by farmers who had paid the then ruling market price for it, or who had inherited it from ancestors who had done so. This was after 20 years of black majority rule by ZANU PF (the Zimbabwe African National Union/Patriotic Front, an amalgamation of the main Mashona and Matabele political parties, ZANU and the Zimbabwe African Peoples' Union, ZAPU).

An exception was a substantial area of land that had been bought with funds donated by foreign governments for resettlement purposes. Government officials and ruling party functionaries had somehow managed to occupy 3,5 million hectares of this, and, generally, grossly mismanaged or totally neglected it. This was typical of the corruption and inefficiency rife in the country by that time. It appeared that the land had not been allocated to its occupants according to their qualifications or abilities to run a farm, but on the basis of party or tribal loyalty, or in exchange for a bribe. Most of the land was run down badly, and not properly farmed.

Even the white farmers accepted that ZANU PF had exercised for-bearance, up to then, as regards the land issue.

By that time (early in the year 2000) the bulk of the commercial farming land had been bought legally by the current, mainly white owners. It might have changed hands lawfully many times, and in many or even most cases after majority rule, under a ZANU PF government and under a constitution approved and extensively modified by that party. The owners had not taken it by force or stolen it from anyone. There are still a few white farmers, from no more than a dozen families, owning land in Zimbabwe, who have inherited it through an ancestor to whom it was allocated by the Chartered Company. Even they can argue that their ancestor was allocated the land for services rendered, and in accordance with the only effective law governing the country then.

The farmers could argue that there was not an accessible fertile piece of ground on Planet Earth that had not been seized by conquest time and again, and which did not remain in the hands of the last conqueror. Should the Americas be handed back to the Indians? England returned to the Anglo Saxons from the Danes and Norman French who had invaded it, or to the earlier Celtic inhabitants? The descendants of some of these last-mentioned deprived people had lived in Cornwall for only one and a half thousand years, and might be glad to have their many times great-grandparents' lands returned to them. How far do you go? Even the Celts had invaded Britain, most of Europe and much of Asia in their heyday. They, too, had had predecessors with an earlier claim to those lands.

The white Zimbabwean farmers could also claim that it was just as well for the country, and especially for its black citizens, that the whites had taken over its management. There had been absolutely no prospect of the nation developing to any significant degree under Lobengula's rule, in terms of health care, education, commerce, industry, human rights or agriculture. In fact most of today's teeming millions in Zimbabwe would probably never have been born had modern medical treatment not been available to the bulk of the population, and tribal warfare not been curtailed. The 275 000 whites living in Zimbabwe in the 1960s were probably as numerous as the black occupants in the 1890s. They could, further, claim that they had treated the blacks of Zimbabwe a great deal better than the blacks would have treated them, had their roles been reversed.

The above gives some idea of the two main opposing points of view regarding the land issue in Zimbabwe. Both have facts and logic to recommend them. Other voices are recorded later, and the authors would like you to consider them all as objectively as you can, so that you can form your own opinions. Then you may be in a position to make a decision regarding what needs to be done to bring matters to a sensible and just conclusion. You should be able to weigh the moral issues, as well as the strictly legal aspects and decide what outcome would most benefit the majority of the people.

This Land is Our Land

Let us now attempt to lay all bias aside, and to look at the situation objectively. I say "attempt" as this is very difficult to do, given man's natural disposition to see things from his own point of view, even if he is not directly involved in an issue. Feelings of kinship, shared racial or national background, circumstance, creed or ideology, as well as direct personal association can kindle feelings of involvement or empathy and lead to bias.

It cannot be believed that the "natives" in question, even in the 1890s, shared the British enthusiasm for the colonisation of their land. The Boers of that decade in South Africa certainly found problems with colonisation, resisted it heroically, and were forced to accept it only after a brutal war in which forty-six thousand died, half of them Boer non-combatants in concentration camps. They rebounded half a century later to force their own unwelcome ideology, and their view of the proper distribution of the wealth of the country they shared, on its other, more numerous, inhabitants.

The indigenous Zimbabweans, likewise, would not have acquiesced willingly and knowingly to an arbitrary allocation, by invaders - today we might call them illegal aliens - of extremely valuable resources that dispossessed and disadvantaged them so utterly.

Unfortunately for themselves, the whites had, very early on in their occupation of Zimbabwe, sown the seeds of their own overthrow. There were two wings to the colonial presence in the country. As well as the military and commercial invasion under Rhodes, there were the missionaries. Many had entered the country before Rhodes' emissaries, and they continued to arrive after the pacification of the territory. Their aim was not wealth or land. They wanted to convert the Africans to Christianity and to educate them. They were not out to enrich themselves at anyone's expense. They believed that they were doing the work that God had chosen for them, and they did it very efficiently and totally selflessly. They and their successors in black education, many not missionaries but civil servants still under white rule, and many of them not especially religious people, did their job so well that, by the 1960s, Zimbabwe had the most highly educated populace in Africa.

Lobengula had tolerated the missionaries, considering them to be mentally deficient but harmless, as long as they did not convert his fighting men to an impractical religion which actually insisted that they behave meekly, loved their enemies (no less!) and learned to turn the other cheek. Despite this disturbing eccentricity, however, it had to be said in their favour that they had been useful in treating his gout. The missionaries often had advanced medical training, or took pains to acquire skill in that field.

Prior to the initial defeat of the Matabele, and to that of the combined Matabele and Mashona uprising, they had made few converts, and virtually none among the Matabele. After that, they made many. The natives had discovered that the pacifism they had noted and been amused by in the missionaries' declared beliefs appeared not to be taken too seriously by the white man's God, nor by his soldiers or businessmen. There was more to Christianity than had initially been apparent. Further, for the less fervent, a declared conversion to Christianity was little to pay for an education, which was soon to become highly valued.

Many of Zimbabwe's post-independence black leaders were educated at mission schools. Successive white governments helped to fund missionary schools and hospitals from taxes paid by white taxpayers, and set up government ones. The health and education of the indigenous people was given a high priority, though it must be admitted that much more was spent, per capita, on the separate and better facilities for whites.

The educated African, aware of his own abilities and learning, found it difficult or impossible to accept a white as being, inevitably and purely because of his colour, his natural superior and his overlord. The literature he was given access to, which was initially almost entirely written by whites, often led him to believe differently. More than that, he became conscious of his own identity, his abilities, his self-image, his worth, his pride and his ambition. He would not be a slave or a disenfranchised cipher in his own country, hewing the wood and drawing the water for the privileged invader. The demographic arithmetic in place told him that he did not need to tolerate this unnatural and inherently uncomfortable state of affairs.

In direct conflict with their accepted duty to educate the African (was this the rumbling of a conscience?), our objective paragon might say, the whites took the wrong approach in their efforts to develop the country. They opted for promoting white immigration as the key to progress, as opposed to encouraging the development of the skills of the indigenous people, and permitting a meritocracy to grow in which colour did not matter. They did not seriously attempt to build up or allow the natural development of a black middle class - not until it was too late. Thousands of blacks who gained a high standard of education were forced to compete for a hopelessly inadequate number of jobs in black education or black health care.

There was little else open to them. They were not considered for the jobs traditionally held by whites in commerce, industry or the civil service, although they often had far higher academic qualifications than those holding the jobs in question. There were definite and rigidly enforced ideas as to the "place" in society of the "native", however educated he might be. Thus, until the late 1970s, when change became inevitable, one seldom came across a black bank teller, post office clerk, shunter or driver on the national railways. These jobs were effectively reserved for whites, in a form of unofficial apartheid.

There were two entry levels to the police force, one for whites, and another, lower, for blacks. Whites with four years' secondary education were accepted as Patrol Officers, whether they had passed their General Certificate of Education Ordinary Level exams or not. Blacks with at least two years' secondary education (they, in the later years, often had passed "O" Levels or even Advanced Levels) were accepted as Constables. The highest rank they could aspire to was Sub Inspector, in theory below that of Patrol Officer.

A huge pool of discontented, unemployed and well-educated people formed. They soon found something to do. The armed struggle was to absorb them gleefully.

Restrictions on ownership of land, entrenched in the Land Apportionment Act of 1930, promulgated long before the right-wing Rhodesian Front came to power in 1962, constituted more than a hint of an apartheid state. The election of the RF was followed shortly afterwards by the Unilateral Declaration of Independence (UDI) in November 1965, and the implementation of a blatantly racist constitution. Since both were designed to perpetuate white power, there seemed to the African Nationalist to be no alternative to war. It was a war that could never be won by the whites, given the numbers involved and the fact that no country in the world but South Africa supported the rebel white government.

In the early 1960s Nationalist leaders turned their backs on conventional political action, believing that there was no chance of winning political control for the majority by peaceful means. They began to wage a campaign of violence. Early efforts at insurgency, starting with an abortive attack on a white-owned farm in Matabeleland in the early 1960s, were not a serious threat. In the first decade of the war the security forces had little trouble in getting intelligence from the rural people regarding the presence of insurgents. Thousands of freedom fighters or terrorists, depending on one's point of view, however, were given military training in Russia, China, North Korea, or in former colonies elsewhere in Africa. Zambia and Tanzania became bases for training and stationing of the armed forces of ZANU and ZAPU (Zimbabwe African People's Union), the main Nationalist parties. A large fighting force was being built up.

As the death rate on both sides in the war escalated (mainly of blacks who were not combatants) inter-community relations inevitably suffered. Where there is the threat of death, there is fear. Where there is fear, there is hate. Where there is hate, reason surrenders to emotion. Our instincts for survival take charge. People think, or rather feel instinctively, in terms of "us" and "them", even in a civil war, and lose track of the root causes of the conflict. Balance and discretion are stifled, and men cleave blindly to the totems, the simplistic icons, the standards, the slogans, and the jingoist rallying-calls of their ethnic or social group, their army, their country, their race. "We" are always the good guys. Our ego and our survival-centred instincts tell us this must be so.

Without this conviction, how do we justify our self-serving actions, the things we feel we have to do to get by in this world, to survive, to dominate? Since right must be on our side, of course, the others must therefore be in the wrong. To believe or behave otherwise is suicidal, disloyal to our group and, therefore, to ourselves.

Desperately afraid and therefore, defensively aggressive people did long-lasting harm to the future of inter-race relations in the country. They lashed out blindly and foolishly. Sometimes physically, or more often and equally hurtfully, verbally, they attacked people whom they considered to be the enemy because of the different colour of their skin. They had dared to challenge "us" for what was "ours". They were a threat to our possessions, our lifestyle, or even our lives. The snake strikes instinctively, out of fear, not malice.

Often the more sensible and less aggressive individuals, liberals on either side were labelled and denounced by their peers as traitors to the cause, sell-outs, as not supporting the war effort. Everyone who did not rally to "our" flag was an enemy, a traitor. Attitudes hardened. You need a Nelson Mandela to rescue a country from that sort of schism. For a while we thought we had one in Zimbabwe.

The enlisting of the spirit mediums to the Nationalist cause in the mid-1970s gave the liberation struggle wider legitimacy and broader support among the black population. From now on, the inhabitants of the rural areas generally supported the Nationalist guerrillas. The security forces no longer were able to get information from tribesmen as to the whereabouts and activities of the enemy. The insurgents were, as prescribed by Mao Tse Tung, able to move among the people like fish in the water. They infiltrated virtually all the tribal areas.

The unexpected handing over of Mozambique to its indigenous people by the Portuguese in 1974, following a change in government policy there, opened up a vast and important new front for the insurgents. The United States put intense pressure on South Africa to cease support for the rebel regime in Salisbury (Harare). The resultant demand by South Africa that the UDI government come to terms, and their embargo on imports into Zimbabwe, caused a shortage of nearly everything, particularly ammunition, and forced a settlement on the white government of Ian Smith.

Drastic changes made under the power-sharing Bishop Abel Muzorewa/ Ian Smith Zimbabwe-Rhodesia government in 1978, though most significant, had been too late, and were seen by blacks as being a desperate effort by the whites to hold on to what could be salvaged of the status quo.

Under ZANU PF rule from Independence in1980, and for 20 years thereafter, change was accelerated, and blacks took charge at virtually all levels of government. Most of the mainly white senior civil servants were replaced before their black successors were trained to perform their functions efficiently. The civil service expanded exponentially, and its efficiency crumbled. Though thousands of well-qualified, competent, and often dedicated recruits were enlisted, their managers were political appointees with no experience or relevant expertise. Deprived of the opportunity to learn on the job, and to work their way up through their organisations, they could not be expected to succeed in government. Nor, in the main, did they. Morale and the work ethic suffered as the efficient saw others with the all-important connections promoted over them.

Faced for decades with a situation where they had been denied jobs solely because of their colour, the new black rulers were highly suspicious of employers who rejected apparently qualified job applicants who were black and equipped on paper for a job, but who lacked experience in the field. The feeling was that if one had a good enough academic qualification, one could do any job. This was not always the case. A brilliant student with a doctorate in social studies, but no industrial experience, might know nothing about managing a factory that produced bicycles. A talented few among such students might be able to adapt to the new environment without training in the field. Many more could not, and state-owned enterprises suffered drastically as a result.

Since the members of the new government had received most of their military training and equipment from the communist East, they had acquired of necessity a leftist philosophy during their struggle for power. True to the pattern of an inefficient socialist state, the ruling party became both a major investor in business enterprises, and a hindrance to efficient business management. Government-owned businesses, known locally as parastatals, such as the National Railways, the state fuel-importing body, NOCZIM (the National Oil Company of Zimbabwe), the Cold Storage Company and the Cotton and Grain Marketing Boards which, in the past, had been relatively efficiently run, were on the brink of collapse. They survived only on government handouts.

Poor management, nepotism, cronyism, inefficiency, a lack of financial discipline, unnecessarily high staff levels and rampant, unashamed and unpunished corruption had destroyed them. Experience, honesty and efficiency meant nothing. Inexperienced and inefficient people who might have paper qualifications from obscure tertiary educational establishments and the essential party card, or an acceptable tribal background, replaced competent managers. The nation suffered in silence. Ordinary men dared not question the heroes of the liberation struggle.

The government's failure in virtually all aspects of governance eventually became so obvious that it became generally unpopular. Nevertheless, the ruling party was severely shocked to lose a referendum on a new constitution in February 2000. It was the first time in 20 years that it had lost an election of any kind, and it faced parliamentary elections four months later, in June. The possibility that the government might lose these elections to the Movement for Democratic Change (the MDC), a party originating from the Trade Union Movement, which had sprung to life and instant maturity only nine months before the referendum - and which had opposed it, was of grave concern to the ruling party.

A new strategy was needed - a new issue to patch up the sorry image of the party. The repossession of the people's land was to be the key to the people's hearts and votes. Within three days of the referendum result, people professing to be war veterans began invading farms across the country. It appeared that, twenty years after independence, they had suddenly discovered that whites still owned most of the best farming land in the nation. Many farmers and their numerous employees were forced off their land. A massive campaign of occupation and intimidation was launched on the commercial farming areas. The government and the police force professed themselves unable to defend the farmers, farm workers and their families from the violence as it was "political", and not something they could deal with. This violence was to spread to the towns.

The mantle of Robin Hood had descended upon the eager shoulders of ZANU PF. The party would take the commercial farmers' land and give it to the poor! What a brilliant idea! For comparatively uneducated and economically deprived people, this was a strong argument to vote for the benefactor. Access to land was all-important to them. These rural folk tended not to be as well educated as their relatives in the towns. They were not as aware of the immense damage that the destruction of the commercial farms and a breakdown in law and order would do to the economy and to all those who were not the most direct beneficiaries of the largesse of ZANU PF. Those chosen few were the top officials of the party.

Though the party claimed that the war veterans (most of whom were far too young to have carried arms in the liberation struggle) had acted spontaneously, this was not supported by the reported facts. The occupations and violence were instigated and directed by the government, and the perpetrators were transported, supplied, sustained and paid by government agencies under the control of the ruling party, using taxpayers' money. This has been conclusively documented by media from all over the world and by the independent press in Zimbabwe.

The violence being visited on the farms caused huge damage throughout the economy.

The commercial farming sector, the country's largest employer and a major foreign currency earner, was under siege. Banks feared collapse as a massive volume of farming debtors failed to repay loans. Consumers were afraid to spend, and businesses shut down. Tourism, a major source of foreign currency, declined by an unsustainable 80%. It seemed that private property rights throughout the nation were worth nothing. Government leaders boasted of their intention to seize mines and businesses for redistribution to the party faithful.

Fearing a total breakdown of law and order and general anarchy, foreign investors fled the country. Local people who had cash available did not dare risk it in business - it was invested in high-interest-bearing savings accounts. Foreign donor governments cut or terminated aid to Zimbabwe. Almost overnight the country became a pariah in the international world of diplomacy, trade and finance. Business confidence dropped to an unprecedented low, and unemployment soared to a disastrous 60%.

The farm invasions and the associated massive intimidation of huge sections of the electorate worked to a degree. Opposition candidates were effectively barred from campaigning in many rural areas. ZANU PF scraped through the June 2000 elections with a minority of the total vote cast, but a small majority of parliamentary seats, as the opposition was divided.

Some had hoped that the pressure on the farms would ease after the elections. This was not to be. The campaign for the next presidential election, which must, in terms of the constitution, be held by the end of March 2002, was already under way. Discredited thoroughly, ZANU PF could not hope to win an election on the merits of its governance of the country over the past twenty-one years. Its only chance of winning would be by intimidation and by playing its two remaining cards.

One of these was the race issue. ZANU PF needed a scapegoat for its mishandling of the economy, and proceeded to whip up indignation among the black majority against the tiny white minority, blaming it for all the country's economic ills. The reality is that whites still own or manage many of the surviving healthy businesses in the country and their enforced removal would see a collapse of most, resulting in a further serious degeneration in the economy, to no one's benefit. The "white" card is being played cynically, as Hitler played the Jewish card in the 1930s.

The racial antagonism issue is a highly effective gambit used by the party, and it has served them well in the past. They have invoked it at every election since independence, only to bury it conveniently after winning another landslide majority in an election in which an ever-decreasing percentage of a disillusioned and bored electorate bothered to vote. In the 1995 election only 30% of the electorate cast a ballot. There was no effective opposition at that time to ZANU PF, and therefore no need to vote.

Most white Zimbabweans do not appear to be aware of the deep resentment felt by their black countrymen at the way they have been treated over the past century, nor do they feel that there might be some justification for this. They have succumbed to the usual human stratagems of denial and transference of unpleasant aspects of their behaviour with which we all justify our less palatable actions. They should learn to be sensitive enough to be aware of this feeling on the part of most of their countrymen, and of its causes, and make adjustments to their attitudes accordingly.

Evidence of this black resentment was seen at a pre-parliamentary election debate in June 2000, in Bulawayo. On this occasion, the only major support shown for the ruling party candidate by the mainly-black audience was when he referred disparagingly to "some people who think that they are superior to others". Whites who doubt that this bitterness exists can confirm it with their black friends or associates, though they may find that many blacks are hesitant to discuss the matter. Their traditional black culture is very sensitive about hurting people's feelings, and they try not to do so.

The government's other card is land. The party is unashamedly offering land only to ZANU PF members. This is blatant and deliberate bribery. The land they offer, however, will not go with full tenure, with title deeds. In the best (or worst) socialist tradition, it will be held at the discretion of government officials, who are likely to be allied to ZANU PF. This strategy will tend to keep the occupants toeing the party line. However, it will also mean that there is no major asset available to offer as security for the financing of crops. Farmers, traditionally, have pledged their land to their bankers to finance their operations. This facility will not be available to the resettled farmers, as they will not own it. The capital necessary for intensive farming will not be available.

Today, there are two self-evident truths accepted by most parties involved. Firstly, the racial balance in the ownership of land in Zimbabwe is still largely as decreed by Rhodes, and reform of this is urgently needed. It is not acceptable that the whites control as much as they do at present.

There must be a massive re-allocation of farming land. Blacks who want to and who have the training, experience and the ability to farm (those who are reasonably likely to make a success of it) must be assisted to do so on suitable land. Many blacks have earned a Master Farmers' certificate, which is available and highly respected, and a number have succeeded in establishing themselves in resettlement areas such as that in Gokwe. Zimbabwe is still a relatively sparsely populated country, and there is plenty of land to go around for those who genuinely wish to farm and who are able to utilise it.

Secondly, common sense dictates that this redistribution must be done in an orderly, legal fashion, and in such a way as not to ruin the economy and impoverish the people of the country. As the Roman Marcus Tullius Cicero said more than 2000 years ago, "The welfare of the people is the ultimate law." The government of Zimbabwe is currently ignoring this principle, and is busily engaged in flooding good farming land with inexperienced people who will ruin it.

With this prime imperative in mind - the welfare of the people - the restoration of the rule of law in Zimbabwe must be the immediate priority. When people can be sure that they are not going to be murdered, raped, assaulted or intimidated by those who are paid for that purpose by the government, they can start to look at solutions to less urgent problems that have been with us for generations. Only when the Police and the armed forces revert to their traditional role of protecting the basic rights of the people, will foreign and local investors have the confidence to start rebuilding our economy.

Thereafter, the government can begin to negotiate with the international community for the aid already promised to implement a legal land reform programme in a rational manner. Massive relief of our crippling foreign debt will only be considered by the world's economic powers to a Zimbabwean government which is serious about reforming its economy.

The most virulent African nationalist or dyed-in-the-wool white liberal cannot deny that the white Zimbabweans, prior to majority rule in 1980, had done a remarkable job in creating a highly efficient agricultural sector, a thriving mining industry and a strong foundation for a healthy commercialised and industrialised economy. Their accomplishments were a tribute to their high level of competence, innovation and energy. The advances they made in Zimbabwe were a significant example of the contribution the much-maligned British Empire made to modernising under-developed countries. Such progress was beyond the capabilities of the uneducated indigenous people, acting on their own, in the 1890s. It can, of course, be argued that the black Zimbabweans could have been guided and assisted, rather than frog-marched, along the road to development, and that they should have been treated with much more respect.

The whites did not, of course, accomplish these miracles alone. The indigenous people performed the physical work required. Those who differ on the solutions for our country today must recognise that the country's great strides forward were achieved with this teamwork. Future success lies in operating as a cohesive force.

The seizure of the country by the whites can be defended only on the grounds that it helped to build the wealth of the nation, for the benefit of the bulk of the people. While the whites, in control of the economy, benefited most, the majorty also benefited substantially.

Laws evolve or are created by men to order their affairs for the good of society. No nation can afford to flout its own laws, or it will revert to chaos. In addressing our land issue, it is imperative to acknowledge this. The government must ensure that the moral and legal rights of all parties are enforced and protected in such a rational way that no one suffers unduly, so that the progress our people have made is not destroyed. Making the rich poor will not make the poor rich, earn desperately-needed foreign currency, or provide food for the people.

Commercial agriculture, largely under white ownership, is the largest employer in the country, and a major earner of foreign currency. Provision exists in our law for land reform, and even for a massive and compulsory seizure of land in the commercial farming areas. A legal and equitable system for implementing it was agreed to by the Government of Zimbabwe and by major international donors at the Harare Conference in 1998. This would have been funded by foreign aid, and would not have crippled the economy. Productive farms would not have been taken from efficient managers. Had this programme been implemented, the immense harm that has been done by the breakdown of law and order accompanying the land invasions would not have paralysed our country.

The damage to the image of the country has been immense. It has also resulted in the almost total destruction of the once flourishing tourist industry, the boycott of Zimbabwe by investors, the withdrawal of aid and financial support by the international community, spiralling plant closures and job losses. The commercial farmers, the local and international business community, and the world's major economic powers all endorse the agreed system of land reform, based on paying farmers the market value of the land and assets they give up, on a willing seller, willing buyer basis.

Even ZANU PF agreed to this in 1998. The donors would have met the cost. Land would have been allocated to those capable of using it to best advantage, and not just to every itinerant person who claimed it, and who could produce a party card. It is possible to achieve land reform without destroying the basic fabric of our society - the basic economic infrastructure. Once destroyed, it will be very difficult to rebuild.

It is important to note that the mere possession of currently or recently fertile and productive land with a potentially high yield does not of itself guarantee wealth. The land has to be worked and managed properly. The operation has to be financed. The product has to be marketed efficiently. Only people with the training, experience or skills can achieve this. Those that can put the land to effective use for the benefit of the nation should own or manage it.

No advantage to Zimbabwe or its people can accrue from destroying the highly efficient commercial farms that are the country's most important asset, and the largest employers in the country. The nation and her people will not benefit from the pretence that the violent seizure of productive farming land by undisciplined mobs can lead to effective land redistribution. A better way has been carefully designed, and all interested parties, including ZANU PF, the farmers who occupy the land now, and the foreign powers that will pay for the process, have agreed to implement it.

The promotion of massive state-sponsored and often flagrantly racist violence, ostensibly to obtain land for the poor, but in reality to buy votes for a tired and discredited political party so that it may retain power, can only bring ruin.

To counter this, an awareness of the dangers inherent in the path we have been driven along is developing among the different ethnic and social groups in the nation. Our people are realising that they have common interests which transcend racial and social boundaries. They are becoming aware that being different from one another does not necessarily mean being enemies, and that we can easily tolerate linguistic, racial and social differences which, considered logically, are really not a barrier to working together or to understanding and liking one another.

Zimbabweans have come to realise that we *can* co-operate in the cause of progress, that we need to harness the talents of all our people for our mutual benefit, and not handicap ourselves by arbitrarily excluding whole segments of our population on spurious racial grounds. We know we must resist the schemes of those who wish to create divisions among us for their own gain, in order to divide and rule. We know that in unity there is strength.

The people of Zimbabwe are truly becoming one nation. We are tired of being divided and defined as black or white Zimbabweans, as though colour were the ultimate and infallible guide to character. All we want is to be Zimbabweans, working together to build a prosperous, peaceful and united country.

▮◦◇◦▮▰▰▮◦◇◦▮

The time to build has arrived
the time to build together, and to build each other.

Nelson Mandela

MEMORIES OF A DESIGNATED FARM

The song and the land are one.

Bruce Chatwin

y father grew up in a small town in South Africa. Encouraged by his father, he dreamt always of becoming a doctor. One day, when he was only twelve, that dream was shattered. His father, whom he loved and respected deeply, died, leaving his mother with limited funds to piece together a new life for herself and their three children.

By the time my father was midway through high school, the money was finished, and he had to take on a job in the magistrate's office to help support the family and educate his two younger sisters. He was devastated, but there was no other option.

The light returned to his life when he met and married my mother, only to be doused again when he left for North Africa to fight in a war that he never spoke about to us, even in later years. On his return, he was given the opportunity of buying a virgin farm in what was then Southern Rhodesia for two thousand pounds. He borrowed the money, packed his meagre belongings and headed north a few months before my birth. When I was strong enough to travel, my mother flew up with the three of us children to join him.

Although I remember little of those early years, apart from the warm shafts of sunshine which drifted through our open bedroom window each morning to wake us, I do recall stories of elephants coming down to the river to drink, and of devastating floods that swept the pump away.

What I remember most about my father was the headaches. When one of these came on, he would need absolute quiet and a darkened room. He had very little patience, so we always kept out of his way. Fortunately we had over 13 000 acres, so it wasn't difficult.

In later years the doctors finally discovered that he had a brain tumour, which must have started growing when he was a youngish man. He also had Buerger's disease, which is an allergy to nicotine. But he didn't know this. So, in addition to ranching cattle, he grew tobacco and maize. He also smoked - Gold Leaf Cork-tipped - about fifty cigarettes a day.

My mother was one of those extraordinary, selfless people who wanted to help everyone, make everyone happy and keep the peace. She loved literature, poetry, music, her garden and long walks in the veld, where we would find all sorts of wonderful treasures to bring home. There were the pure white lilies that flowered just before Christmas, the bright red bottle-brush, tipped with yellow sunshine pollen - the sun almost always shone on our farm - and the tiny blue and white vlei bells which grew among the rocks and in pools of shade close to water. Mum also loved the three of us children dearly: I think that is what kept her going.

None of the doctors my father visited knew about Buerger's disease, so he was treated for everything they could think of, including gout. They didn't have scanning equipment then, so nobody knew about the brain tumour. Even the witch doctors couldn't help.

When my father was ill, Mum would organise the farm workers, make sure that the tractors had been refuelled, and shoot any cobras which may have crawled, surreptitiously, into the house.

She also monitored the tobacco barns. Late at night, in the pale light of the moon, she would slip on her shoes, pick up the torch that was waiting at the door and walk down the long gravel road to the barns.

The worker on night shift would be there in the smoky blackness, stoking the furnaces with new logs drawn from the high wood stacks behind the barns. As he threw each log into the fiery red coals, a shower of sparks would erupt, igniting the flames and creating a halo of light so that the worn bricks glowed a deep crimson.

Inside the barns, the air would hang, moist and still. Above, tied on long, thin poles called matepes, the tobacco would be suspended, layer upon layer, from just above head height right up to the top of the barns. When the barns were being stacked, the workers would climb up the long cross poles and stand at staggered heights so that the man at the bottom could pass each matepe, with its precious load of tobacco, from one to the next until it was placed neatly at the very top. Stacking the barns took a long time.

The temperature and humidity level in each barn was a critical aspect of the curing process and had to be controlled carefully. An old thermometer hung below the tightly packed rows of leaves, registering the efforts of the stoker and the effectiveness of the wet sacks placed over the raised internal flues. As you entered, the air wrapped around your body, enveloping you with its soft, warm touch. The aromatic smell of leaves transforming slowly from a fresh yellow-green to papery gold held, for us as children, the mystique of the gifts carried by the three wise men: gold, frankincense and myrrh.

When Mum was satisfied that everything was in order, and that the man on duty would stay awake for the rest of the night, she would walk back along the empty road to the house, accompanied by one or more of our dogs.

She was one of the most caring people I have ever known. She took on everybody's problems, gave them sound advice, tended tirelessly to Dad and had endless patience with us. She also used to teach bible stories to the workers in the farm village so that, in her own small way, she could pass on a message of hope that would transcend the grinding drudgery and physical struggle of life on a virgin farm located thirty-three miles from the nearest town.

Even as children, we worried about her. Worried about the way she had to share her time between us and Dad, taking care that our allocation never exceeded his. Worried when she sat late into the night trying to figure out how to pay for fencing, doctors' bills, the monthly groceries and school fees. Worried, just as she worried, when the rains didn't come...

When my father was too ill to keep the farm going, he sold it to our neighbours and built a house in Marondera, a small town south-east of Harare. I remember driving away from the farm for the last time in our old grey Land Rover, with my white cat curled up on my lap and the dust churning behind us. My heart was numb with the loss of my childhood haunts and the wild beauty of the ranch.

My family never returned to the farm - it was a closed chapter in their lives. But, whenever there was an opportunity, my husband and I would stay with our friends on the adjoining farm and they would take us down that long, sandy road back in time. Understanding my need, they would walk with us to the river, wander through the vleis where the tiny blue vlei bells still grew and give me space to reunite with the baobab tree which had grown tall and broad in the intervening years. The last time we visited the ranch was just three months after it had been designated - it was one of the first in the country to be on the list.

It was a strange feeling to be driving back for the last time. The reservoir was cracked and empty, the farmhouse had been abandoned and the garden had disappeared in a tangle of weeds. There were patches of oil where the diesel engine had stood and the door of the shed sagged on its broken hinge. A couple of roosters scratched listlessly near the chicken run. Already most of the game had been shot out and the fences that my father had erected with loans paid back over many years had been stolen. The lands where tobacco and maize had stood tall in the good years were now shoulder-high in weeds. The tobacco barns I remembered so well, which towered above you, touching the clouds if you lay flat on the ground, were forlorn and cracked.

I am glad that our mother is not alive today. I am glad that she cannot see the devastation on our ranch where thousands of indigenous trees have been chopped down. Where nobody lives now because this land was never ideal for small-scale cropping. Where the limited soil that was arable has been washed away because it no longer shelters in the protective presence of trees that had stood for years, sometimes even for generations.

Our mother was always frugal and detested waste. The escalating wasteland that is today's Zimbabwe would have destroyed her.

IN THE BEGINNING

 will never forget Sunday 5 March 2000 when it all began. We had spent a lovely weekend in Harare with my brother who was out visiting from Bosnia. We had celebrated my mother's eightieth birthday and had taken her to a restaurant for a special meal. My brother had bought her one of those plastic badges that you pin to your jacket lapel. She was not very pleased about wearing something that said "I am 80 today", but she did receive much special attention at the restaurant because of it!

On Sunday afternoon we travelled back to the farm wondering whether we had been invaded. We drove up to the main farmhouse on my husband's parents' farm at about 3.30 pm and were told that the war veterans had arrived early in the morning and had been sitting outside their front gate all day. The farm manager had told them that they could not stay, so they had moved to our adjoining farm instead. I was aware of a sinking feeling in the pit of my stomach, but I felt less afraid than I had anticipated. It is amazing how one's mind goes onto "auto pilot" in times of crisis, and that is exactly what happened to me.

We drove home to our farm expecting to find a large crowd at our gate and were pleasantly surprised to find no one there after all. We drove the truck into the yard, unloaded our two dogs and luggage and waited. We could hear shouting, singing and dancing not far away, and were sure that the war veterans would arrive at our gate at any moment. We had such a sense of foreboding, as we waited and wondered how it was going to work out. Would they become violent? How should we react? Should we pack up again and simply leave, until all this blew over? We had absolutely no idea what their reaction to us was going to be. Each time the noise grew louder, we thought, "This is it. They are coming." But they didn't come.

Time dragged on as we waited nervously. At about 5.30 pm six of them arrived at the gate. This was a relief, as there were about sixty of them at the bottom of the hill! Their leader was a very thin, little old man. He had brought five very large "body guards" with him, and these men just stood with their arms folded, staring blankly at us. The little old man told us that he had come to take some land, and would we mind sharing this land with him...? It was an amazingly bizarre situation! He was extremely polite and not at all aggressive, but very assertive in his demands. The strategy the invaders collectively adopted, was to attempt to intimidate in whatever way they think could of. Their first tactic had been to sing loudly and to dance at the bottom of the hill for an hour and a half, before coming to speak to us. It had worked extremely well, we *were* intimidated, and it was such a relief that only six of them had come to the gate. It was also a relief that the conversation on both sides had been friendly and polite. We were trying to establish a relationship with them, so that they would not want to threaten us in any way. Our adrenaline was pumping, our brains were racing and our stomachs were sitting in our shoes!

After a half-hour conversation they left and rejoined the crowd at the bottom of the hill. I cannot remember what the discussion was about, but I do know that my husband was very good at changing the subject and that he never actually answered a question. I was really proud of him.

The police came and a reaction unit from our area arrived. There was more talking and the police told us that, basically, there was nothing they could do. We should just stay calm and let the invaders do whatever *they* wanted to do! We knew that this would be the outcome of any discussion with the police, but we were just grateful that we were not faced with a violent crowd. So many other farmers were having a terrible time with threats and insults from farm invaders. That night we could hear them singing and dancing for hours. I wondered whether they would ever turn violent and whether they would arrive at the gate at three in the morning, shouting abuse at us...

The next day was much the same. We could not see them at the bottom of the hill, but we could hear them loud and clear. During this difficult time we had such amazing and loving support from friends and neighbours. The week went by with our visitors demanding food, water and other basic necessities from time to time. Generally speaking, however, they were quiet and peaceful. This first week was the hardest to get through, as we had no idea what they were going to do next. My husband decided on the following Monday to put guards up at the top of the farm to try to stop any further invasions. The next day we had a telephone call from the CFU (The Commercial Farmers' Union) to warn us that the police were coming out to our farm because they had had reports that our guards were shooting at the war veterans and that I was setting my dogs on them! This was crazy. I have one fox terrier that has no idea what her teeth are for, apart from being there to eat bones and to catch rats. The other dog is an Aussie Blue puppy, only nine months old.

The incident terrified me and made me realise how manipulative these people could be. I realised that we should never underestimate them, and that we could not delude ourselves about what they thought and felt about us. My dogs are very important to me, and I was so afraid that I would not be able to prove the invaders wrong and that the police would insist our pets were put down.

When the police arrived, however, the whole thing was sorted out. In fact, the one policeman burst out laughing when he saw my dogs, realising that they could do very little damage. He asked the head war vet what he was up to, and the little man could find nothing to say, so he just slunk away. The rest of the week was very uneventful and quiet by comparison, with the invaders chopping down trees and singing and dancing as usual.

I decided that the only way I was going to cope with this was to spend time on peaceful and quiet things, so I started doing some embroidery and painting. I found these activities very satisfying - they were a great help and kept me sane during this very difficult period. My dogs became even more important to me and I spent a great deal of time with them, playing, walking around the garden and just enjoying them. I could no longer take them for walks and this I missed a great deal. They both seemed to understand and never once asked me to do so, as they used to. It was uncanny. Animals are very perceptive.

On Sunday 11 March our visitors held a party. The music was very loud, with much singing and beating of drums. At first we thought, "This is it... they will arrive at the gate any minute..." Once we began listening to the music, however, it was surprisingly pleasant and peaceful. The tone of the singing and the drums indicated that they meant no harm, except, perhaps, to intimidate us a little. I sat outside, under the wonderfully warm, star-filled sky and listened to them for a while. On the Monday they arrived at the gate again with another demand - I forget what it was this time - but after the conversation I told them that I had really enjoyed their music on the Saturday night. At first I thought that I had said the wrong thing (in fact I thought I had been really stupid), but in retrospect the comment worked to our advantage as, from then on, the music stopped. Since it had not affected us in the way they had hoped, they realised there was no point in continuing.

How long were we going to exist like this? There was a danger that, living under this kind of stress and tension, we would lose our sense of perspective. It was vital that we attempted to see at least some of the humour in the situation. During the next couple of weeks the invaders started to build their little shacks around our house - again trying to intimidate us. We learned to pay them very little attention and to ignore everything they did. The destruction of the trees for their shacks was criminal, and there was nothing we could do to stop it and nothing the police would do either. I packed up all our valuables, and each time we went to Harare, I would leave another box at my mother's house in the city. We ended up with only the basics in our home on the farm, so that, if we had to leave in a hurry, we would not be abandoning everything.

Looking back over the past year I wonder how we got through this very bizarre and stressful time and realise that God was never far from us. We have had to move off our farm and onto my in-laws' farm, where things at the moment are fairly quiet. Intimidation and destruction continue throughout the country and we have no idea how much longer we will have to accept the situation. But we believe that there is light at the end of the tunnel, that there will be change and that our lives will get back to normal sometime in the future. We all just have to remain focused and positive. Life is an ongoing journey of self-discovery summed up well by TS Eliot in his poem, "Little Gidding":

> *We shall not cease from exploration*
> *And the end of all our exploring*
> *Will be to arrive where we started*
> *And know the place for the first time.*

FARM INVADER

Our party must continue to strike fear in the hearts of the white men, they must tremble.

President Robert Mugabe

 have a story to tell. I tell it because I believe people should know what made me, and those like me, the young "war veterans", behave as we have done now for more than a year. I would like people to understand us, as I think that a lot of bad things are being said and written about us. This is not fair. We should have our chance to let the people of Zimbabwe and foreigners, who like to criticise and interfere with our affairs, know who we really are and why we have done what we did.

I must explain that these words you are now reading are not all mine. I am speaking this, not writing it, to a white man in a smart office. My English is poor, as I only went to school for a few years and was never taught to read and write the language properly. I picked up bits and pieces of it here and there, however, and I have told this story in my words, mainly in English, but aided by a translator who speaks siNdebele, and who interprets things when there is a problem with the language.

I have insisted that I be allowed to read this story, have it re-translated back to me when I cannot easily understand it, and change what I do not like. The words may not all be mine, but what you are reading is what I want to say. This *is* my story. The meaning of it is mine, if not the exact words. It is the truth. There is not enough money to make me lie about these things I tell you now.

I was born in Bulawayo some time early in 1977. I missed being "born free", that is, born after Zimbabwe became independent under a black government after 18 April 1980 by only three years. My birth was not registered at the time. It never was registered accurately. My mother came to town as a young girl, aged fifteen or so, already nearly ready to give birth to me.

I do not know who my father was, and I do not think that she knew either. If she did, she never told me. Her parents had chased her from her home in rural Matabeleland, the exact place does not matter, when they found that she was pregnant. She should not have been. She was not married or betrothed in terms of our culture. Her parents were very strict, I believe, being old-fashioned, traditional people who had never adopted Christianity, and she was a great disgrace to them.

I came to understand that they did not think that I, although their daughter's child, was part of their family. In our culture, children are held to be totally of the father's blood, not of the mother's. My mother came to town to stay with her older sister, who was married to a factory worker. Her brother-in-law tolerated her there, as long as she paid her way. Her sister was the only friend she had in the world.

My earliest memories are of sitting on the dirt verge at the side of the road outside a beer-hall in Makokoba Township, Bulawayo. The beer-hall was the Main Beer-hall, the Big Bar, as it was often called. It deserved its name, and I knew it well. I do not rely on my childhood memories of it. I have lived around it for most of my life, and it is huge. Tens of thousands of revellers have passed through its gateways every weekend for a hundred years. My mother made a living roasting meat and mealies (Indian corn on the cob) which she sold to people passing by, often on their way to and from the Big Bar.

Makokoba, the Old Location, as it is still often called, is the oldest African township of Bulawayo, and started to develop right after the white settlers got there more than a hundred years ago. They built themselves large houses to the west and south of the town centre, built kias (very small houses on the premises, out of sight round the back) for their domestic workers, and built the "Location" to house the black employees of their businesses.

I grew up in Makokoba for the first several years with my mother. She was a clever, though not at all educated, hard-working person, and managed to send me to school for a few years from when I was seven years old. She died when I was ten, in 1987, and that was the end of my schooling. She had never been healthy, and had always had a disturbing cough. She never had a relationship with a man that I knew of - I think that she just did not like them, or was afraid of them. Looking back, I think that she had had a very unpleasant experience with a man early in her life, and that the man (whom she would never discuss with me) must have been my father.

On my mother's death I found it impossible to live with her sister. She was kind enough to me, but her husband resented my presence in the house. My mother had paid her share of the rent, and he did not seem to think that I could contribute. He did not give me an opportunity to prove that I could. With three children of his own to look after, and his wife contributing a little by sewing and mending clothing, he felt that he could not afford an unproductive passenger such as I was likely to be.

Life became very unpleasant, and I felt that I was always on the verge of being given a beating I did not deserve. I was never actually hit by my aunt's husband, but always felt threatened by him, and the tension was almost worse than actual violence might have been. I knew a number of kids in the area who were regularly beaten by their fathers, especially or only when they were drunk, and their situation was preferable to that of those of us who were fatherless. Occasionally I heard my uncle refer to me as "that child with no totem", a reference to the fact that my father was unknown, and that it was therefore not known who my ancestors were, or what my clan or my totemic symbol was. That was a serious matter in our ancestor-orientated culture, and I did not like to be reminded of my outcast status.

There were a number of orphaned or runaway children of around my age who lived outside the beer-halls, surviving by selling food, sweets, and fantastically contrived wire toys, picture frames and a hundred other legal gadgets, and by dealing in other less innocent commodities. I knew many of them well, as we had worked and played football together for years in the Old Location and around the nearby Manwele and Mashumba beer-gardens. Both were built on the banks of a stream between Makokoba and Mzilikazi, and had wide lawns all around them. I had been a keen footballer, and was well-known among the other youngsters for this. I was one of the stars of the pick-up, impromptu, soccer games we played whenever we had the opportunity.

We used to climb over the wall of the open-air stadium at Stanley Square in Makokoba, and watch the boxing matches on Sundays. Ambrose Mlilo and Langton "Schoolboy" Tinago were our heroes. I became one of the leaders in this adventure, and it was in this exercise that I first started to test how far I could break the law and get away with it. It was quite easy. The municipal police, if they saw us climbing over the wall, were never fast enough to catch us, even if they cared enough to try.

I moved out of my aunt's home. I had my mother's cooking grill and a few hundred dollars in savings she had managed to scrape together. I was able to increase this amount by careful management, buying mealies and meat in the dark of the very early mornings from the markets, and cooking and selling them in the evenings and weekends around the beerhalls. I slept under trees in the beer-gardens at night after the municipal police patrols had gone, or on the verandas of the little shops in Makokoba and Mzilikazi.

It was not easy, but I survived. Sometimes I managed to rent a lean-to shack against the walls of houses, or just slept on the verandas of the little shops around the townships. The people there were obliged by their culture to be hospitable and kind to children and they often helped us, until we grew large enough to be a threat to them. We urchins helped one another out with information on likely spots to find shelter, food and work. We had to do this in order to get by. Without our network, life would have been much harder for us.

The main language in the townships was siNdebele, the Zulu language of the Matabele, whose ancestors had come from Zululand in South Africa. Some also spoke English, and we street-kids used to practise speaking English with one another when there was little work to do. I read the local newspapers when I had the money available to buy them, or when I could find or borrow old copies, and this improved my English a little.

Many of the residents of these suburbs were from Mashonaland, or of Mashona descent, and we practised their language also. It was polite and good for business to be able to speak to our customers in the language they preferred to use, and we enjoyed learning the languages anyway. We were proud of our ability to speak different languages. It was like a game or a hobby to us, and we could never understand why most of the whites we met, apart from farmers, could not speak the local languages.

I did not often meet white people in the African townships (as some called the high-density areas), of course. I came across them in the town centre of Bulawayo. I started to go there during the daytime on weekdays, when the business of selling food outside the beer-halls was slack. Out of curiosity, and for the easy money, a gang of us would make our way east into the centre of Bulawayo. We would beg for handouts from white people there, mainly women shoppers, or offer to guard their cars for them when they left them unattended to visit the shops. I was amazed to see that these whites were actually prepared to pay us for this service, or just to give us money because we asked for it. Sometimes I made more money from this activity than from my main business.

For years I managed to earn enough money to pay for food and a poor sort of lodging, but times were getting harder and harder. Gradually, and inevitably, as a result of poverty, I became involved in criminal activities. I found it difficult to descend to this, because of my mother's influence, which, I found, still governed my thinking a lot of the time. Not all of it, or I might not have done so well for myself. She had had a very strict moral code, and would never have stolen or cheated the drunkest and most unpleasant of her customers. I found it difficult to live by her standards, and eventually had to bend some of them. I never, however, completely escaped from her influence. I still can feel her presence, and almost see her, when I am faced with a moral problem. I find this to be quite a nuisance.

As the 1990s drew to a close there was less money around. People drank less and bought less food outside the beer-halls. There seemed to be fewer whites in the town centre. There were more street-kids competing for fewer customers. There were now hundreds of AIDS orphans on the streets, a lot younger than we were, and able to generate more sympathy from our targets - the affluent shoppers. I was part of a small gang of young men my age, in their late teens or early twenties, and we started to steal and rob.

Our first venture into dishonesty on a commercial basis was shoplifting. Three or four of us would work as a team. Some would distract the salesmen and security guards in shops on the western, down-market, side of the town centre, while the others stole from the racks or counters. This was quite profitable, but risky. The shopkeepers were on the lookout for people like us, and we could not safely go back to the same place again. We could sell the stolen property at our regular "stalls" or places of trade, or to people we came to know who made a living by buying and selling stolen goods.

We also became expert at stealing from cars parked in the town centre, snatching handbags or clothing through open windows or unlocked doors. It was amazing how often people left their doors unlocked and their windows open with valuables on the seats. Sometimes we worked the decoy trick there as well, with one of us distracting the driver while another did the snatch-and-run.

There were many drunks in the evenings making their way home from the beer-halls, particularly at the weekends and after pay-days at the end of the month. As we grew older and bigger and more desperate, and as times got harder, we graduated to more serious crime by ambushing them in dark places, beating them unconscious, and stealing their wallets and watches.

We developed our own, I think, exclusive, technique. In Bulawayo's high-density suburbs a lot of people carry knives. More, I hear, than is the case in Harare. We, Matabeles have a warrior heritage, and do not like to go unarmed. The townships are dangerous places, after all, with so many territorial gangs about. We had a few frightening experiences with people who were not as drunk as we had thought, and who were prepared to fight for their pay packets. At that stage we would attempt to hold and overpower our targets, and quickly lift their valuables and wallets.

On a few hits, as we called them, members of our gang suffered minor stab wounds. We were left with no option but to anticipate violence and to take the cash from an unconscious person. We would strike our victim on the head with a stone without warning, and take the money from his unconscious body. Stones were our chosen weapons. It was easy to hide a stone in one's hand before an attack, to throw it away if a police check was expected, and to find another for the next "customer". I used to find good-sized stones and keep them at my room until I needed them for a hit. These would do the job and stun a "customer", without cutting him too seriously. We always used to strike with the flat side of the stone, to minimise the damage we did.

We carried knives for our own defence - folding, non-locking pocket-knives with a blade not more than three and a half inches long, and therefore legal, but did not use them as tools of our trade. We would have been categorised as a much more serious grade of criminal had we used them in our work. We would have seriously injured or killed scores of people, and the police would have been forced to hunt us down like wild dogs on a cattle ranch. On the odd occasion when an intended victim fought back or threatened or frightened us and thereby made us angry, he would usually suffer more. On one embarrassing night, we, all four of us, were put to flight by a mature and sober man with a heavy stick, who gave a few of us nasty bruises.

Even the bulky Sidludla, who could normally be relied upon to stand his ground and give better then he got, was knocked to his knees. Having staggered to his feet, he managed to run away. On that occasion we had smoked more dagga (cannabis or marijuana) than we usually did before getting on with business, and we made an effort to cut down on its use as a result. A small amount of dagga was normally useful in giving us confidence: it made us less afraid and more calm than we would otherwise have been. We looked upon that incident as a training exercise, and learned from it. No more did we mix too much boom (Afrikaans for "tree", hence the tree of knowledge, and township slang for dagga) with business.

We were proud of the fact that we never had killed anyone, though I think we were very lucky. We had been forced into crime, but we observed certain limits, and tried to minimise the damage we did. We would not be worse than we had to be to survive.

"The Stone Gang" began to be feared and dreaded throughout Makokoba, Mzilikazi and Barbourfields townships. If not quite famous, because our names and identities were not known, we had at least achieved notoriety. Police patrols were stepped up in the area, and we began to feel threatened, as it appeared that they were there to apprehend the Stone Gang. The police even increased their plain-clothes patrols, I think mainly to catch us.

We had a few near escapes, and on one occasion avoided arrest only by throwing a few suspiciously large bundles of cash away behind some rubbish bins before we were checked by a police CPU patrol (Crime Prevention Unit - a group that operated in plain clothes, not uniforms). If the police had found us in possession of that large stash of money they could have arrested us as suspects or confiscated the notes, knowing that we could not justify possessing them, and would not report them. We went back and found the money later that night, fortunately.

We had become used to earning a lot more cash, and had rented ourselves proper places to live in during the 18 months or so of the Stone Gang's operations up to February 2000. We now needed more cash to fund our more luxurious standard of living, and had to attack more drunks to finance it. We could not see ourselves going back to a situation where we had to struggle to sell our meat or mealies in a shrinking market, and live in shacks or in the open. We were victims of our own success. We did not want to expand our activities to another area, where resident gangs would have objected violently to our presence. It looked as though we would have to carry on robbing until we were caught. It was that or starvation, or near starvation, and the police were bound to get lucky and catch one or more of us soon. We tried to live on less, and make fewer hits, but it was hard to get along.

The war veterans saved us from arrest or destitution. In late February 2000, a man in his forties approached me while I was selling my mealies and meat outside the Main Beer-hall. He knew my name. "Stix", he said, "Would you like a job that pays real money?" "Stix" was my nickname, and was taken from that of a South African football player I had admired as a child, though my legs were not thin like sticks, as his were. The stranger said that he had been told that I was one of the main "youth" leaders in the area. I think he meant tsotsi (thug or criminal) gang leaders really, knowing my own local claim to fame.

I was concerned that I was getting to be too well known, and was a little suspicious of him at first. He looked like a policeman to me, and I had a nose for that sort of person. He explained that he was a government official, was a war veteran himself, and that he had been tasked with recruiting people to work with the war veterans. In view of my poor prospects at that time, I found his proposal interesting.

Our gang - Sidludla (literally the fat one, though he was more muscular than fat), Rocky and Johnjo, as I shall call them, and I joined the war veterans. We were not fully recognised by the actual war veterans, who were much older than we were, and who had fought in the liberation war, which ended in 1980, when we were small children. We did not receive the monthly pension that the war veterans did, at that time $4 000 per month, and did not have their benefits of free medical care and education for their children, not that that mattered to us, as we had none. We were given free food and accommodation, however, and paid well by the standards we were used to. Of course, none of us, my friends and I, had ever been employed in a normal job before. What we received, and we were paid fairly regularly, was a lot of money to us. Above all, we had security. We did not need to fear the police any more. We slept better for that.

At this stage I must mention that I have to hide some facts for security reasons, and for my own safety. There are some who would not want me to be giving information out about operational matters, and those I would not like to provoke. I cannot give details of how I was trained, or where, or by whom, or especially where I operated while I was a "war veteran". There are also a lot of survivors and relatives of deceased people about, and others who have been injured or offended, and I do not want them to find me.

We received our basic training at a camp, and this included instruction on how to kill with knives and clubs, and unarmed combat. We boys from the ghettos, I thought, could have taught the instructors quite a bit. They did not seem to know anything about fighting with stones and little about knives. We were also taught the political background of the freedom struggle for Zimbabwe and our history and Socialist doctrine, which I found to be attractive. I liked the idea of everyone contributing to society according to his abilities and receiving benefits according to his needs. I could not see it operating in the Old Location, my beloved Makokoba, however, where a practical attitude was more common.

I had not realised until these history lessons just how brutally and, more hurtfully, with how much arrogance the whites had treated us blacks after invading our country. I had not realised that the whites I had had dealings with in the Bulawayo city centre were quite as sinister as that. On looking at the facts, it was incredible that they could have had the insolence to believe that we would allow them to treat us as they did, stealing everything of value in our country, and expecting us to accept this as though their God had decreed it. Our ancestors certainly would not have accepted this, and I don't think their God had any right to speak for us. From what the whites say of him, he would not in any event have approved of their actions in our country.

After completing our training, which came naturally to the Stone Gang, we were driven in 4x4 vehicles to a commercial farming area in Matabeleland, near Bulawayo. This was in early March of 2000. Our mission was to repossess farms that were currently occupied by white farmers. We, in our group, would not say that they owned this land. It had been stolen from our ancestors a hundred years previously, and it was our task to take it back for the black people of Zimbabwe.

Our instructions were clear and, generally speaking, we followed them strictly. We were not to attack or harm the white farmers and their families. We were, however, to harass them verbally on any and every occasion we came across them to make them realise that they were not wanted on the farm or in our country. We were told that the farms had been designated for resettlement under the government's fast track resettlement scheme. Assaulting or killing the whites was not something we were permitted to do. If it were considered necessary, other more senior, and more heavily armed cadres would make that decision.

The farm workers were a different story. We were encouraged to intimidate them, and to re-educate them so that they would understand that they should support the ZANU PF party in the approaching parliamentary elections, which were to be held in June of that year. We could beat them up when it seemed to our leaders, real war veterans who had fought in the liberation struggle, that this was necessary, and it often was. These people had to realise the consequences of selling out to the enemy. It was our task to see that ZANU PF won the elections, and that the Movement for Democratic Change (MDC) sell-outs and whites did not.

I had known that there had been a referendum on a new constitution that February, just days before we were recruited. I had not registered to vote, as I had not been politically aware at the time. The government had backed the new constitution, but had been defeated in the vote. This was a serious matter. The remaining whites in the country, it had been explained to us in our training, were plotting with some renegade black trade union leaders and the British to hand the government of the country back to the whites. The object of these people was to re-colonise Zimbabwe. All the benefits of 20 years of independence would be lost.

Our revolutionary government, however, was not going to stand by and let the British, the farmers and the black sell-outs steal the fruits of independence. The war veterans and we young cadres were going to be deployed to frustrate their schemes.

This was obviously a critical situation, and my friends and I felt honoured to be given the opportunity to help the nation, and to be paid for it as well. I felt that my mother would have approved of what I was doing. For the first time in our lives we felt that we were doing something important, something for the country. None of us would have wanted the British back, or for our people again to be enslaved.

It was a good feeling to be part of a noble cause. It was also a relief to be on the side of the government, for a change. We now had the power of the state behind us.

We no longer had to fear the police patrols. They feared us, if anything. You cannot imagine how great that made us feel! We, who had been fugitives from the law for years, were now above it. My friends and I were not armed with firearms, but our leaders, the more senior of the older war veterans, and the members of the security forces who operated with us, were. We felt that we were really empowered. We were the enforcers of the state, authorised to do as we liked. We were the government's agents, and being paid to do the things the police force in Makokoba had hounded us for. This was heady stuff indeed for children of the streets such as we had been. It was not surprising that sometimes we overstepped the mark, and behaved as the young criminals we once were until plucked from our slums by the government to be its instrument of change.

We spent a month in the Matabeleland commercial farming area, terrorising the owners and employees on farms that had been designated by the government for resettlement, and on many that had not been. We forced farm workers to attend "pungwes" - all-night sessions of singing ZANU PF political songs and shouting political slogans. They seemed to be thoroughly cowed. It looked as though there was no chance that these people would dare to vote for the opposition in the elections in June. It was disappointing later to note that nearly all of them had done so.

I was surprised to see that no one was killed during the operations in which I took part . We used limited force only. This had been emphasised in our training. Several black farm workers were beaten up quite severely for not being more enthusiastic in supporting us. This was especially likely to happen if we had been hitting the alcohol or dagga harder than usual. We worked with dozens or sometimes hundreds of youngsters like ourselves and many other older people, men and women, who were there as hired hands, as we were, and with smaller numbers of real war veterans. There were others who were really in charge, and who organised our deployment and our payment and food.

Sidludla, Rocky, Johnjo and I had been disciplined even as criminals on the streets of Bulawayo's western areas, and had inflicted only the harm necessary to get the job done. We tried to retain this moderate

42   *Voices of Zimbabwe*

attitude while working the farms. Our little group did no serious injury to the farm workers, but others among our ranks were not as restrained. They did not have my mother to contend with! We still put our message across effectively, and I often wondered how far we would go if we faced serious resistance. All the people we dealt with seemed to realise that it was best to humour us, and did not mount any serious opposition.

I was surprised that we were so unopposed, because our activities often stopped work completely on the farms we invaded. We would set up shacks and peg out plots on fields of carefully tended crops, take over barns and houses, and deliberately make it impossible for the farmers and their staff to operate. On several farms we totally disrupted the farmers' operations. Admittedly, we often moved on in a few days or weeks to another farm, and when we came back we would find that most of the harm we had done had been repaired as far as it could be.

We specialised in cutting down trees. We needed these to make shacks, but some of our associates were doing this in a commercial way, with trucks carting off huge loads of valuable timber to sell to timber mills or for firewood. We knew that this tree felling really depressed and infuriated the white farmers. Some of the trees we cut down were a hundred years old, I was told. We cut down a lot more trees than we needed for our purposes, just to let the farmers know who was boss now. They reported us to the police, but no action was ever taken against us. We were the government. We had never known such power.

After a month or so, a new mission was planned for us. We were offered the opportunity of going to Mashonaland to assist in the campaign there, which was much more high-powered than in Matabeleland. Farming is much more intensive in Mashonaland. Matabeleland has fewer commercial farms and a lot of them are cattle ranches, with relatively few farmers or farm workers. Mashonaland has a higher rainfall, a lot more irrigated farming land, and is much more densely populated. Many of the farms there are organised like factories. The elections would be decided in rural Mashonaland, we were told, and we were needed there.

We from the Stone Gang, as I indicated earlier on, could speak some Shona as well as English and siNdebele, and this made us highly suitable for transfer to Mashonaland. We would be paid more for leaving our home area, and this influenced us to accept the transfer. We were happy to leave Matabeleland anyway, as most of us had family connections there and feared the reaction of some of our relatives to what we were doing.

Again, the useful 4x4s transferred us to Mashonaland. Where these all came from I am not sure, though many were government vehicles, and some belonged to various non-governmental organisations (NGOs) funded by foreign charities. I wondered if the donors knew to what use their funds were put. Early in April 2000, we arrived at our base camp in the centre of a rich tobacco farming area. We were to spend the next few months there, and would help to shape the course of Zimbabwe's history.

I do not want to go into the specifics of our actions in this period. A lot has been written in the independent press in Zimbabwe about our activities. I have seen a few of the articles myself. I see no necessity for me to detail the various things I did to influence the results of the elections. It would serve only to focus attention on myself and my comrades. At some time in the future that might not be to our advantage.

In general terms, we made it impossible for the opposition Movement for Democratic Change (MDC) to campaign effectively in most of rural Mashonaland. In many areas the MDC did not succeed in holding one meeting while I was there. We did our job well. I am sure that in many other districts in the period from March to the elections at the end of June 2000, the MDC candidates were no more successful than in ours. We would interrupt them and harass and assault them and their supporters. Many thousands of them must have been beaten up.

I am amazed that the tally of deaths only reached a reported 35 in that period. I am also surprised that only five of them were white farmers. When you consider that there were tens of thousands of us going about beating up MDC people, and that hundreds of us were armed with firearms and thousands with axes, sticks, pangas (machetes) and so on, you must realise that it could have been much worse. If you are from the opposition party, you must realise that we have been very gentle so far. Be grateful. Do not think that we will always be so. This applies particularly if it comes to the stage where we are in actual danger of having the forces of law and order turned against us, and investigating our activities during the past year or so. That might happen if the MDC comes into power. We cannot allow that to happen.

It came as a great surprise to all of us that the MDC nearly won the parliamentary elections in June 2000. It turned out that we had been too soft, and had allowed the opposition too much leeway. I am glad to see that the pressure on the rural areas to support ZANU PF has been maintained and intensified since the June 2000 elections. We are now properly organised, and will see to it that things are more rigidly controlled next time. It seems that the pressure will be maintained up to, and, I hope, after the Presidential Elections, which will be held by the end of March 2002.

We are now moving into the towns, hotbeds of support for the MDC and the other enemies of the state, the whites and other neo-colonials. There will be few MDC rallies there in the run-up to the election, and the proper result can be guaranteed. We will see to that.

Already we are politicising the urban black workers, and taking control of the labour movements in the factories. No worker with a grievance will bother to go to the unions, which have been subverted by the MDC, for assistance in labour disputes. We are dealing with those directly. The capitalists who run the economy of our country have been spoiled. We have been too soft on them. No more. If they want to exploit our labour and resources, we will see to it that they pay for the pleasure.

I have been a street-kid in Makokoba. I do not want to revert to that status. I prefer being a "war veteran" and an agent of the government. I have pegged out a few plots of land that I intend to keep. I own valuable assets, and my cousins from Makokoba are looking after them. Who can take them from me while I am shielded by the Party? We are here to stay.

We will not go back to our hovels in the ghettos - not in a thousand years. I have good authority for saying this. We have the guns. We have the military organisation and the support of the government system, the police and the army. Who can mount an election campaign against us in the areas we control? These areas are growing by the day and will soon include all the industrial and commercial suburbs in the country, as well as all of the countryside.

Who in Zimbabwe can stand against us? We will not fail.

❙•⇌•❙⊠❙•⇌•❙

FADED COLOURS IN THE WIND

You think you own whatever land you land on;
the earth is just a dead thing you can claim;
but I know ev'ry rock and tree and creature
has a life, has a spirit, has a name.

You think the only people who are people
are the people who look and think like you,
but if you walk the footsteps of a stranger
you'll learn things you never knew you never knew.

Have you ever heard the wolf cry to the blue corn moon,
or asked the grinning bobcat why he grinned?
Can you sing with all the voices of the mountain?
Can you paint with all the colors of the wind?

From Walt Disney's "Pocahontas"

 liding effortlessly across the crisp blue canvas of the African sky, a towering cumulus cloud obscures the sun for a few moments. High above in the syringa tree, two Meyer's parrots engage in idle conversation punctuated by the plopping of the unripe berries they discard. Beyond the colourful sweep of the garden, a green pigeon preens itself in a gum tree planted perhaps by the first owner of the farm. Butterflies saunter across the lawn and a bumblebee drones on the red salvia. The air is warm and still.

I am on my own. Alone on a farm in Zimbabwe's Karoi district which has seen brutal attacks on farmers and farm workers in recent months. This is the area where Marshall Roper was surrounded by twelve war veterans and struck across the face with a machete. Photos of his agony were beamed around the world and filled South Africa's television screens. Their objective: to stop him from planting tobacco and, ultimately, to drive him off his farm.

Targeted because of their courage and commitment to law and order in the face of anarchy, the Karoi farmers have been especially hard hit by the government-promoted land invasions. The attack on Mr Roper sparked off a demonstration by 3 500 farmers, their workers and Karoi residents, who gathered around the police station to insist that law and order was restored in their district.

Highlighting this incident, a leader article in The Farmer magazine of 3 October 2000 commented that all Zimbabweans could learn something from the people of Karoi. *"War veterans have no legal status, no official status and no mandate from the people. Therefore, in terms of negotiation, they do not exist. While they're illegally camped on farms, they're squatters, and while they're committing acts of barbarity they are criminals. Either way, to acknowledge them is to condone illegality. It is bad enough that the State has chosen to condone illegality, it would be worse still if Zimbabweans did too."*

The leader continued: *"Like those beaten, raped and murdered before him, Mr Roper will remain as proof that land reform in Zimbabwe has been derailed for personal gain...(but) the tide has turned; Americans are considering punitive legislation against Zimbabwe; world opinion is united in its condemnation of President Mugabe and his ruling ZANU PF party and Zimbabweans themselves no longer believe a word their government tells them..."*

What do the people of Zimbabwe believe? I hear so many conflicting points of view in this country where I grew up and which remains an integral part of me.

Last night the moon was full, rising above the dam in silver splendour while the sun dropped beyond the outline of the tobacco barns in a wash of vibrant coral.

At nine o'clock the lunar eclipse began. Slowly the earth's shadow grew from a bruise on the eastern edge to a dark sliver. Within just over an hour, the night had darkened perceptibly and the transformation was complete. Through our binoculars, the moon glowed like embers behind a translucent veil and the stars slid back from the wings, multiplying in a carpet of diamonds against the charcoal sky.

For us, lying on our backs on old sleeping bags, the event was a scientific miracle to be debated at length. And for the squatters and war vets occupying the barns and newly erected huts less than two kilometres away? Was it an event to be feared? One they associated with witchcraft - an evil omen? Or did they fail to notice the new colours of the night reflected in chipped enamel basins as they collected water for the dawn.

This morning we drove down to see the maize and tobacco lands. Seated in two well-worn canvas chairs on the back of the truck, with Brutus and Matrix at our feet, Shirley and I scoured the bush for birds and watched rows of late tobacco slip by into the distance.

Rounding a corner, the familiar tobacco barns came into view: tall, brick structures that by now should be filled to capacity, releasing soft columns of smoke into the early sky. Inside, the air should be damp and still, a thermometer hanging below leaves curing to potato-chip crispness in the unrelenting heat.

On the farm's only red soil, small plots had been staked out, with maize and cotton planted in irregular rows. To the right, men and women wearing drab, torn clothes and expressionless faces stopped their hoeing to watch us. On our left, two oxen trudged along, dragging an ancient plough, while the man driving them slung his long whip across their backs mindlessly. Standing apart from the rest, two men - one with a large black hat - and a woman, took up a defensive, proprietary stance. This man was the leader, heading up a group which had been driven onto the farm at the orders of Karoi's District Administrator.

The truck rolled on until we reached farm workers clearing weeds between the sandy ridges of a tobacco field. Caught in no-man's land between the war vets and the farmer who had, for many years, provided them with a livelihood, they too were expressionless. Three children played a game with sticks, and a fourth, who was left out, was sobbing loudly. A young girl carried a baby on her back: I wondered if it was hers. She looked at us absently and moved on. The days of singing to the rhythm of the hoe were gone. The splashes of colour as workers moved along the tidy rows, topping tobacco, were a memory.

On the way back, passing the barns, I saw a huddle of squatter children. Their faces reported the story they'd been told: that we were intruders and the land they were occupying was rightfully theirs. The biggest child, a young boy, jerked a finger in the direction of the people who could afford to own - or ride in a truck.

For a moment my old canvas chair became a throne and I, who as a child had reaped tobacco barefoot with our workers and experienced the pain of poverty when the long droughts came or the hail struck, sweeping away a farmer's hopes and bank balance in a brief instant, was a privileged white to be driven away.

The truck changed gear and we were once again passing the divide between the red soil and the sand. Alone among her tilled clods, a woman set aside her hoe to watch us. Her clothes hung loose and shapeless; I was too far away to see the expression on her face. Slowly she lifted her hand shoulder-high in a tentative greeting. Was she reaching out over the growing divide? Was she acknowledging the pain of taking and losing land? Did she wish that things were different? I longed to respond, but she was a "war vet", a squatter. And my friends, who had struggled for years to buy and build up the farm, were now under siege. They had lost a tremendous amount; they could lose everything. My hand stayed by my side. We drove on.

Sometimes, when I consider what tremendous
consequences come from little things...
I am tempted to think there are no little things.

Bruce Barton

ESCAPE

...Come, my friends,
'Tis not too late to seek a newer world.

From "Ulysses" by Alfred, Lord Tennyson

nly four more weeks. The days drag by. I can't wait to board that plane and fly to England. I can't wait to leave stress and anxiety behind. I can't wait to say exactly what I want to say, without having to look over my shoulder.

I have lived in Zimbabwe all my life. But at the age of twenty-one, I have decided that I would rather be anywhere else than here in Zimbabwe.

I have been working for the last three years. You slave away all month just to watch your pay cheque dwindle down to nothing, as you hand out your money to various departments of the government for "services" rendered. It is now, now that it is *your* money that you are giving away, that you realise what puppets we all are. You pay your rates and taxes, which you have to queue for hours to do - for what? The roads are full of potholes, the verges are never cut, the streets are covered in litter and the town just looks dirty...need I go on? Yet, nobody argues, questions or demands. We all go along with our lives like hypnotised mummies accepting that we are getting no value or service for our money. If you paid for a full tank of petrol and were then sent away with an empty tank, would you just drive away and accept this? Why should we? Why should we be any different from anywhere else in the world?

I love my sport. I play hockey and squash and I go to the gym twice a day. At the gym I can give vent to my frustrations by losing myself in the exhilaration of music and exercise. After a particularly energetic spin class at 6 am, I am ready to face the day ahead. I enjoy chatting to the people at the gym - they are a very pleasant group, and I have more in common with them than I do with the pub and disco crowd.

At one stage, I thought I would further my studies - possibly do a course in Business Management. But when I found out how much a course like that would cost, I threw the idea out of the window. It is very difficult for a young person in Zimbabwe to further his or her education with no financial support. There are no grants, bursaries or loans for us.

During my final year at school I did a scuba diving course. This was a very different experience - even though we were being taught the art of diving in the school swimming pool. I used to dream of ocean depths and fascinating marine life. But who can afford to travel to South Africa or to Mozambique? Who can afford to buy the wet suit and the rest of the equipment one needs? Perhaps one day I will be able to dive in Europe and see a little more than the bottom of a swimming pool.

I have waited for a miracle. I have waited for change, which has not come. I cannot wait any longer. It is time to go. It is time to travel and realise my dreams and ambitions. I have never been to the United Kingdom before, but it certainly sounds as if it is the place to be, if you are a young person looking for opportunity, success, money, travel, adventure, excitement, or simply to better yourself.

I know that life is not going to be easy. I receive e-mails every day from friends who are overseas. Some of them are homesick and talk about the cold. Alan was saying that he misses the friendliness of the people in Zimbabwe. He says that people seldom greet you when you come to work. Zimbabweans tend to smile more often than many people overseas do. He says he is sick of living in carbon copy, cupboard-like rooms and houses. He misses space. He misses driving everywhere and hates queuing for buses and tubes. His girlfriend, Mandy, comments that all people seem to do is work and worry about money. It is like living in a bank, she says.

Jane says that she loves the efficiency. It is wonderful to walk into a shopping mall and know that you are likely to find what you are looking for. To be faced with eight varieties of whole-wheat bread is something to look forward to! Choices. What a pleasure! Jane knows that I love photography, and says that I will be able to afford to buy a decent camera in England. You'll only have to save for a few months, she says, and you'll be out taking photographs of London's landmarks. If I stay here, I'll never be able to a buy a good camera, let alone a new car.

And yet...as everybody says, "there is just something about Africa". When I leave for gym at 5.30 am, the freshness of the morning and the promise of the new day overwhelm me. I even composed the opening lines of a poem yesterday morning:

Across the lush green grass of the race track
The morning mist settles...

Yes, there is something about Africa. I have my family, my animals and that "bit of Africa" that is a part of me. Perhaps, in England, I will finally find some answers.

THE NEW COLOSSUS (*Emma Lazarus*)

Not like the brazen giant of Greek fame,
With conquering limbs astride from land to land;
Here at our sea-washed, sunset gates shall stand
A mighty woman with a torch, whose flame
Is the imprisoned lightning, and her name
Mother of Exiles. From her beacon-hand
Glows world-wide welcome; her mild eyes command
The air-bridged harbor that twin cities frame.
"Keep ancient lands, your storied pomp!" cries she
With silent lips. "Give me your tired, your poor,
Your huddled masses yearning to breathe free,
The wretched refuse of your teeming shore.
Send these, the homeless, tempest-tossed to me,
I lift my lamp beside the golden door!"

COLLECTOR LETTER

Dear Mr Collector, I'm baffled, I fear -
Can't make no sense of my taxes this year.
I see from the handout you kindly provide,
I've got to pay taxes - no Zimbo can hide.

But the budget I've seen - so cleverly wrought -
Shows I've got to pay a lot more than I'd thought.
On anything over sixty thousand per year,
Up to forty percent for your coffers I fear.

Then the surcharge kicks in, another thirty percent,
If eight forty thou. I can save from the rent.
Then, again, the AIDS levy - it's hurting me sore -
So little is left - it's three percent more.

And if any's left over to buy myself food,
It's fifteen for sales tax - d'you think that is good?
I'm afraid it's a fact, our country's expiring,
It looks like we're doomed; the economy's frying.

You take forty, plus thirty, plus three plus fifteen -
How dare you do this, I think it's obscene -
It's eighty-eight percent, is that not a crime?
MPs don't pay taxes, is their lot not sublime?

As if that's not enough - please confirm that I'm right -
Sixty percent duty for your buddies in white,
For lots we import that we can't get in Zim.
That's one forty-eight - no wonder we're grim!

And more than that, it is sad to relate,
There's a new "carbon tax" at a hellish rate,
Three thousand six hundred a year must I pay,
To run my twin-cab - what more can I say?

Then - last nail in the coffin - there's death dues as well -
You fiend - you're hounding me right into hell.
I pay a lot more on what I've managed to hide,
You won't let me go rich to the other side.

If you were making good use of my dough,
If I saw some return - some quid for my quo -
I'd feel so much better - it'd deaden the pain -
But it's cash for the Congo or corruption's drain.

So there goes my profit, I'm sadly distressed,
You get more than I earn - you really are blessed!
Well I hope you're happy now you got all the loot,
And I'm happy I'm giving your country the boot,

For Mr Collector, I've had it with you,
Likewise with your party, whatever its hue!
I'm off to Alaska, a much harsher clime,
But where they know taxes like yours are a crime!

NB: The above is a slight exaggeration. The actual tax rates per annum
are as follows, from January 2001:

⊠ From $60 000 to $180 000 - tax is from 20% to 40% on a sliding scale.

⊠ Over $840 000 there is a 30% surtax on the amount payable.

⊠ There is an AIDS levy of 3% on tax payable, excluding surtax.

⊠ Sales tax is 15% on most items for "end users", sometimes more.

⊠ Many Customs duties are 60% ad valorem, and sometimes more.
The duty on special items such as passenger cars is higher.

⊠ Members of Parliament, who make the laws, don't pay income tax.

⊠ The real (street) rate of exchange for the US$ is about Z$160.
Twenty years ago it was Z$0.66. Since Independence we have lost
96% of the value of the Z$.

⋮⋯⟝⋯⋮⊠⋮⋯⟞⋯⋮

VOICES OF A LOST GENERATION

I think we are in rats' alley
Where the dead men lost their bones.

From "The Waste Land" by T S Eliot

 here is no one to tuck them into bed at night. No one to read the stories from which our childhood memories are made. No one to place a cuddly toy in their arms when the nightmares come. There is no one.

Their bedrooms are the darkened streets and dingy passageways that the moonlight shuns. Their food comes from dustbins - if they are lucky - or from creatures which lurk in the dark corners, struggling themselves to survive.

These are the children that society discards. The majority know their parents, or have relatives, but mounting social problems have forced them to take refuge on the streets, swapping abusive family relationships for abuse of a different kind.

In the twilight of lost childhood, these children are forced to become adults without experiencing the security of a stable family life - and without experiencing love. Instead of supporting each other, there is sodomy. Instead of sharing food, they share glue. Without identity, they merely exist: the faceless and voiceless children of a lost generation.

Originally, Zimbabwe's infrastructure catered for the needs of the population. Since Independence, infrastructural investment has been minimal, despite rapid population growth. In many areas only one pre-school existed during the '80s. There has been little progress since then. Today, a solitary pre-school cannot hope to cope in a crowded township, nor can a single youth centre.

Development has been stifled by a lack of responsible planning on the part of national and local government, city councils and society at large. Economic hardship has compounded the situation, resulting in grinding poverty for many families. Without money or food over a long period, parents become depressed, venting their aggression on those without a voice.

Those organisations which have taken it upon themselves to care for the children are under-funded and under-staffed. Despite the fact that the task is often thankless, they continue their work under extraordinarily difficult conditions, visiting the streets at night when the children are vulnerable and afraid. It is then that they are more likely to admit the truth about their situation and accept an offer of help. While it is risky to venture out late at night, the youth workers are committed to doing everything possible to save the children.

It is one thing to remove a child from the street, it is another to remove the street from the child. In many cases, the freedom of street life continues to haunt those who struggle with the restrictions of a safer lifestyle.

Where possible, children are encouraged to return to their families. Advance counselling helps them to forgive the injuries they have suffered and equips the parents or guardians with parenting skills. Despite their limited resources, many rehabilitation centres are committed to providing the children with free education and free skills training. Assistance with income-generating projects helps family units to survive.

"We believe that survival lies in a strong family system," explained a family worker. "Destroy this and you destroy the fabric of society." In certain parts of the country, we find that unity exists, regardless of the problems. In other areas, it's a case of each person for himself."

"What we need in this country right now is integrity. Where are our ethics? Where is our vision? When a country has no vision, the people perish. With a vision, there is hope. As a nation, we need political, economic and social vision. We need to rise and aim at a future. There is much that we could teach the rest of the world - in certain instances we could even become role models. However, every social programme we use today is an import. There is no time - or money - to develop our own systems based on our cultures, traditions and environment. Other countries provide funds for social projects; our government provides nothing, despite the taxes we pay."

Although the problems they face are daunting, these family workers never lose hope. The job of "working with dry bones and trying to bring them back to life" can be distressing, but the success stories bring their own rewards. Part of their success lies in their efforts to emulate the natural environment. "If you remove all things natural, you destroy a child."

With money, the family workers believe that they could remove all the children from the streets. "How can a country allow the children, who are its future, to be nurtured by the streets? Every child deserves a childhood. After all, each child is just a child."

⁞•⇨•⁞▷◁⁞•⇨•⁞

J'ACCUSE

It is easier to sail paper-boats on lily ponds,
To plunge like a gannet in the sheltered sea...

Than to travel in the mind to that place
Where the map becomes reality, where cracks
Are gullies...
... and the shaped grey rocks

Are no longer the property of wandering painters,
A pleasant water colour for an academic wall,
But cover for the stoat-eyed snipers...

I can no longer hide in fancy: they'll hunt me out.
That map has mountains and these men have blood...

Now is the future that I never wished to see...
I was quite happy dreaming and had no fear:
But now, from the map, a gun is aimed at me.

From "It Was Easier" by Ruthven Todd

accuse most Zimbabweans of contributing to the present state of affairs in this country. You are so preoccupied with yourselves, your immediate families and your own selfish pursuits that you have lost sight of the bigger picture. You have forgotten the poor, the helpless, the abused and the victimised. You are terrified of standing out from the crowd. You are afraid, and you have lost your self-respect and your dignity.

Government of Zimbabwe, we used to respect you. During your first ten years in power, you achieved much that was good. You improved health care for the people and saw to it that we received a good education. We thank you for this. But things have changed. You have changed. You no longer care for your people. You no longer care about your people. We are expendable. You set your thugs upon us to beat and torture us and to kill us if it pleases you. What type of rulers order the elimination of their own people? I accuse you of having drawn about yourselves the cloak of evil, and together with your late colleague Hitler Hunzvi, of having embraced the powers of darkness. Remember: "The evil that men do lives after them..."

You war veterans, who fought in the second chimurenga (revolution) against Ian Smith's whites to liberate your country, what are you doing now? Why are you fighting your own people to keep another evil system in power on the pretext that you want to liberate your land? How does killing white and black opposition supporters liberate land?

I accuse Shona Zimbabweans of turning their backs on their black cousins when the Matabele genocide took place. Some researchers have estimated that as many as twenty to thirty thousand lives were lost. Today it is you who are hungry and afraid, and that is why you are ready to shout about democracy.

I accuse White Zimbabweans of continuing to feel superior to blacks. The majority of you still have not accepted the fact that this is Zimbabwe not Rhodesia. You have not learned our languages and you persist in being condescending to us. Yes, we appreciate your help in donating to worthy causes, but do not forget to treat your workers in your businesses and on your farms with respect. Without our labour, your enterprises would not prosper. We must work as a team. Acknowledge us, understand us, value us. Have you ever considered the fact that we want to be more than merely "happy employees"? We want to be creators and owners of wealth, employers and captains of industry ourselves.

Black Zimbabweans, we must learn to speak out against injustice of any kind. We must stop feeling inferior and we must accept ourselves as people with democratic rights. It is not enough merely to be concerned with food and shelter and the basic necessities. We must not put up with corruption (it is not enough to laugh and shake our heads in disgust). We have to do something about the people who disappear and who are never seen again.

If there is a man who ought to be emulated for his principled stand, it is Nelson Mandela. He is able to take the emotions out of issues and argue solely on principles. As Stephen Covey points out: "Principles are like lighthouses, they do not move." The boat approaching the lighthouse must change course, no matter what its size.

You all stand accused. What about me? My friends tell me I have a big mouth and they ask whether I am afraid. Some people think I am arrogant. Others feel that I take unnecessary risks. "Albert," they say to me, "You have a lovely young family. You have an excellent job, a house and a car. Keep your mouth shut!"

I cannot keep my mouth shut. I am an intelligent, confident person. I am also black. But I am a person first and a black second. I am afraid, yes. But I am not too afraid to speak out. I cannot imagine my children growing up without me to guide them. Yet, at the same time, I have to speak out for the sake of my children and for all the other children of the country. If I do not, what sort of place will they inherit? What will their future be?

People ask me about my religious beliefs. "Why do you start off every meeting you chair with a prayer?" they say. I do not attend church on Sundays because I found that church-going could often be suffocating. I feel that churchmen and women should speak out against evil. This does not happen often enough. But I do believe in God and in the power of good. When I pray, I am asking for God's help to fight against the great evil that our government embodies. So many people fail to understand the importance of the spirit world in black culture. It is incredibly powerful. So I am praying for my protection as well as for the protection of all who are present at our meetings.

I have accused you all of apathy, of self-interest and of lack of concern for our country. Now I exhort you all to change. Be proactive, work within your sphere of influence and let's teach our children to stand up for what is right. Fight racism, tribalism and corruption. Let us make this the great nation it can be.

▮◄⇔►▮✕▮◄⇔►▮

People often say, with pride, "I'm not
interested in politics." "They might as well
say, "I'm not interested in my standard
of living, my health, my job, my rights,
my freedoms, my future or any future..."
If we mean to keep any control over
the world, we must be interested in politics.

Martha Gellhorn, American journalist, 1984

THE EXILE

The voice I hear this passing night was heard
In ancient days by emperor and clown:
Perhaps the self-same song that found a path
Through the sad heart of Ruth, when sick for home,
She stood in tears amid the alien corn...

From "Ode to a Nightingale" by John Keats

 t the age of 29, I feel I should have reached a point where I am ready to settle down and prepare for the rest of my life. At least this would be the normal course of action for most young adults, certainly in First World countries. Living in Zimbabwe, however, changes a person's perspectives. You cannot plan any future in Zimbabwe because you don't know if there's going to be one. A young person on an ordinary salary can forget about owning his own house one day, because property maintains its real value and wages don't go up in line with inflation.

It is with growing alarm and despondency then, that young people of all races watch their peer groups disintegrating as everyone who can, those lucky enough to have the right passports anyway, make that frantic dash to the West, looking for greener pastures. Those less lucky manage to "make a plan" - the well-known Zimbabwean saying that epitomises life in Zimbabwe where anything can happen and does, and people have to learn to adjust to constantly changing situations. Aspiring emigrants try every trick in the book, in an attempt to find a way of leaving the country, be it through ancestry entitlement from some long-dead relative, or by claiming refugee status in Canada. The result is that there are very few people left behind. We now have a tiny white community where the average age is between 50 and 60. The people in this age group are too old to make a move elsewhere. The young whites left, live in an " incestuous" society, where everybody knows everybody else and minds everyone else's business. Unhealthy in the best of circumstances.

Peter Godwin, author of "Mukiwa", says that Africa is no longer a place for the white man. The white person has "had his day", he says. It would appear that he is being proven right. We have only to look at the many scourges ravaging this beautiful continent. The evil, corrupt, bigoted, totally selfish old men, whose only interest is to enrich themselves at the expense of their own people, are the worst of these infestations. What sane person would willingly annihilate everything around him and not give a damn, as long as his personal wealth increases? Yet this is the tragic legacy of Africa, and it seems to happen unchecked in numerous countries on this continent. Power corrupts. The leaders in question appeared, at one time, to have wonderful ideals. They announced their aims with conviction as being health care, education and housing for all their people. Why then do they destroy what is in place already, and make things worse rather than better?

Those of us now living overseas, who grew up in a close-knit, friendly society, and in an environment that is secure and spacious, have to adapt quickly to the jam-packed, competitive, cut-throat, hustle and bustle of the First World. We eke out a living in the cold, cramped cities of the UK, or we try our luck in Australia and the USA. The problem is that the grass is never greener, at least it isn't for me. Some people really come to terms with living abroad and learn to love the different way of life, but I think most of us miss the untamed beauty of the African bush and the splendour of the rugged terrain which is unmatched anywhere else. I miss the teeming herds of antelope and the amazing diversity of our African wildlife, with which no other continent can hope to compete. I miss that incredible, distinct smell of the first rains and the sunsets and the sounds that are peculiar to my country. A fury grows within me, as I helplessly acknowledge that we are letting these evil people do what they will to one of the last Edens on earth. They are raping it and getting away with outrages on a masive scale: we must not allow this sacrilege to continue.

Perhaps Mr Godwin will be proved right in the end, and Africa will fall over the edge of the abyss and sink into oblivion, becoming a black hole on this planet. I, however, would choose not to see a bleak future. With the emergence of viable opposition parties in Zimbabwe, we have a chance, a burning beacon on the horizon that is hope itself, and I pray with all my being that good will triumph over evil. Zimbabwe could become the Switzerland of Africa and an example to all the other nations on this tragic continent.

Every day I spend abroad, I feel guilty that members of the opposition are going through Hell for the love of their nation. I want to do something to help. I want to get off the fence and return to my own country. The people of Africa must be taught to expect certain standards of behaviour - standards that characterise the difference between the Third World and the First. In the USA, President Bill Clinton not so long ago, held up air traffic for a short while because he was having a haircut. The furore and the fuss that was made by the press and the public was incredible, and Mr Clinton apologised. This small offence is nothing compared to what happens regularly in Zimbabwe, where an aeroplane may be commandeered without prior notification by high-ranking government officials and without an apology. What a vast contrast in attitude. The difference is that people in the First World will not tolerate treatment of this sort, while in Africa, it may be accepted. These thought patterns need to change.

I love Zimbabwe and I hope and pray that we young people, both black and white, can all return soon to enjoy a prosperous and peaceful lifestyle in our own beautiful country.

Is the grass greener?

QUEUES AND QUEUING

his activity has become a way of life in today's Zimbabwe. If you are not queuing for petrol or diesel, you are queuing at the bank, at the post office, at the clinic and at the revenue hall to pay for your water and various licences. Imagine the number of man hours we all waste waiting, waiting, waiting...

It drives us crazy with frustration and desperation, when there are so many worthwhile and more profitable things to do. But we have no option - we have to feed our cars and trucks, we have to draw money and we have to seek treatment if we are ill.

How we appreciate it, if the queue is well organised and those who are queuing are kept well informed, especially if we are one hundred and twenty-seventh in line. Is it worth waiting, or will the fuel run out before we get to the pumps?

We all dine out on queuing stories. Some of these are amazing. Some are frightening, others are hysterically funny. We keep sane because we attempt to retain our senses of humour. We find ourselves able to cope with stress of this nature by trying to focus on the positive.

Interspersed in the pages that follow, you will have glimpses of Zimbabwe's queues and the people in them.

LET'S QUEUE IN ZIMBABWE

Let's queue in Zimbabwe, we'll show you some fun,
But if you won't queue I'm afraid you'll have none.
We queue to pay rates, and taxes and water,
At the ATM you may wait `till next quarter,

If you're from Paris, from London or Rome,
You've never had fun like this while at home.
For where is the challenge, the cherry on top,
When you can find it all quickly at any old shop?

Let's queue in Zimbabwe, the bank is the best,
A pensioner pushed in - treated him like the rest,
Just like Super 12 rugby, of the man on the ground,
If raked by the Kiwis, only pieces are found.

The fuel queue's a shocker, it's life or it's death,
You fight for your place, if it takes your last breath,
A guy pushed by my auntie, I'm afraid it was grim,
She called in her hit squad - her gardener nailed him.

Nothing to beat it - adrenaline rush to the head,
When you've got a full tank, you can go home to bed.
You know you can cruise for a week or ten days,
When you land a full tank, you're in quite a daze.

It's a sign of the times; because of the stress,
I've got acne again - my skin's such a mess!
But I'm really quite happy, to be like a child,
For when you're past 40, that really is wild!

We love our Zimbabwe - here you can't go to seed,
You must fight tooth and nail for all that you need!
You stay sharp and stay young, and if lucky you hoard.
We love this our country, where you never get bored.

64

PATRIOTISM

...Each new morn,
New widows howl, new orphans cry; new sorrows
Strike heaven on the face...
...Bleed, bleed, poor country!
Great tyranny, lay thou thy basis sure,
For goodness dare not check thee!

From "Macbeth" by William Shakespeare.

y brother, sister and I grew up in a country called Southern Rhodesia. We lived on a farm our parents had christened "Solitude", far from even the smallest village. It was a hard life for our parents in the 1950s, but for us children they were "golden-tawny days". We remember the wonderful freshness of those early mornings, the raindrops on the grass, the distant lowing of the cattle and the smell of the tobacco curing in the barns. We remember the river coming down in flood and the brown water swirling higher and higher until it broke the banks near the house. We remember the magic of Christmas. We remember the sound of a car gradually getting closer and closer, while we wondered who was coming to see us. We remember the fear and excitement of a cobra in our bedroom.

Many years ago, we were proud to be Rhodesians. Somehow, there was something very special about our nationality. We were the best. We had that pioneer spirit, we had guts and determination. We were the brightest jewel in Africa. Or, so we thought. In many ways we were. But it was an exclusively white concept. The blacks barely entered the equation. They were there, and we were concerned about them in a paternalistic way. It was our duty to make sure that they had food, clothing, shelter and medical care.

Aged 17, I went off to university in South Africa. I had been a boarder at school, so it wasn't too traumatic. I was amazed to find myself in an unmistakably liberal environment. So many of the students were activists and were agitating for an end to apartheid. My mother had warned me that, as a Rhodesian, I was both a visitor to South Africa and an ambassador for my own country, and I was, absolutely, under no circumstances, to get involved in any form of politics.

This was perfectly correct and convenient, as far as I was concerned. My only feeling of political conscience was irritation. Our residence committee had decided that every Wednesday evening we would give up either fruit or bread, on alternative weeks, and this would be a form of protest and a contribution to the poor and hungry. I found this infuriating, since I was always hungry myself. I really resented being forced by these conscience-stricken liberals to give up bread and oranges - especially bread.

And then there were these embarrassing women, who insisted on standing on street corners, dressed in black. This was a more serious and more daring protest against apartheid. Many of our own female students (South Africans, not Rhodesians!) had embraced this cause, and used to miss lectures to join other women in the centre of the city.

The lecturers were also very liberal and very anti-establishment. This was the time of the Vietnam War, something else I knew nothing about and was hardly aware of. But the lecturers talked of the horrors of war, and contrasted the terrifying realism of Siegfried Sassoon and Wilfred Owen with the cloying, romantic and unrealistic patriotism of Rupert Brooke. And the horror of war, indeed, seemed more real than Brooke's noble and idealistic words.

When UDI was declared, I was very excited at our courage and boldness and The Natal Witness took a photograph of a few other Rhodesian students and me sending a congratulatory telegram to Ian Smith. How we resented the Brits, who had sold us out.

I finished university and returned to Rhodesia, got married and became a teacher. The African Nationalist Parties, ZANU and ZAPU, had embarked upon a "liberation war", which was largely futile until the mid '70s, when, with assistance from the government of recently independent Mozambique, they began to make serious headway in infiltrating and enlisting the aid of rural black people.

The years went by, and it became increasingly clear that Ian Smith's Rhodesian Front regime was not going to work and that it was based purely on white self-interest. My husband and I joined the Rhodesia Party, which had noble ideals, but these were never consummated. They and the Centre Party seemed to have the best interests of the country at heart, but they could not convince the white electorate that the rigidly racist RF had little chance of holding the reins of power for much longer.

Then the election of 1980 took place and Robert Mugabe became the leader of Zimbabwe. The white population was absolutely stunned. We had been led to believe that the transition from Zimbabwe Rhodesia to Zimbabwe would be a gentle one, since there was no doubt as to who was going to win the election. Bishop Abel Muzorewa, a mild and Christian man, would be taking over - it was a foregone conclusion. Instead, the man elected to the most powerful position in the country was one of the leaders of the "Liberation Struggle". "Terrorists" had become "Comrades" and "freedom fighters" overnight.

We whites wondered what would happen to us. Should we leave immediately or wait and see, as we had done so often in the past? Mugabe impressed us, at first, with his conciliatory attitude and with his apparent desire for peace and prosperity for everyone. Those who had "taken the gap" to South Africa often secretly wondered if they had done the right thing. Their friends in Zimbabwe were fine, it seemed. Not much had changed, they still had their pleasant homes, their businesses, their boats on Lake Kariba, their holidays outside the country.

And the years went on. We, whites took a back seat. We were there, and yet we were shadows. We would look upon this Zimbabwe and shake our heads at inefficiency, and at corruption (still at this stage, on a minor scale), arrogantly and patronisingly. "Wouldn't happen if we were in charge," we'd say to one another. "See how standards have dropped. Shocking, isn't it?"

In the background, during this period, there was an on-going power struggle between the ZANU PF and the ZAPU forces. These were the days of Gukurahundi, where thousands of innocent rural Matabele people were slaughtered in a terror campaign mounted by the ruling party. I know so little about this. I am ashamed. Only now is the extent of the atrocities being made public by human rights activists. The present government will, I am sure, "reap the whirlwind" in the not too distant future.

The closest we came to any sort of action was the battle up the road near the Hill Top Motel in Bulawayo. Mortars were fired and we spent a couple of hours crouched in the shower, as it seemed the safest place in the house. Amazingly, the children slept through the noise and confusion. It sounded as though a war was being waged in our back garden, but it was actually about a kilometre away. The next day the people of Bulawayo were confined to their homes, as they waited uneasily to see what would happen.

The Unity Accord sorted out these problems, ostensibly, and the years went on. Corruption became more and more blatant, and more and more, a fact of life. We would shake our heads, becoming immune to each new revelation, each new scam, each new manipulation or embezzlement. And the people became poorer and poorer. Jobs became more and more scarce. A chosen few people in the higher echelons of politics and society became more and more powerful and increasingly prosperous. News of wild spending sprees abroad reached us in Zimbabwe, and we shrugged in contempt, distancing ourselves further from these outrages.

At the beginning of the year 2000, suddenly, our political consciences were awakened. Suddenly, we could do something, and suddenly, we had to do something. And we did. The government lost the referendum on their proposed new constitution. This would have entrenched the power of the ruling party. They had expected their cowed subjects to allow them to do anything they wanted. They were shocked at their defeat. The people, who had been submissive for so long, had stood up and had voted "No". It wasn't only "No" to the proposed new constitution. It was "No" to everything that had been going on. "No" to corruption. "No" to bad governance. "No" to exploitation. "No" to poverty. No. No. No. The people had found their voice at last.

Suddenly, with the advent of the MDC (The Movement for Democratic Change) which had arisen from the populist trade union movement in September 1999, there appeared to be a chance for something different - for change. A change for the better. A chance, at last, of electing an honest and competent government. The referendum result seemed to add credence to this view. Suddenly, there was hope for the future. It seemed that there was, after all, a limit to the tolerance of the electorate for the gross corruption and folly of ZANU PF. They could no longer hide behind their status as the liberators of Zimbabwe.

For years we whites had felt helpless and detached. For years we had been a small minority whose important and valuable role in business, farming and the various sectors of the economy was resented by the ruling party. For years we had had to listen to the sneering "-isms": colonialism, capitalism, imperialism, racism etc. (Not of course, communism or socialism). Our voice had not been meaningful, because of our small numbers. We could only be spectators.

The nation held its breath. What would our President say after the beating the government had taken? How would he respond? His apparent reaction was that he had accepted the verdict of the people. He publicly stated that the people had spoken and that the government would respect the will of the people with regard to the "No" vote. This was far from being the case, for action had already been taken to preserve the power of ZANU PF. The election was only months away and the government had realised that it had completely misread the feelings of the people. It did not have the support it thought it had. So ZANU PF unleashed against its own people the dogs of war. A calculated terror campaign was put into effect to subdue and crush Zimbabweans, and to annihilate them, if necessary.

The government decided to make land its call to arms. White farms were invaded, farmers attacked and black farm workers victimised, intimidated and brutally assaulted. So-called "War Veterans", most of them in their twenties, were employed by the government to occupy farms to prevent farmers and their employees from working to provide food for the nation and tobacco to earn much-needed foreign currency. Murder, rape and mayhem became the order of the day. In the towns, MDC supporters were assaulted. Petrol and diesel supplies faltered and often ran out altogether, and queues of every type of vehicle imaginable snaked about the streets. Life became chaotic.

We know the outcome of the June election. And we know what has happened since. And we know that the next step is the Presidential Election in 2002, or sooner. We know that what we have seen so far is only a taste of what is to come. The MDC has called this year "the end game".

But what really happened during the months of February to June 2000 and the months since then, when all the violence and terror was unleashed? We, the people of Zimbabwe, have developed a sense of unity. For the first time, the majority of blacks and whites have found themselves with a common purpose. This is survival. This is the desire for change. This is "No" to the perpetuation of corruption, of misuse of power, of being ground into the dust beneath the feet of an arrogant, amoral few.

We, whites, have found our voice again. We have learned once more what the word "patriotic" means. No longer will we stand as observers, looking through the window like the creatures in "Animal Farm", watching Napoleon and the other pigs behaving disgracefully. No longer will we countenance the idea that "some are more equal than others". They are not. We want to make a difference and be part of a new and proud Zimbabwe. We want to be counted and do what we can to help. No longer will we be lotus-eaters, dreamily shuddering at chaos in a distant, detached fashion. We belong here, we are part of what is here and we want to help to make it work.

SAVANNAH TALES:
IT'S COLD IN THE SAVANNAH

Looking down at a pool of water, depthless
Reflecting the hollow in my once-being
A soulless echo of a used-to-be life.

 uring the day when the sun burns hot and angry on the dry savannah plains and refreshing rain and a cool breeze are a distant thread of dream unreachable for the ordinary animal, Lutala and I are on the run. We shimmer through the tall grass like the mambas and the cobras have taught us, burying our tails between our legs like the cowards we have become. We run from sun-up till sundown and we do not stop for food or water or shelter. During the night we sleep in makeshift hollows scraped into the ground as the dogs have taught us. Sometimes the rain comes and our hollows flood and we are swept across the plains and sometimes the wind is cold like ice and our fingers are so numb we can't tell if they exist until the dawn.

Each morning we wake up, shake off the drops, flex our fingers and move on. It is a hard life but it is the only one we have now. They say Kugona committed suicide, but whoever heard of a rabbit killing himself. He was found hanging from a branch of the big msasa tree at the edge of the clearing and no one really understands how he got there. The tree is so high, unclimable for us tiny creatures, and when did they teach rabbits how to tie knots and where did he get the twine that hangs only from the trees in the forests at Hwange? So many questions and no answers that make any sense, but I know he was murdered, and why.

Jongwe, the bespectacled self-proclaimed herald of the savannah, screeched a long and irritating whine into the dawn. "Ceetzehns orv thee Sarvannah! Ceetzehns órv thee Sarvannah!" (He has taken to saying everything twice as if he could make us believe it the more times he says it or make him believe it, I'm not sure.) "Ceetzehns, we hehv reezorn to believe thaht there are tretahs amongist us. Tretahs amongist us. We weel storp eht nutheeng, we weel noht leave any storn untehned, storping eht nutheeng, nutheeng, to mehk sure thut theez tretahs are brought to justeece, justeece I seh!" By that he did not mean the courts of law or the upholders of the law but a two-headed baboon called Justeece. Let me tell you about Justeece.

He used to be on our side, once long ago, believing in truth and fairness and equality, content with his one head. Then Biguana, our "honourable" life-emperor of the Savannah gave him another much bigger head and Justeece suddenly required more space in which to live, more food for his second head and before long, his second head had bullied his much smaller, far too timid first head into submission. Of course, as in all good fairy-tales, the second head was evil and insane. Justeece climbed all the way up the social ladder until he was second in Biguana's favour only to Jongwe, the bespectacled chicken and H-h-h-hyena. Together they formed a seemingly invincible team, Justeece letting the rule of law slip through his fingers, Jongwe writing and reporting wild fantasies to cover up the truth and H-h-h-hyena committing all the crimes that Justeece never saw because the eyes of both heads were only open to the pictures that Biguana wanted him to see.

So it was that on that fateful day, twenty honest, upright citizens of the savannah, rabbits, bats, elephants and chimpanzees, were rounded up and herded through the grass into the clearing where they keep the starving lions. Kugona was one of these animals.

It did not seem possible but Kugona escaped somehow, his small frame flitting through the tall grass bordering the clearing and his tiny rabbit legs flying far and fast through the red dust. It took them two days to recapture him. We found him hanging on the msasa tree the next morning. Everyone says that the Hyena-Baboon comradeship silenced him or punished him or killed him by mistake while trying to beat a confession out of him. Jongwe says Kugona killed himself because he was a "tretah" who couldn't bear to live with his "tretahrous" ways any longer. Funny, but I believe Everyone.

When Kugona died, Lutala and I decided that this struggle could no longer be fought in daylight, in the open. So we ran. We need to get to safety now, to the caves that Biguana is afraid to enter because he fears the mudzimus of all the animals he has killed, and when we reach the caves, we will begin to plan our secret war.

The savannah grows more dry each day, the leafless trees a constant reminder of the great fire that burned the birds' houses down, and the lake is no longer a lake, just a few scattered pools here and there, under guard of the baboons and the hyenas. There is very little left for us to lose, our pride, our dignity, our beloved vleis. Lutala and I and the hundreds of other animals we've met along the way realise that each day that Biguana stays in charge of the savannah we lose a little more. Someday it might be our lives. Worse than that, it might be the whole savannah, the place where we have lived and loved since time began.

We cannot let this happen. There will be an uprising. We have decided. Rabbits, bats, monkeys, elephants, snakes, every animal that crawls or flies or breathes, every animal that believes in truth and justice, will fight and we will not be quelled. We will shout loud and long and hold our heads high and our sticks and stones even higher and we will prevail, make no mistake. It may take a long time but we won't give up or give in and we will not starve to death as Biguana hopes. Contrary to expectation, we have discovered an alternative food supply to peanuts. Our friends, the elephants have introduced us to Amarula and Masawa and just yesterday Lutala discovered a round, swelled cactus filled to the brim with water. Even my lips are showing signs of promise.

Farisai

From our correspondence...

Dear "Farisai"

"Savannah Tales" was sent to me over the e-mail a couple of months back and I think it's a very moving and beautifully written piece. Your phrase, "We shimmer through the tall grass..." will stay in my mind always... We would very much like to include your story in our book...

The reply:

Thank you for your letter. I am touched by your words of encouragement and to realise that the words I write are touching the hearts of people I never imagined they would reach...

Farisai

"I like the dreams of the future better than the history of the past."

❈❖❈❈❖❈

...AND MY TRIBE IS SCATTERED

Woman of the fields, woman of the rivers,
Woman of the great river banks,
O, my mother, I am thinking of you.

Enoch Nyalunga "Cries of the Heart"

he plane is hot and humid. I settle down in my window seat with a briefcase full of work. So far, so good. The seat next to me is empty - perhaps I'll have the whole row to myself! After working until the early hours, I am exhausted.

My train of thought is disrupted by the air hostess, who helps an elderly lady down the aisle. She drops with difficulty into the seat beside me and smiles, mopping the perspiration from her brow, and searching for a place to put her well-worn handbag.

Despite the heat, she is dressed in a thick woollen jersey, a well-padded anorak and a hand-knitted woollen hat. Perched on top at a careful angle is a smart black felt hat.

"Tsk, tsk, tsk," she exclaims, shaking her head. "It is too hot!" "Can I help?" I say. "You will feel better if you take off your jersey and anorak." After a slight struggle, both garments are stowed safely in the storage area above and the felt hat rests on the empty aisle seat. The woollen hat remains firmly in place. I am curious.

"Where have you been?"
"Canada."
"Who were you visiting?"
"My daughter, she is a nurse."
"Did you enjoy it?"
"Yes, Canada is number one!
It is cheap. Too much.
$20 for a nice dress.
Nice food. Cheap.
Canada is good.
But too much rain. And it is cold.
I get very sick. (Her cough is hollow).

But there is money
And my daughter is happy.
Zimbabwe ... it has changed.
Too expensive
People starving. No food.
No money.
No job.
Before, when I was small, it was good.
King George was good.
The *Mukiwa prime minister was good.
This government is not good.
Today no *gwaai, no beans.
No pumpkins - before plenty pumpkins.
Today no jobs, no food.
And no pension.
Before there was pension.
I have no pension...
I have nothing."

For a few moments we both ponder in silence. Then she draws back
the broken zip on her bag and tucks her papers away neatly into a
brown envelope.

"You have children?"
"No - no children." (She shakes her head in sympathy).
"Me - I have four."
"I go one month to one, one month to another.
Three months in Canada.
My daughter likes Canada.
But it is cold.
Only $5 for meat - too much meat!
And vegetables, many vegetables.
Here I eat spinach. And cabbage.
Sometimes pumpkin. No meat.
There are no jobs.
No factories. No businesses.
Rent is too high.
No money, no school.
The children suffer."

The air hostess brings food. Yogurt, a roll and a meusli bar. I offer the
meusli bar to her and, behind her thick glasses, her eyes light up with

delight. She packs it carefully into the bag with her bar and I wonder what little child will peel back the paper with even greater delight. With the generosity of one who has so little, but is accustomed to share, she passes me her yogurt. I hesitate and then take it. She needs it more, but I do not want to appear rude. We sip our tea in silence for a while.

"Can you open?" She passes me the chicken roll wrapped in thick protective plastic. I hand it back and she munches thoughtfully, her small fingers misshapen with arthritis. These are fingers which, over the years, have crocheted and knitted clothing for children and grandchildren, for family members, friends and those in need. Today it would be difficult.

The plane drops steadily and the trees in the vast expanse of bush before the runway take on individual forms. She reaches for my hand and holds it tightly. "Going down is not so good. I am afraid."

I tell her that flying is quite safe. That it is safer than travelling in a bus. She smiles and continues to hold my hand tightly.

The plane drops heavily onto the tarmac and comes to rest outside the airport building. She peers through the window to see if her family is waiting.

"Can you open?" I hesitate. "No, this window does not open." She laughs cheerfully at herself and the air hostess comes to help her from her seat. I carry her jersey and my luggage as she walks painfully down the stairs, helped by the friendly hostess.

When she is seated comfortably in the wheelchair, I take her hand and wish her a safe journey. She smiles with the satisfaction of one who has travelled a great distance, who has seen wonderful places in another world, but is pleased to be home.

❖ ❖ ❖

⊠ Mukiwa - a white person

⊠ gwaai - tobacco

WHERE HAVE ALL THE FLOWERS GONE?

 t's Sunday morning. I lie in bed, dreaming I'm with my son and his friends in London...

What do you think they are thinking about when they are creating chaos back home? Surely they can see that everything is going down hill.

It is not going down hill for them. They're still fine; it's only the rest of us that are affected. They want to stay in power, because, if they don't then they will start suffering.

Maybe, but things are going to start hitting home for the average person pretty soon.

Well, the way I see it, whatever happens, things will seem better in the rural areas in the short term. Presumably people with new land will be better off initially than they were, and the places they left will be less crowded. The problem will only show itself when things get so bad in the towns, that people are forced to return home to the rural areas.

I wonder how long that will take.

Well, it may take a couple of years.

How do you think that things will turn out?

I reckon that, if they lose, the situation will change quite quickly, but if they win, then things are going to take much longer. I still think there will be change, but it will be a more difficult process.

Will it be worth going home to?

Depends on what you want.

What do you mean?

Well, if you want fast cars, plenty of money and something to do on a Saturday night, then I would say no. But if you want to enjoy nature, live a simple life with a wife and a few kids, then I would say yes.

Exactly.

When all this is over, I want to settle back home.

Me too, but only when it's safe, and things are looking up again. You know what? Living here gives you a little more perspective, and I am wondering if maybe I should consider Zambia or Mozambique.

Ja, that is a good point. I have never been to either place.

What! You have lived your whole life in Zim, and have never been to Zambia?

What can I say? We always spent our holidays in South Africa. One problem back home is the chicks.

Have you noticed that most of them are doing better than we are over here, and they are all doing much better than they could ever do back home? Who is going to want to come home with you and live in the bush?

Hey, you're right.
Well, I think you should save as much money as you can. Maybe money
will buy you happiness.

6 o'clock, Monday morning. I yawn and stretch over to press the button on top of the coffee maker. I doze for another few minutes and then turn to touch my husband's side. Empty. I know where he is. By the time the coffee is brewed he's back...

Nothing. Maybe tomorrow.

This routine is repeated almost every morning. Our son has been gone six months now. He's good at keeping in touch. He e-mails two or three times a week, so we still feel part of his life. We're happy that he's there - in London - seemingly doing well, but we miss him. We're beginning to feel our age, our isolation.

Tuesday morning. At the local shopping mall. There are plenty of whites here - white faces, white hair. Most of the shops give 10% off for pensioners. There are many familiar faces...

How are you, George?
Oh, I've just got back from overseas. Went over to see the boys. Both
are working in London now - doing well. David's married, as you
know - that nice girl from Harare. Remember he met her at a sailing
regatta? Met up again in London. Oh, yes, there were plenty of kids
there that you would remember from our sailing days. They stick
together those kids - give each other a lot of support. Help each other
to settle down. It's hard over there, hard to fit in, get established. A
lot of them live together, rent one of those big houses, and then share
out the bedrooms - sometimes there are fifteen of them in a house. Yes,
they stick together, have good times, but, do you know, every man jack
of them - at least the ones I spoke to - dreams of coming back - one
day.

Wednesday morning. I'm in town alone, shopping. I see an ex-pupil from way back, but I recognize him immediately.

It's Martin, isn't it? Martin Sibanda?
Yes, ma'am. I've been away for six years, studying and working in
Canada. I'd love to return to Canada or the States. Life there is stress
free. Race doesn't matter in Canada. No-one cares who runs the
country, as long as one's prosperity is guaranteed. Politics there is

seldom discussed - there's no need to agonize over such matters. Yes, compared to the situation here now, life was wonderful there. But of course I missed Africa. Imagine growing up in the sunshine and then having to cope with being indoors most of the time during their long winters. That first winter I felt disoriented and muddled. I used to set my alarm an hour earlier than I needed, just so that I'd have time to wake up properly and try to adjust. When I realized I was suffering from vitamin D deficiency, I began to go outside and walk in the snow, even though the temperature was minus twenty degrees!

I hate it here now. I'm repulsed by the death rate caused by AIDS, by the corruption and the poverty. I hate the way people seem so resigned to their fate, and all the time more people are leaving. In my spare time I coach the under 15 rugby team at our old school. I don't mind spending my own money helping those boys to get the practice and competition they need. But sometimes it all seems futile. Just as my tight five were getting really good, I found out four of the boys' mothers are nurses and they're all emigrating either to the States or England at the end of this season.

Wednesday afternoon. Bridge. Four aging women, all with children out of the country, their hopes of being with them, here, in the land they all love, perhaps watching grandchildren grow up, fading into dreams. But it's particularly sad today as Sam is leaving. She's been lonely since her husband died, and now she's decided to join her son and his family...

I'm dreading the thought of living in Jo'burg. Just the idea of driving in all that traffic turns my knees to jelly. But James says he needs me to help him in his new business, and it will be so good to be with little Lawrence. As you know, since Tony died, he's become the light of my life.
How's Michael?
Well, he worked all the hours God sent in London, so that he could go over to Canada and be with Naz over Christmas. Her folks just couldn't afford to bring her back to Zim this time. Naz wrote and said that he was beside himself when the 'right kind of snow fell', and he dragged her out of the warm flat to help him make a snowman in the middle of the night! By the time they'd finished it was six feet tall, and it survived for two months! He made snow angels, too, but was only allowed to do them when Naz wasn't around. I suppose the sight of a six foot seven inch man, lying in the snow and moving his arms and legs around to carve out the shape of an angel, would have attracted attention! When he had to leave to return to London he left sweet little notes for Naz everywhere - reminding her to eat properly, to check the

door was locked etc... She only found them much later - in her slippers, or the pocket of her coat.

The one in her bus pass caused a lot of embarrassment. When college restarted she just opened the pass and gave it to the bus driver without thinking. When he began to give her strange looks she checked. There was Michael's note, saying: "I love you - look after your back!"

What's your Paul doing now?

Oh, he loves it in London. He's working hard, still temping, which he likes, because he can make up his salary by working so much overtime. He and his mess-mates rented a cottage in Wales over Christmas. They were lucky, too, as they saw snow for the first time in their lives. He phoned us at two o'clock in the morning, just to tell us how beautiful it was!

But it was good to hear from him in anyway. It was the first time our family had ever been apart over Christmas, and I missed him so much.

Thursday morning. Coffee with a friend in town...

Oh, I loved it in Birmingham. I would have stayed - I was promised a temporary teaching post there. It was so wonderful to be with the boys. Jabulani is running his own mess there. I couldn't believe how spotless and organized it was. He obviously learnt more from his time at boarding school here than just academic subjects! There are six of them in the mess, including Vusa, and they take it in turns to shop and cook - wonderfully organized. I couldn't believe it. Jabulani has just finished his degree at university, and Vusa is starting a course in computers - you remember how good he is with them? Jabulani has a Bosnian girlfriend. I didn't get to meet her, but I guessed it was serious. I wonder how she will fit in here if he marries her?

Why? Does he want to come back here?

Of course. Although he was born in England, he's a true Zimbabwean.

Friday afternoon. Relaxing at home, reading the weekly newspaper. The news is depressing as usual. I skip to the letters page. There's one from a girl called Nomazwe...

What are you people doing in Zimbabwe? Why can't you solve the country's problems?

Why do I have to be here in London? I have a good education. I have 'A' levels.

And yet, I'm here away from my family. I have to clean offices - high-

rise buildings in this alien city, so that I can send my mother £100 a month. Without this, what would she live on?

Saturday morning. The phone rings...

Can I speak to Noma's grandmother?

We call Evelyna. We know she's expecting the call. Her son-in-law phones every Saturday. He and Sezeni are settled in Jo'burg now, but their three children are here. And it's time for school fees...

What did he tell you, Evelyna?
Ah, he said the money had been stolen - there in Jo'burg. He can't send anything yet. But school starts on Tuesday, and Noma's doing form four. Without the fees, ah! she can't go back.
Oh, it's three and a half thousand a term for Noma's school and then there's the books - another five thousand. Then there's the other two children - they're both in school now. What'll we do?

Sunday morning. I lie in bed, dreaming. I'm with my son and his friends in London...

Hey! Good to see you.
You too! What's up?
How long have you been in London?
A few months. You?
About four.
Enjoying it?
The weather is pretty depressing at this time of year, but once you get used to it, it's not too bad.
Ja, to be honest, I thought it would be worse.
Been out anywhere good?
Just a couple of pubs, nothing special.
Not exactly our Ivy League back home.
I was sick and tired of going to the same old place every weekend, but, you know what? It was actually a great pub.
Ja, and the chicks!
Sure, but they're all over here now.
You're right. There is no one left back home.
I heard that Gillie might be coming in a couple of months.
Gillie! Things must be getting bad. That guy had only just got back from South Africa and he had all those grand ideas of what he was going to do.
Well, that's what I heard.
Do you know that it takes me about an hour to get to work and an hour

to get home. There just seem to be no hours left in the day.
I know what you mean. Time just flies by in this place, because it's just work, sleep, work, sleep. No time to relax and enjoy yourself. Just ask guys who've been here two or three years. They say it's as if they arrived yesterday.
It's a recipe for midlife crisis! One moment you are in your twenties, the next you're forty, and you don't know where those twenty years went!
Anyway, when are you going home to see the folks?
Next month. You?
Maybe May. I tell you what. The first thing I'll do when I get home is go straight to Cape to Cairo for a big rump steak.
Sounds great! You're right. I have had to walk past those Angus Steak Houses every day on my way to work, and I'm dying for a steak.
Ja. You know what I'm looking forward to? Sun.
For me it's not the sun, so much as the heat. When you are at Lake Kariba, sitting in the hot sun with a cold Castle in your hand, there's nothing better.
Somehow, beer always tastes best on the Lake or on the Zambezi. Once, when we were coming back from Shabani at night, we were feeling a little thirsty, so we pulled into the Why Not Bar, and we ordered some beers. They took them out of a huge chest freezer. Mmmm they were beautiful.
Man, that's mean. Tell me, what are we doing so far from home?
Waiting!
Waiting?
Most of us are waiting for Zim to hit rock bottom, and then they'll realize they need us again. Then we can go home and start from scratch.
How long do you think it will take?
Not long, I hope. But I met some people who left when it was Rhodesia, and they're still waiting.

And so the weeks pass, and we go on waiting. Waiting for the madness to end, for the rule of law to return, for the politicians to realize that, in losing our young people, we're losing the real wealth of our nation. We're waiting to show the world that we're all Zimbabweans who love this land and that we can be united by a common purpose: to rebuild our beautiful country and bring our children home.

KARIBA

Stillness ...silence ... emptiness
Is broken by the murmuring
Of birds as misty vapours rise
Before the early dawn.

Silver water stretches
Till it merges with the sky to form
Unlimited horizons widened
Endlessly beyond.

Hugely round and orange
Comes the slowly rising sun to touch
The naked whitened branches
With its glow.

Skeletons of forests
Reach in frozen supplication,
Silent protest at their stolen
Right to grow.

This day will bring strong winds to hurl
Their force unstemmed across the lake
To sweep the water into waves
Of ocean strength till in their wake
Is debris flung in careless piles,
The action of a monster child
Whose temper rages for a while,
Then vanishes to show a smile.

The great Zambezi valley,
Bathed in sunlight holds the sleeping power
That wakes to wild destructive rage
Or nourishes a flower.

ZIMBABWE'S WILDLIFE HERITAGE

*This we know: the Earth does not belong
to man, man belongs to the Earth.
All things are connected like the blood that
connects us all. Man did not weave the web
of life, he is merely a strand in it. Whatever
he does to the web, he does to himself.*

Chief Seattle in a letter to US President Franklin Pierce, 1855

was born in Bulawayo, Southern Rhodesia in 1946, the elder of two children. My parents were also born in Southern Rhodesia and my Scottish grandparents were early settlers, arriving in 1899.

Zimbabwe has been home to me for 54 years and I make no apologies for being white, as I consider myself a true Zimbabwean.

While I'm sure the years before 1946 would have had their periods of uncertainty, I look back over the past 45 years from about 1955, and realize that this wonderful country has always been in the grip of one crisis or another.

During the '60s and '70s I was privileged to travel to some of the remotest areas of Zimbabwe, where I was able to enjoy and appreciate the splendour of our wonderful wildlife, for me one of our finest natural heritages.

It was during the mid-eighties that my already considerable interest and concern for wildlife and the environment developed, and I joined the Matabeleland Branch of the Wildlife Society of Zimbabwe. This organisation had been formed in 1927, its prime objective being to promote the welfare of wildlife. This was to be the beginning of a serious involvement for me in numerous crisis situations affecting our wildlife.

Geographically, Bulawayo, my home town, lies more or less in the centre of Matabeleland Province, where there are many national parks, the largest of which is Hwange National Park, which I rate as one of the finest. In addition, the province has, as a result of limited agricultural

84

development, numerous game farms and conservancies.

There are eleven National Parks in Zimbabwe. I have visited all but Gonarezhou, situated in the southeast. I am obviously more concerned with the parks in Matabeleland, these being Victoria Falls and Kazuma Pans in the north, Hwange, midway between Bulawayo and the Victoria Falls, Matopos south west of Bulawayo and Chizarira situated on the edge of the Zambezi escarpment overlooking Kariba and the Zambezi valley.

Once I joined the Wildlife Society of Zimbabwe in 1986, my interest in Hwange National Park increased dramatically. Probably the most significant influence was my regular participation in the annual Game Count Census in the Park organised by The Matabeleland Branch of the Wildlife Society. This enabled me to visit some of the remotest and most beautiful places. My love for the Park grew, and I was fortunate enough to experience wonderful sightings of some of the world's most interesting wildlife and birds. This, for me, was totally exhilarating.

Sadly, however, Hwange (and the rest of the parks in Zimbabwe) started to deteriorate to a horrifying degree after independence in 1980. Each time one visited the parks, it was more and more evident that management structures were disintegrating, as an unsympathetic central treasury saw fit to reduce financial assistance and squander money on what it thought to be more important issues. It also became apparent that within the headquarters of the Department of National Parks and Wildlife Management, internal squabbles were the order of the day, with most members of the Department, from the director down, concerned only with personal gain. I felt that this would lead to the complete breakdown of the parks. They were just not interested. It was crisis management by basically uncommitted executives.

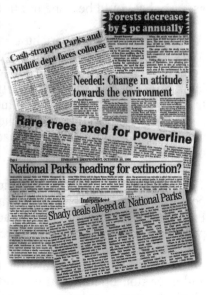

On numerous occasions I was approached by men in the field pleading that I try to do something to rectify the appalling situation that was developing. Many of those who appealed to me were extremely capable, dedicated men whose only thought was for the well-being of the wildlife and the environment. This attitude of responsible concern certainly didn't filter through to their superiors, most of whom were political appointees.

It became evident that Hwange was heading for a crisis, as there was inadequate funding and poor management, and the aging equipment responsible for the game's water supplies was deteriorating. In addition, the accommodation facilities, road conditions and the whole infrastructure were nothing less than a disgrace. Although these aspects were not directly related to wildlife, it was extremely embarrassing, for a Zimbabwean to witness the outraged attitude of tourists, many of whom indicated they would never return to Zimbabwe. In the early 1990s Hwange experienced a number of poor rainy seasons and droughts which depleted the surface water and underground reserves. It was quite clear that we were going to lose thousands of animals if the situation wasn't rectified.

I had recently become Chairman of the Branch and our committee decided to do a complete survey of all the boreholes in the Park to assess what could be done to alleviate the shortage of water.

As Parks could give us very little information, we were given permission to conduct the survey ourselves and eight society members in three vehicles departed from Hwange Main Camp, in June 1994. Ten days later, after covering approximately 1250 kms in the Park, we returned to Main Camp, completely disillusioned and horrified at what we had seen. Out of a possible 54 boreholes that could be pumped, only six were running, with four of these being maintained by local safari operators.

The Parks management had sufficient funds to operate only two. But perhaps for me, the worst shock was when I approached Nyamandhlovu Pan, some 10 kms from Park headquarters. This probably is the most popular pan in the Park from a viewing perspective. I found numerous vehicles parked there and irate tourists swarming about the viewing platform, frustrated because the pan was absolutely dry. The pump had been non-operational for some considerable time. In particular, elephants were becoming increasingly agitated at the situation, their probing trunks investigating every little recess in the mud for the slightest moisture.

I returned immediately to Main Camp headquarters to enquire as to why and how this situation had occurred, only to find, as was normally the case, that the warden in charge could not be located. I returned to Bulawayo, and the following day was, to my amazement, able to contact this individual by phone to register my concern about Nyamandhlovu Pan. I was absolutely bewildered when he said that he was unaware of any problem at the pan. This clearly indicated the direction in which the Park was heading. It also occurred to me that, way back in 1928, when Hwange was first proclaimed a National Park (in an area about which very little was known) the first Warden of Hwange, Ted Davison, in his first two years, covered 2000 miles on foot and on horseback in the Park. He experienced extreme difficulties, which included marauding lions, lack of water and malaria, in order to learn as much as he could about the Park. And here, the current warden, with a Landrover at his disposal, parked in front of his office, was not aware that the most popular viewing pan in his Park, a stone's throw away, was bone-dry. This was a crisis. We had to do something. We had to get involved.

As in any situation of this urgency, the first priority was finance. How and where were we going to get the hundreds of thousands of dollars required for such an exercise? Fundraise, yes, but this would take time and the amounts raised would probably be meagre in relation to what was required. We had to find sponsors, people who were sympathetic to the cause. It was decided that our initial approach would be to the safari and tourist companies, operating not just in the area but countrywide, and so the huge task of contacting every possible source to assist in financing the resuscitation of game water supplies in Hwange commenced.

We had to move quickly, as the situation was desperate. We probably still had five months before any meaningful rainfall could be expected and we were certainly going to lose animals. How many depended on how soon we could commission the pumps. There was no time to start ordering new engines. We had to repair the existing engines and pumps which were all well past their prime, having been donated to the Hwange National Park by the Indian Government in 1986 as part of a government to government aid programme. An unexpected reaction from potential sponsors was that they felt that this was not their responsibility, but that of the government.

Tour Operators were being charged high licence fees, and various questions were being asked. Where was this money? What was it being used for? Why was the Park in this desperate situation? We all knew the answers, but this was not the time for questions. We had to save one of the finest game parks in the world. One suggestion was that government was deliberately withholding assistance in an effort to prove that the parks were a liability and should be opened up for resettlement. I, personally, felt this was unlikely, since the parks were vital to our tourist industry.

Fortunately, as time progressed, we were able to convince the sponsors that we needed their help. Donations and sponsorship came in from all sections of the tourist industry and from numerous other donors, whether they were involved in Hwange or not, and work started on patching up the pumps and engines to get us through to the rainy season.

I discussed the situation in Hwange with the then President of the Wildlife Society, and we decided that a full report be written and a meeting organised with the Minister responsible for Environment and Tourism, detailing the seriousness of the situation. The report was duly completed, and the President of the Society and I met with the Minister in July 1994.

This meeting was very cordial, with the Minister expressing shock and surprise at the report, and indicating that he was unaware of any problems in Hwange. He did report to Parliament about the seriousness of this situation shortly after our meeting, only to be shouted down, and asked why he was so concerned about animals, when there were a number of areas in Zimbabwe where people were in the same predicament, which was a fact. My answer to this was that people can appeal for help, animals can't.

With finances now more readily available, rehabilitation work continued with committee members of the Branch, all of whom were volunteers, spending much of their spare time delivering and collecting engines and pumps, purchasing oil and diesel, and ensuring pump attendants' rations were received. Unfortunately, there were still the few who criticized our actions, insisting that nature should take its course, and if the animals were destined to die through lack of water, we should not interfere. I felt that man had introduced all these artificial pans to supply water to the animals as far back as the 1930s for the benefit of the tourists, and since the animals had become reliant on them, we had an obligation to ensure that water was available for them in the dry winter months. Assistance and support increased almost daily, and it was on one of my trips to the Park that I met a British volunteer soldier who was a part of a twelve-man team from the Royal Electrical and Mechanical Engineers. He told me that they had all paid their own airfares to Zimbabwe and had teamed up with National Parks to assist where they could concerning the problems being experienced in the Park. During their two-week stay in Hwange they had managed to repair a number of pumps as well as five motorcycles. On their departure, they commented that they were full of admiration for what the Park's staff had managed to achieve given the limited equipment available to them. They did, however, find the working conditions unsatisfactory and unhealthy, since workers were often literally swimming in diesel and had to use the most basic of equipment.

It was significant that the Minister of Environment and Tourism, whom I'd met about a month before, when commenting on the British volunteers assisting parks said, "Nobody appears to have the faintest idea how many boreholes and pumping stations there are in Hwange National Park, let alone how many are actually operational. Independent sources cite between 60 and 69 while nobody at National Parks headquarters could volunteer an answer apart from saying 38 were in the Main Camp area." He continued,"This is alarming to say the least, given the on-going water crisis facing wildlife in what is one of the largest national conservation areas in the world." He obviously had not read my report to him where all these details were given following our survey.

Unbeknown to me at the time, Cable News Network (CNN) was also in Hwange covering the situation and interviewing members of the Royal Engineers, who must have indicated that I was in the Park. The following morning CNN asked whether I would be available for an interview.

This interview was shown on TV worldwide the following day on eight consecutive hourly news bulletins. Almost immediately, I received phone calls from friends in various parts of the world saying they had seen it. From something that had been initiated quite by chance, we now had got our message across to the international community.

Work on the engines and pumps continued furiously, with most of the help at this stage coming from local people and companies.

Out of the blue one morning, a very concerned lady called Nancy Abrahams, phoned from New York. She had been to Zimbabwe some years before and had visited Hwange National Park, which she indicated had been the highlight of her trip. She had heard of our problems in Hwange and was devastated to think that all those beautiful animals, and, in particular, the elephants " maybe gonna die" and she wanted to help.

I indicated that it was very likely that we could lose large numbers of animals, but that we were doing our best to prevent this from happening. Her immediate reaction was, "This just can't happen. A friend and I wanna send you US$20 000. Please send me your banking details so that I can transfer the money as soon as possible." I was completely taken aback. Here was someone, who had never met me, and yet she was prepared to donate US$20 000, which, at the exchange rate at that time, was almost Z$200 000 for what she considered to be a very worth-while cause.

Barely had I replaced the receiver when the phone rang again. It was Nancy. "I've changed my mind," she said. My immediate reaction was, "We've lost the money." She then went on to explain that she and her friend had decided to increase the US$20 000 to US$30 000, so concerned were they about the possible loss of the animals, particularly the "ele's". "You just can't let them die," she said.

Well, this was the start of a wonderful friendship, not only for myself but also for a number of other committee members. We were later to meet Nancy and her husband and daughter when they came out to Zimbabwe, and we were able to show them what we had achieved as a result of their generosity and concern.

This wonderful gesture by Nancy Abrahams paved the way for us really to resolve our problems, and by November 1994 at the start of the rains, we had 29 pumps running, as opposed to a situation five months previously, where only six were operational.

News of the Hwange water crisis was now being reported on almost daily through one medium or another to our advantage. We had averted a major disaster. The committee had realized, however, that these actions were only temporary measures, and did not actually resolve the problem. Engines and pumps had only been patched up to see us through to the rains. This was not a long-term solution.

Unfortunately the 1994/5 rainy season was not good. The rains fell late and were not very significant, which is often the case in this drought-prone area. It appeared that '95 would be as serious as '94. We needed now to embark on a more permanent programme. While we were well aware that the engines and pumps needed to be replaced, on closer inspection we found that many of the borehole casings had corroded, having not been renewed in some cases since the 1930s, and the boreholes had collapsed. Pipes and rods had exceeded their life expectancy, but probably the most serious concern was that the water table had declined noticeably, with some boreholes having dried up completely.

Early '95 saw a strategic management workshop being held in Hwange attended by about 50 concerned stakeholders. Over the four-day period there was a final consensus of opinion that the basic problems were inefficient water management and inadequate funding. Such conclusions were nothing new, we had detailed these problems in the report given to the Minister the previous year. Of extreme significance was how little information and knowledge National Parks had on game water supplies, and this was clearly why the Park was in its present predicament.

We had now embarked on a major refurbishment programme. Donor agencies were approaching us continuously to offer assistance, for which we were most grateful, and a local borehole-drilling company offered reduced prices, as well as passing a huge credit of several hundred thousand dollars for work they had done. Slowly we were starting to see the fruits of our efforts.

It was during this time that I was approached by the Australian-based TV station, Discovery Channel, about the situation and asked if they could do a 15 minute documentary on the Hwange crisis, which they had heard about. Their main concern was that I was to guarantee they would be able to film the hundreds of animals, in particular, elephants, which were suffering from the drought. Since we had just participated in the annual Game Count Census where, because of the limited water in the Park, we were able to have our largest animal count ever, I saw no problem with their request.

Ironically, during the two weeks following the game census, a fair amount of rain had fallen in the Park just prior to my arriving to meet the Discovery Channel team. I was sure that I knew exactly where to look for all these hundreds of animals. I found to my embarrassment, however, that, now there was plenty of water available, the animals had dispersed, and after three days of visiting every likely place, I had located only six elephants. Sadly, we did discover 17 elephant carcasses at a seep called Nehimba. At these seeps the elephant excavate small holes just large enough to place their trunks into, so that they can drink as the water slowly seeps in. It is extremely time-consuming and an elephant may remain drinking from the limited water supply for many hours, while the others wait their turn. In this case the animals that had died, were probably so exhausted and stressed that they were unable to move on in search of water, and eventually had succumbed and died while waiting their turn.

This was the worst tragedy that I witnessed during this drought period. We received very few other reports of deaths, so our efforts were now being rewarded. I reported this to the authorities and, after a subsequent newspaper article, I was severely reprimanded through the press by the Deputy Minister of Environment & Tourism, who claimed I had "a hidden agenda", as he had not heard of any elephants dying. What exactly he meant by this, I still do not know.

By now game water supplies were starting to improve, a number of engines had been purchased, pumps and piping had been replaced and a number of new boreholes drilled. National Parks' staff were assisting in every possible way and men were being trained in the maintenance of equipment. This exercise continued through to the start of the rains in November '95. As a result of the good rains experienced that season, the workload eased somewhat although drilling continued, and by the start of the 1996/7 season, game water supplies were adequate. Subsequent years also have seen good rainfall in the Park, which has ensured that the crisis situation of the early 1990s will not occur again in the foreseeable future.

We have, however, continued assisting parks up to the present time in the drilling of new boreholes in other areas. This is to help in dispersing the wildlife from the traditional areas in an effort to allow the environment to recover from the huge concentrations of game, which have had devastating effects on the surrounding areas adjacent to the pans. A welcome decision in 1996 was made by Government when it was decided that parks would operate commercially and all money generated would benefit the Department directly instead of going to the central treasury. It was hoped that this arrangement would assist parks to overcome their problems related to the shortage of funds.

While initially no real benefit was seen, the financial situation of parks certainly did improve in later years, although probably not as significantly as one would have liked. The decrease of tourism within Zimbabwe recently, due to the current political instability of the country, will no doubt create additional financial shortages.

Tragically, while game water supplies were of paramount concern in our parks, yet another sinister event was taking place within Zimbabwe. Owing to relentless poaching, the rhino population was decreasing dramatically, and the rhino was well on the way to becoming an endangered species.

In 1987 the rhino population of Zimbabwe was estimated at 1000 animals. By 1992 there were only 430. Another crisis was upon us. Almost all the rhino on the African continent, north of Zimbabwe had been eliminated and now the scourge had arrived in Zimbabwe.

Rhino horn has for centuries been a valuable commercial commodity. It is used as an aphrodisiac and to make handles for daggers for sale in the Middle and Far East. Zimbabwe, with the parks experiencing severe financial constraints, was a prime target. Anti-poaching patrols had ceased and the infiltrators took full advantage of this. The perpetrators of the new war were men armed with automatic weapons, who crossed from neighbouring countries into Zimbabwe. The onslaught on the rhino became almost uncontrollable.

Certain programmes were initiated to try to stem the slaughter of the rhino, one being a de-horning exercise funded largely by concerned people. This did little to save the species, however. In fact, a number of rhino, which had been de-horned, were still slaughtered, to eliminate the chance of poachers later tracking them a second time. As proof that they were doing their job, even though they had failed to produce the horn, poachers would remove an ear to present to their employers on their return to their home countries. The situation was nothing short of sickening.

While illegal hunting had been carried out initially by foreign poachers, it became apparent that local politicians, government employees, military personnel and numbers of parks' staff were now also involved. In July 1992 the local press covered a sensational case involving four members of the Central Intelligence Organisation (CIO) who had been apprehended in Harare with two rhino horns. An off-duty game scout arrested for alleged poaching in Chirisa safari area committed suicide while in custody. These were just two of a number of reports.

By the end of 1993 the white rhino population in Hwange had all but been totally eliminated. Only a few black rhino had survived, probably largely due to their ability to operate in rugged terrain that was difficult for the poachers to penetrate. In the Gonarezhou National Park a healthy population of some 75 animals in 1987 was reduced to ten animals by 1990.

The response to Zimbabwe's poaching crisis was not all passive, however. In 1994 an anti-poaching effort code-named, "Operation Stronghold" was introduced to meet the challenge. Zimbabwe adopted a "shoot to kill" policy which also raised considerable criticism both from inside and outside the country. Some quarters objected to the taking of human lives to protect wild animals.

Unfortunately, despite this hard-line approach by the Department of National Parks and Wildlife Management, the numbers of our rhino were declining. In 1994 recorded poaching incursions were taking place almost daily and the Department's requests for increases in staff, more funds for essential equipment like radios and helicopters, went unheeded. The disparity between the Department's needs and actual means was critical. It appeared that there was a disturbing lack of appreciation of the contribution wildlife makes to the nation's economy among government policy makers.

When it became apparent that the rhino war currently being fought might not be successful, a new approach was decided on and the Zimbabwe Black Rhino Conservation Strategy Plan was introduced. Its objectives were: to conserve viable populations of black rhino in areas designated as intensive protection zones (IPZs); to develop translocated breeding nuclei elsewhere in Zimbabwe; to develop one or more captive breeding centres in the country and to continue supporting the international captive breeding programme.

Impressive as the strategy appeared, this document, after approval by the Director of Parks and the Parks Board, languished in the Ministry for almost two years before publication. The delay stifled implementation of major components of the programme. Parks, however, were able to implement the capture and translocation of animals to three private conservancies (Midlands, Save and Bubiana) and to establish four IPZs in late 1993.

The role of the conservancies was of paramount importance, while the IPZs, particularly Matusadona and Hwange, were considered to have been successful in black rhino recovery. In my opinion, the conservancies played a huge part in ensuring the survival of the black rhino.

Recognising the need to maximize security and intensify the breeding potential of our depleted rhino population, the private conservancies undertook to offer the necessary security, so as to ensure the survival of the species. Like-minded neighbouring ranchers removed cattle fences and collectively converted vast land holdings back to wildlife preserves. In addition, the conservancies developed community-based conservation programmes around their perimeters, which led to direct employment and indirect stimulation of secondary industries, in order to gain support for their rhino and wildlife programmes from the community.

Well-equipped anti-poaching units were deployed in these areas, and for the first time in over a decade, the rhino appeared to have a small chance of survival. The Save and Bubiana conservancies both introduced reward incentives to informants who provided information on poachers.

In a legal sense, the rhinos remained "res nullins" or unowned either by the state or by private individuals. But by virtue of their being a protected species under Zimbabwe's wildlife legislation, there were restrictions on their exploitation and they could only be hunted, sold or otherwise exploited in terms of a permit issued by the Minister.

National Park's efforts to establish and introduce IPZs and the assistance and willingness of the conservancies and wildlife ranches certainly appear to have been successful in re-establishing our rhino herd, which is extremely encouraging. The rhinos could, however, still be easily lost, if vigilance is not maintained.

In 1997 I attended the opening of the CITIES convention in Harare, where a report stated that only 43 rhino had been illegally killed during the period 1990-1995. I found this to be unacceptable and totally inaccurate. Our rhino herds had been decimated.

The first few months of the year 2000 saw yet another crisis developing in Zimbabwe. The government, unable to reconcile social and economic imbalances, embarked on a fast-track land redistribution policy which has gone horribly wrong, and which includes the wildlife conservancies of the country. The government had given assurances that this land would not be included in their programme.

Large tracts of land within many of the conservancies in Zimbabwe have been invaded. It is difficult to understand why, after all these years of hard work by many people of all races who have been working with Government to protect our wonderful natural heritage, we now see animals being slaughtered, and forests and grasslands being destroyed in what appears to be a tragic battle for political dominance.

Many conservationists are unable to operate effectively, as a result of political interference. Poaching and the destruction of our natural resources are now referred to as "political protests" and no action is taken against offenders. In certain instances, farmers involved in wildlife conservation have been warned that, if any further incidents of poaching or bush-clearing are reported, they will be the ones held accountable. As a result, huge financial losses have been incurred, with figures of game losses to date from certain areas amounting to many millions of dollars.

There now seem to be two levels of poaching. The first is the political, malicious level, where the destruction of wildlife, fencing and other assets erodes the farmer's ability to earn a living. Secondly, there is the criminal level, where people who have no legal claim to land are taking advantage of the breakdown in law and order to poach game and fish and steal wire, fence posts and timber for resale.

So, once again, our rhinos and the rest of our wildlife appear to be facing a grave crisis. How long will it be before we see the rhino being targeted yet again by individuals who are concerned only with their own personal financial gain?

The loss of wildlife and property is only half the story. Tourism and many of its related spin-off industries have been adversely affected, with foreign exchange earnings from this sector expected to be about 65% down for the coming year.

I firmly believe, however, that a solution can be achieved through continuous dialogue, with a pragmatic and visionary approach from all involved. Possibly even a neutral arbitrator could be utilized. Not all individuals and institutions linked to government have staked their political future on the present land stance. There are people within the National Parks, the police force and the ministries who have a sensible grasp of what is required, and there are war veterans who understand the need for a responsible and equitable redistribution of land. I have no doubt that there is sufficient goodwill among all sectors of the people of Zimbabwe to resolve these issues. There are so many who love our country's wildlife and who appreciate its beauty.

Every Zimbabwean must protect the country's fragile eco-system before irreparable damage is done. We need to resolve the current political problems in the interests of Zimbabwe and its people, not those of its politicians.

We must accommodate and educate our rural people so that they will consider our priceless natural heritage to be a valuable asset, and one well worth preserving; one that they and future generations will enjoy forever. Less than a century ago our country was a wilderness, almost entirely as nature created it. Today so much of it has been infiltrated, overrun, and destroyed tree by tree, animal by animal and stone by stone, decimated and deprived of all its natural checks and balances.

Are these the last days of our Eden? We pray that this is not the case.

A Further Blow to Wildlife and Tourism.

Zimbabwe Independent

The nation's leading business weekly MAY 11, 2001 TO MAY 17, 2001

Gonarezhou demarcated for resettlement

One of Zimbabwe's foremost national parks, Gonarezhou, has been demarcated for resettlement under the controversial fast-track programme in a move likely to deal a mortal blow to tourism in the south of the country, the *Zimbabwe Independent* has established this week. The demarcation of part of the world-renowned national park, the beacon of tourism in the south-eastern Lowveld, comes barely two months after the signing of a Transfrontier agreement between Zimbabwe, Mozambique and South Africa, encompassing Gonarezhou as a regional conservation area. The sudden change of land use at Gonarezhou, without consulting the other signatories of the agreement, is likely to scuttle the setting up of a vast game park which includes Gazaland in Mozambique and the Kruger National Park in South Africa.

❧⟐▧⟐❧

QUEUES

And then there was this joke that did the rounds.

John had been sitting in a queue for hours. The queue hadn't moved because the tanker bringing the diesel hadn't yet arrived. He was tired and hot and he had had enough. He walked up to the man in the next vehicle and said, "I've had a guts full. I'm going to State House to complain to the President." Within half an hour, he was back, but had to take his place at the end of the queue. His acquaintance walked up the line and asked him what had happened.

"I went to State House," John said, "but I decided there was no point in staying. The queue there was even longer than the queue here!"

THE WISDOM OF THE WILD

The land has been hurt. Misuse is not to be
excused, and its effects will be long felt.
But nature will not be eliminated, even here.
Rain, moss, and time apply their healing bandage
and the injured land at last recovers.
Nature is evergreen, after all.

Robert Michael Pyle

ntermittent gunfire invaded the quiet afternoon. For a brief moment the birds were silent, the incessant song of the crickets ceased, and an eerie stillness settled over the farm.

In her haste to escape from the sounds of devastation, and be reunited with her troop, a mother monkey dropped her very new baby - he was perhaps less than a week old - on the garden side of our security fence.

When I went to collect the laundry from the clothes line, I heard a plaintive cry. There were hornbills on the lawn for the first time ever, and I wondered if the sound came from a mother feeding one of her young.

The hornbills took off, gliding effortlessly across the veld and heading towards the dam where our water birds continue to nest in relative safety.

Abandoning that idea, I followed the sound across the lawn. Over the years my garden has been a constant source of inspiration: an oasis of colour during times of drought and a place of tranquillity during the lean or painful seasons of our lives. Throughout the months since the farm invasions, it has taken on even greater significance as I am no longer free to take the long walks that have meant so much since I first came to the farm, young and full of hope over forty years ago.

The cries grew louder and more desperate. There on a big grey Mexican aloe leaf was a tiny baby monkey. Holding on for dear life, his tiny primate hands clung to either side of the leaf between the thorns, and his long tail dangled down dejectedly. Another heart-breaking mew escaped from his little puckered pink mouth.

Outside the security fence some twelve metres away, a very agitated mama kept peeking and bobbing around the rocks and trees, every now and then giving and answering calls. I restrained myself from touching him in case his mother did not like the smell of humans, and retreated quietly.

From my office window I was able to watch the rescue unfold, unobserved. It took virtually two hours for the nervous mother to duck and dive into position for the final lunge. When she was less than a metre away from him, the most incredible thing happened.

Without the quiver of a branch, or the rustle of a leaf, the whole troop appeared, to act as a decoy. As if responding to some hidden signal, she stood on her hind legs, moved towards the aloe and, with one hand, plucked the infant from the leaf and slammed him to her chest. He clung on so tightly that he vanished almost entirely into her fur. Still terrified, she bounded from tree to tree, making a zigzag retreat.

Shafts of long sunlight stretched across the still lawn. As silently as they had come, the troop moved out. Mission accomplished.

TRUST

Trust resides in every human heart
and one has to search for it there,
and be guided by the truth as one sees it.
But no one has the right to coerce others
To act according to his own view of truth.

Mahatma Gandhi.

 s we grow older and more perceptive, we come to realise that there are few absolutes in life. But there is, in Zimbabwe, one very important single factor of which we need to be aware. This influences everything for good or ill that happens here today. I speak of the relationship between black people and white people.

My great-grandparents, the Reverend Charles Helm and his wife Elisabeth, were German missionaries sent by the London Missionary Society to Hope Fountain Mission (south of Bulawayo) in 1874. They were surrounded by black people, whose language and beliefs gradually became comprehensible and familiar to them. Charles and Elisabeth made friends with their neighbours and tried to be helpful wherever possible.

When their daughter, my grandmother, Erica Helm (later Hepburn) was three years old, she, her sister Jessie (later Lovemore) and their parents were invited to attend a ceremony as guests of King Lobengula. They watched a hundred Matabele warriors in full battle regalia, a few metres in front of them, leaping, stamping and swaying. These men, dressed in skins and feathers, brandishing shields and razor-sharp assegais, filled the air with the deafening and terrifying sounds of war - deep groans and grunts and shrill ululating. Not for one second did the Helm family feel even mildly nervous, although they could have been massacred in an instant had Lobengula so desired.

Charles learnt to speak siNdebele perfectly and was trusted so completely by King Lobengula, that he was chosen to be the King's official translator when other white people wished to communicate with the monarch.

In the Hope Fountain graveyard stands a headstone engraved with the words: "Charles Helm, friend of the Matabele" - words which make me proud to be his descendant.

Over a hundred years ago, Charles and Elisabeth adopted an orphaned baby and brought her up, eventually helping her to find a good husband.

A few years ago, I employed a lady called Berlina, who discovered my relationship to Charles. She told me that the orphaned baby was her grandmother.

I now benefit from the Helm's goodness and kindness. Berlina and I have a relationship based on mutual reliance and affection, and I am trusted by her whole family. This trust exists between many black and white people in this country. It is the one single quality that heals our wounds and keeps our hopes alive.

Yes Baas

Yes, baas, I'm so happy you came to my land,
You built this house, so big and so grand,
It's a pity the kia, the shack where I live,
Isn't really so great, and it leaks like a sieve.

Yes baas, you're so clever, I know for a fact,
You run a big business, with talent and tact.
But when you get home you slip off the tracks
Forget Dale Carnegie, with us you relax!

Yes baas, I've got a good job, I can see,
I'm senior retainer, with three men under me.
But my father's grandfather, who fought for Lo Ben,
Was an induna of note, and led five hundred men.

Yes baas, you're OK, with your Benz and your fleet;
You take us all fishing - oh what a treat!
You loaf in your houseboat in luxury obscene,
I camp on the bank and wash in a stream.

Yes baas, you've great tackle - your fishing's a joy -
You don't bait the hooks - no that's for your "boy".
I carefully cook all the morsels you bring,
And eat what I catch with a stick and a string.

Yes baas, it's great that we travel in style,
We cruise in your 4x4, mile after mile.
You in front with the madam, with music and fun,
Just me and the dog behind in the sun.

Yes baas, you're so kind - you've got lots of cash,
Your foreman got married, you gave him a stash.
But because I rushed home when my father was sick,
You chased me around the house with a stick!

Yes baas, you're a treasure, you pay me on time,
But then what you pay me is not that sublime.
And you got so angry when my tenth brother died,
Yet I've 30 to go, and from them I can't hide.

Yes baas, I know that you're kinder than most,
If it wasn't for you, I'd give up the ghost.
You lent me the money to pay my lease hire,
But I owe you so much - now I cannot retire.

Yes baas, I know that you're fair in your way,
You wouldn't steal nothing, as you often do say.
But your mislaid wallet - later found by your wife -
You swore that I stole it, and threatened my life.

Yes baas, you're a good man, if you judge by the rest -
When you look at the others - not hard to be best!
You never get drunk and "perform" while at work,
But once home you change, you become quite a Turk.

Yes baas, you've heard it's a new country out here -
The Party says now that you whites have to fear.
But remember your bar when Smith was in power,
Your buddies sang troopie songs hour after hour?

Yes baas, you don't hit me or none of that stuff,
But what you do is still quite enough,
You're fair and you're kind and a pearl among whites,
But patronise me again and I'll punch out your lights!

Yes baas, for sure, it's a sad thing to see,
The war vets have raided your factory with glee.
Whatever you think, you can't blame me,
It wasn't me told them that you're MDC.

Yes baas, I've told you before and it's true,
I'm not a war veteran, I'll swear black and blue.
Those that have said it, they just say it to harm.
They'll pay for it later, when I've got my own farm.

Notes for those who have not had the benefit of living in southern Africa:

⊠ Baas   From Afrikaans and southern African pidgin Zulu for "boss"

⊠ Kia   House, often domestic workers' quarters behind a main building

⊠ Lo Ben   Lobengula, king of the Matabele in the 1890s.

⊠ Nduna   Chief.

⊠ Boy   Once used as slang by some people in Zimbabwe for a male employee.

⊠ Tenth brother   Africans have close but extended families, and cousins descended from a common male ancestor are often considered to be brothers and sisters. The numbers of relatives who have to be cared for can confuse whites.

⊠ Troopie songs   War songs popular with the Rhodesian army and their supporters.

⊠ War veteran   A former combatant in the resistance to the UDI government in Rhodesia. Many pro-government militia men claim to be war veterans but are not.

WAR VETERAN

The workers have nothing to lose but their chains.
They have a world to gain.

Karl Marx

 am a war veteran. I shall call myself Black Power, which is, of course, not my real name. I am glad to have been given the opportunity to contribute to this book. I think that people who are white, and who cannot possibly see things the way I do, or blacks who have sold their pride and their souls to the whites for money, will write much or all of the rest of it. I have no expectation that they will manage to present my case fairly, or even attempt to do so. Hence I contribute this, in the cause of veracity.

I was born and brought up in a major city in Zimbabwe. My parents were poor, and, although I had an exceptionally good academic record at junior school, could not afford to send me on to high school. I had to quit my studies then to earn money for my family. I thought at that time that I would never have the opportunity for any further education.

It was quite legal for me, as a black, in Zimbabwe in the early 1960s, to leave school at the age of 11 or 12. Had I been white, school inspectors would have tracked me down and made sure that I went to senior school and took a course suited to my academic abilities, at least until I was 16 years old. Education was compulsory for white children, but not for blacks. If necessary, I would have been given a bursary and, possibly, even been sent to a government boarding school of a very high standard, such as Prince Edward School in Harare, Milton in Bulawayo, Guinea Fowl in the Midlands, or Plumtree in rural Matabeleland.

These schools were for whites only. The Southern Rhodesian government provided an excellent education then, for whites, second to none in the world. No such effort was made for black children such as I. We could go to schools of a lower standard, but only if our parents could afford to send us there. I admit that the fees were greatly subsidised by the settler regime, but much more per child was spent on white education. The master race had to be catered for properly to ensure its continued dominion!

I was very keen to advance in the world, and realised that I needed an education to do so. I felt grievously hurt that I was receiving less assistance than a white child in the same situation. This was my country, to a much greater extent than it was his. He could always go "home" if things did not work out for him. My only home was here. Though not in a formal education programme for several years after leaving school, I made sure that I read the local press avidly, and any books I could lay my hands on.

I had further reason to resent the whites. I had very seldom met or talked to white people as a child, and had spent most of my time in the high-density areas (totally inhabited by blacks), where whites, except for the police or municipal employees, seldom dared to set foot.

One exciting day, when I was about eight years old, my mother took me to the central business district of our city on a shopping trip. This was a great treat for me. I think it was on the occasion of my birthday. My mother took me into a big department store. I cannot remember its name.

I followed her about with wide eyes, drinking in the sight of exotic items, many of which I could not even identify then, since they were beyond my experience. They were appliances and gadgets like washing machines, floor polishers, television sets and other marvellous creations I was unfamiliar with. I was proud of the way my mother managed to find her way around among the crowds of mainly white people on the huge shop floors. She was really enjoying our outing, and led me bravely up in elevators to at least three higher floors. She made a few small purchases and, after placing them in one of the store's baskets, went to the checkout desk. A young white woman, plastered whiter than whites normally are, sat behind the till. She looked at us with an impatient and long-suffering expression on her face as we approached. My mother paid the amount required, and then asked the "lady" for a bag to put her purchases in.

This person then said loudly to my mother, so that anyone (and there were many) within ten metres could hear her, "Don't you know that we don't give bags to Kaffirs?" I had never heard the "K" word before, and did not know what it meant, but saw immediately that it had utterly demolished my poor little mother. She mumbled a pathetic apology in her poor English and scuttled out of the store like the small, wounded creature that she was. I could have killed that till attendant. I would like to meet her now.

Logically, I know now that the "K" word is the Arabic word for "unbeliever", and can apply equally to whites, blacks or any other group of people not of the Islamic faith. It was used by the Arabs for the occupants of the hinterland of Africa, and became generally used for the African tribes of southern Africa by the white colonialists. It came to have a pejorative connotation, I think, only after the Second World War, but it has always been bitterly resented by blacks. Do not expect me to be rational about anyone using this word to demean my people, however. I will never fully recover from this experience. I do not think my mother ever did before she died. She never mentioned the incident to me again. I was too sensitive and humiliated ever to talk to her about it.

This may seem to be making too much of a small thing. I could be blowing this incident out of all proportion. It is, however, typical, of the contemptuous way some whites dealt with blacks in Zimbabwe before we won our independence. "What meat did these men eat that they had grown so proud?" as a civilised white man once wrote. Personally, I never was subjected to quite such a vicious dose of racism again. However, I occasionally did find arrogance and contempt in the attitude of whites towards me in the few dealings I had with them when I first ventured from the black ghetto where I grew to maturity. Some of this may have been sparked by my less than conciliatory attitude, but I make no apologies for that. Let them appease us. They have cause. I'm afraid I came to expect a bad attitude from whites, and may even have imagined it on occasions when it did not exist. That was not my fault, but that of the foolish white people who conditioned me to think that way.

Members of our community would relate an incident such as the humiliation of my mother to hundreds of other blacks, and the resentment would be multiplied enormously, far beyond those directly affected. This sort of tale was very useful to the comrades as a recruiting tool, and I, overcoming my initial distaste, often used to tell my story to a sympathetic and indignant audience, many of whom would come up with their own horror stories of the arrogance of the white man. I wonder how many freedom fighters that till attendant created.

In recent years I have studied the psychology of fear and aggression in the United States. I am sure that the insecurity and deep-seated fear of an outnumbered and unpopular elite, aware of its vulnerability, accounted for the behaviour of that white shop-girl and for many other examples of racism I have been subjected to, heard about or witnessed. That knowledge makes it a little easier to deal with. It does not come close to making it at all tolerable. From a purely personal point of view, I know that I can never forgive the white race as a group for the appalling blow they struck my mother, a total innocent.

Do these people know the damage they have done to their own kin? I remember Alan Savory, leader of a moderate white party (the Rhodesia Party) in the 1970s in Zimbabwe, saying that the racist Rhodesian Front had put the whites in this country in terrible danger. He was so right. How many other blacks have had similar experiences to mine? Why did we tolerate the rule of these people for so long? How can we forgive ourselves for doing so?

They robbed us of our country. They slaughtered our grandfathers (who were armed only with spears and knobkerries) with machine-guns, cutting them down by the thousand like grass before the scythe, like vermin. They did this because the "cheeky blacks" had dared to object to the wholesale theft of the land of their birth, and chose to obey the appeals of our ancestors to resist. Our grandfathers were only obeying the rules of our religion, following the advice of the spirit mediums, and attempting to prevent the theft of their birthright.

Once they had conquered us, the invaders grew fat on the fruits of our country and the sweat of our brows. They educated us enough to become useful to them, but not any more if they could help it. They routinely insulted simple, inoffensive, good people like my mother. Some of them, I am sure, like the "lady" in the shop, did this several times a day. This was an intolerable state of affairs, and I am proud to say that I would help to bring it to an end!

I was saved from a life of ignorance and poverty by the revolution. In my late teens I became a member of ZAPU (the Zimbabwe African People's Union) and then of ZANU (the Zimbabwe African National Union, the majority Shona-speaking faction which split away from ZAPU and became the main political party in the country), in 1964. I attended Party meetings, became a registered member, and took part in demonstrations and rallies. I was strongly built and aggressive, and was seconded to the Party security branch, giving protection to our leaders and, occasionally, punishing sell-outs who gave information to the security forces. This sort of action was regrettable but necessary. We all felt that it was acceptable for us to use violence to free the people, since we had been enslaved by it. I became a regular bodyguard for touring senior leaders of the Party.

The Police had picked me up in 1962, when an informer saw me circulating ZAPU leaflets in the streets. These leaflets called for the killing of white people, who by then I had identified as the cause of our poverty. I was interrogated, fingerprinted, photographed, beaten up in an amateurish sort of a way and detained for further investigation. So were hundreds or thousands of others, and I was hidden in the mob. Insufficient evidence was found to prosecute me, and I was released without being charged after a few weeks on remand. I think that the police were nervous that I might complain of assault if I was taken to court, and they no doubt thought that I had been given enough of a lesson to ensure that I would behave myself in future. They were wrong. At that time, I believe, there was no legal framework in place to permit my indefinite detention without trial for a minor offence. That situation would be rectified within months.

I was lucky in that only the uniformed police and the Criminal Investigation Department had dealt with me. The Special Branch were preoccupied with more serious offenders, and did not know the full story of all that I had been up to, or I would not have got off so lightly. Unfortunately, however, my particulars, photograph and fingerprints were now in the hands of the police. They did not suspect half of what I had done, though they well knew of my involvement in the Party security section, and I was often picked up from then on if there was some security witch-hunt in progress.

Also in 1962, some months after I was first arrested, the white electorate voted the Rhodesian Front government into power. These racists made it very clear that there would be no painless and inevitable progression to majority rule through the ballot box, after a few decades, as might have been expected from their predecessors, the United Party. The blacks would be kept in their place, and would never taste majority rule, "Not in a Thousand Years" they boasted foolishly. The battle lines were drawn. The people would not listen seriously to moderate black voices after that. War was inevitable.

In 1964, as a member of ZANU, I was again arrested on suspicion of committing violent acts in contravention of the Law and Order Maintenance Act. This law was, by then, being used regularly as a weapon against the black nationalists. It denied anyone singled out by

110

the forces of the fascist state the right to due legal process in terms of Western legal practice. I must say that *we* found it very useful after coming to power. It was a necessary evil, for a legitimate government to defend itself with. That did not prevent us from disliking it when it was used against us. It proved to be very helpful in drumming up indignation against our oppressors in some liberal Western states, mainly in Scandinavia, which contributed heavily to our liberation war funds.

There was insufficient evidence available to convict me in court, I think, because the police were not prepared to compromise the identity of certain spies or Special Branch agents who knew what I had been doing, and who alone could give evidence against me. I was not at that time a big enough fish to make that worthwhile. I had been carrying out duties that were necessary for our Party to free the country from white rule. I am not ashamed of them, though I might have been executed by the Smith regime had they been able to prove them. The Law and Order Maintenance Act was invoked against me, and I was sent to a restriction camp.

In the camps I began a new life. These camps were the universities of the freedom struggle. Foreign aid made available to me the education I had been denied as a child. In my early 20s, I sailed through the English General Certificate of Education at Ordinary and Advanced levels. I qualified easily for tertiary education. I had kept a low profile in the camp for the three years I had been at my studies, as I was fully occupied in improving myself. Others, with less to occupy themselves, held the political spotlight, and the authorities must have presumed that I had reformed. I was released from restriction and warned that I would be dealt with very severely if I did not behave myself.

Within a week I had made my way across the border, the Zambezi river, to Zambia, and enlisted as a full-time freedom fighter. I underwent my military training in a secret camp.

My service as a bodyguard for the elite of the Party, while a youngster, paid off. I was remembered by some of the hierarchy, and recommended for a place at an English university before I was sent to the front. At that time there were many casualties among our cadres on the front line, and my early connections and my academic ability may have saved my life. This is something that embarrasses me a little today. Many of our best soldiers died at the front, and I never even made it that far. It was not my fault though, as I was as keen as any to fight the war for freedom.

I am not sure who paid for my education, other than the Party, but there were several of us who attended a respectable college in the English Midlands, and studied for degrees in the Social Science, Business Administration and Political Studies fields. The Party leadership recognised that it was going to need trained administrators when in power. We would not use the dregs of the Smith regime to run our country. After I graduated I was sent to the United States, where I completed a two-year post-graduate course. Then I spent the rest of the war years in the Party offices in England and Mozambique. Those of us in the higher positions of authority were not risked in the war zone. We were needed to organise the war effort, and would form the new government of the liberated Zimbabwe.

Immediately after liberation in 1980, I joined the civil service of the new nation of Zimbabwe, and became one of its young lions. Today I run an important department of my Ministry.

I am sick to death of reading obviously biased and dishonest reporting of the situation in this country in the state-controlled press. These people are presenting my case, but doing it so badly that they are an embarrassment to me and to the Party. They should tell the plain truth and not try to justify themselves in terms of a moral and economic system that has no place in Africa. I am nearly as tired of them as I am of reading the better-written diatribes in the independent press that our Government permits to exist in this country. The writers of these reports would like their readers to believe that they are concerned about the essential welfare of the bulk of the people of Zimbabwe.

Those of us who have endured the pain and the humiliation of living in our country under a racist white government know that this is a lie. Any person, organisation or group which seeks to perpetuate the economic domination of our society by whites, by blacks who behave as whites, or by the capitalists of the western world, is not concerned about the black people of this country.

We are our own masters. We are not slaves. We will run this country in our own way, as we want to run it - in an African way. If that does not conform to the wishes and standards of people in other parts of the world, that is just too bad. We do not prescribe their political medicine for them. Who are they to prescribe for us?

In February 2000, the people of this country started to take back the land that was stolen from them more than a century ago.

They have my blessing in this. The land must in the end, like the means of all production, belong to the people. We cannot accept that the invaders (who hold us, the black indigenous people, the historical owners of the land, in contempt) own the vast bulk of the best farming land of this country. Should Cecil John Rhodes' vision for Africa be ours? Should we accept his division of our land into white and black sectors? Please! Be reasonable. If this continues to be the case, what does our national sovereignty mean, what is the point of independence? Where is our self-respect? The people must control the land. The people must own the land.

People ask - are we going about this the right way? Our country is a part of the world. We must deal with it, and it must deal with us, so that we may realise the benefits of our membership of the global community. We must use the comparative advantages of our cheaper labour and our bounteous natural resources to produce goods for sale in the West and in South Africa.

They say that we must gradually pass through the phases of economic activity pioneered by other non-western, non-white countries. I recognise that international trade is necessary for our country, and that it suits us to deal with the capitalist West. That is where the real money is, and we must tap into it and emulate the success of countries such as Japan, Malaysia, Singapore, Thailand and the territories of Taiwan, Hong Kong and South Korea in trading with them. That is the only practical way forward.

This, however, does not mean that we have to copy and obey the alabaster icons of the Western World in every detail. It does not mean that we must slavishly think exactly as they do. Fair enough, the rest of the world must see us as being a suitable place for them to do business. If we are not, they will not have anything to do with us. They will not invest in our country. They will not give us aid. They will not write off our massive foreign debt. We need them and their money. We must not frighten them away. We must use them as they have used us in the past.

In the end, we must and will reach the state where we educate our labour force and work our way up through higher levels of industrial competence and technology. Then our workers' standard of living will be comparable with that of first world countries. Will it not be wonderful when we have a standard of living higher than that of the United Kingdom? They are slipping on the ladder of economic attainment. We can rise on the backs of foreign entrepreneurs. That is fine as regards the commercial side, but we must control the land where our fathers are buried.

The western powers are prepared to finance the purchase of our land back from the white settlers. "Let them do it", some say, "It will not cost us anything." Much of this purchase price will remain in Zimbabwe. It will help to build the African Renaissance mooted by South African President Thabo Mbeki. We will end up with the land anyway, or as much as we can profitably use in the short term. Over decades, we will gain all of it. We, for a change, will be getting something for nothing - if only we are willing to write off a hundred years of oppression forever or for some future reckoning.

I am not prepared to do that. That oppression wounds me deeply yet; I feel an intense personal hurt when I see the people who brutalised us viciously for nearly a century until only 21 years ago still lording it over us, still in control of the means of production in our country.

Let them keep some of our land for now - enough to run the agricultural industries whose exports earn us the foreign currency we need. We never have claimed all of it. There is still plenty of space. The whites can have half or a third of "their" farms for the present. We will take the rest for our people to farm and own and occupy. They will revel in their ownership, knowing that it came about despite all that the white man could do to prevent it with his machine guns and his courts.

I am prepared to use their expertise until we can do without it, which will not be, it seems, for some years to come. The settlers did do one important thing for us. They gave us the gift of the English language. Thanks to the missionaries and to the strenuous efforts of the Party since independence, we are the most highly educated country in Africa. We all speak English, the language of international trade. Foreign manufacturers should be flocking here to build up our economy with their investment and their expertise. Once again - let us use them. There is no profit in our boycotting the world. Let it in. It can only help us. To do this, to compete with the capitalists at their own game, we must be seen to be a suitable haven for investment. The rule of law must apply in Zimbabwe. My comrades on the commercial farms must be made to realise that. We need a massive propaganda effort to convince the world that we really do have the rule of law here - already - now. Much has been made of the killing of six white farmers in the past year; yes, six. Is this an outrage! How many of us did they kill? More white farmers than that are killed in a week in South Africa, from what I can make out. That is not outrageous. It is regrettable, I accept that, and I agree that it seems that many or even all the killings were unnecessary. They constitute a very bad blow to our image as a civilised nation.

Our war veterans must exercise the discipline they showed in their successful struggle for Zimbabwe. They must be stoic in the face of the provocation of the farmers, who have stubbornly refused to acknowledge that the blacks have a right to the land. They must resist with discretion the colonialist courts, who recognise only the letter of the foreign Roman Dutch law, and not the spirit of natural justice. We will soon change those courts.

We must process our recapture of the land we need through the courts, if possible, but if not, we can do so in the way the whites took it. The whites now know who are the bosses here. Our comrades who invaded the farms taught them that. It was a lesson they needed. It is now time to exert self-control, and present a smoother face to the West, until we no longer need to pander to them. The enemy has seen that we have muscle. He respects us more than he did. We will take the rest of the land at our leisure. We must not forget that, after the disastrous collapse of the Soviet Union, there is only one Superpower in the world. Let us work with Uncle Sam and his cousins in the United Kingdom and with the other money mongers of the World as long as it suits us to do so.

Forward the revolution. Let us make Zimbabwe great, and, above all, black! The whites must know that, though they do occupy much of our land, it is only at our pleasure. We can take it away when we want to. And we will. In the lonely, dark reaches of the night, when I cannot find peace in sleep, I often hear my dead mother demand it.

OPERATION EYES FOR ZIMBABWE

I have heard your voice for two days and now I can see you.

Old man from Zhombe

During March and April 2001, twenty ophthalmic surgeons came from the United States and from within the country to provide cataract operations free of charge to thousands of desperate Zimbabweans who could never have afforded the operations.

here is a well-known saying, "Fools rush in where angels fear to tread." When I was asked to co-ordinate the "Eyes for Zimbabwe" programme in our area, I never for one moment envisaged the enormity of the task.

My first priority was to phone our local doctor to seek his advice about a venue. I knew that the Kwekwe General Hospital was overloaded with patients and did not want to put more pressure on them. He kindly arranged to have a meeting with his partners and they agreed to let us use Stanley House, a private clinic.

Once the initial arrangements had been made, he approached our Rotary Club, which sponsored a series of advertisements in our local newspapers. Many hundreds of posters were printed in English, Shona and Ndebele, and the word was soon out around town.

The next step was eye-screening lessons in Harare. Initially five of us attended. The following week, my husband took a health worker and two nursing sisters from the Zivagwe Rural District Council to Harare for training.

We bought duplicate books for enquiries and bookings for use at Stanley House, and a second set for the Rural Council Office, where the daily screening would be done. We also arranged for screening to take place on various farms. Free accommodation was provided by one of the lodges and the local hotel arranged a room for staff or elderly people requiring post-operative care. The Catholic Hall was offered as a further option for elderly patients. Since additional operating staff were needed, I visited the hospital and they agreed to help us.

Assisted by two volunteers, my husband transported boxes and boxes of glasses and medicines to Kwekwe. Finally, we collected a consignment of microscopes and other vital equipment from Harare, arriving home late and exhausted after the three-hour journey.

Streamlining the entire operation was my greatest concern. We had no idea what the response would be, never having undertaken a project of this magnitude, but we knew from other areas that a number of clinics had been swamped.

The desperate shortage of fuel was an on-going problem. By the grace of God, we managed to get petrol and diesel delivered to our farm on 30 March, and that enabled us to keep going. By the Sunday evening we were as ready as we could be, given the difficulties facing our beleaguered country. Food had been organised for the nursing staff, doctors and helpers, as well as for post-operative patients and any poor or destitute people needing further assistance.

At three o'clock on the Monday morning, while it was still dark and cold, people began arriving at Stanley House. And they kept coming. The steady trickle swelled until there was a flood of expectant patients milling outside. Soon after dawn, a truck appeared with bales of hay, boxes galore and helpers. When I arrived with other helpers and the microscopes, and saw the size of the crowd, I had to suppress a sense of total panic. How could Stanley House continue to carry out its normal duties faced with such vast numbers of people?

Our first priority was to restore order. In addition to the room allocated, Stanley House agreed that we could take over their theatre. A number of staff members were brought from the nearby hospital to assist and, while they were re-sterilising the theatre, we began sorting out the supplies. We were concerned about all the patients waiting outside - soon the sun would be fierce - but there was nothing we could do.

Fuel shortages delayed the doctors from Harare, who arrived only at lunchtime. Meanwhile I had also organised for the Anglican Hall to be used for post-operative patients because it was quiet and we could serve food with less difficulty.

Once the doctors were set up, screening proceeded at a rapid pace. In the meantime, another room had been taken over at Stanley House to confirm cataract cases and two hospice staff were methodically going through all the medicines.

Despite everyone's efforts, there was growing chaos outside, as more people kept arriving. Our poor driver had done over a hundred trips to and fro, here and there, getting food for staff and helping wherever he was needed. There were thousands of questions from everyone, but somehow I managed to keep in focus - the good Lord was with me... Eventually we closed down for the day and drove home exhausted.

Next morning we arrived early at Stanley House and, to our absolute horror, discovered even more people. Dear God, what could we do? Quick decisions and action. We must move the screening to the Anglican Hall... and the glasses sorting. All operations must be done at Stanley House. Phone another doctor to help with the screening... By this time the queues were kilometres long!

I called on a remarkable ophthalmic doctor, Dr Patel, to assist us. When he arrived, he saw the panic in my face and said, "Calm down. I have done many eye camps in India. Let us restore order like this: outside, you must have one line of women, one line of men and one line for the children - each group should be examined in a different hall." His arrival was a Godsend and now the lines were moving more efficiently. People were having final screening for cataracts and pterygiums. Some were referred for minor operations; others were sent elsewhere for glasses. The lensometer had still not arrived and my lady helpers were becoming dizzy with sorting.

By the Tuesday evening, both of the Harare doctors were exhausted and talked of a Wednesday departure. The list of cataract operations on our schedule was so long that it was essential to locate substitutes. My husband undertook to find a plane, so a friend lent us his and enlisted the support of a pilot to collect a team of doctors currently working in Chiredzi.

The new team was led by Dr Solomon Gurumathanu, regarded as a top ophthalmic surgeon internationally, whose brainchild was the "Eyes for Zimbabwe" programme. He was ably assisted by Dr Ravi from the United Kingdom, with his extremely efficient team. The Deseret Foundation was involved in this remarkable project.

On the Wednesday, the crowds were even greater and we constantly ran out of dilating drops, this and that, size 7.5 gloves and so on. My helpers were wonderfully supportive and had completed hundreds of cataract screenings. By now, operating had been switched to the Kwekwe General Hospital and, within one and a half hours, the new team was at work. It was incredible to watch their dedication - it gives us such faith in Africa. Dr Gurumathanu, who was born in Rusape, south-east of Harare, was giving back to the country through the exceptional gift that he had been given.

Late on the Friday evening, I took one of the operating teams home. Next morning, when we went for an early walk in the peace and quiet of our beautiful ranch, they were lucky enough to see our complete black rhino family - mother, father and two young calves.

By mid-afternoon on Saturday it was all over and we could return home in the knowledge that the programme had been a success.

It is only when the frenetic pace of a project such as this is over that you can appreciate the full extent of the miracle. During the rest of the weekend, many expressions of gratitude and memories came flooding back...

An old lady, dumped at the clinic with her bag and walking stick, had no idea where she was and became very confused, so we took special care of her. She kept saying, "I can imagine what you look like ... this is God at work." When she finally went home with sight, she was proclaiming a miracle.

Another elderly woman who was given glasses simply danced and danced with utter joy - she could finally see again...

Thanking my husband, an old grandmother who was absolutely delighted with her glasses said, "I can see you at last... and you are very good looking!"

Perhaps the most touching comment of all was from a wonderful old man who lived in Zhombe. After his cataract operation he came to me and said, "I have heard your voice for two days, and now I can see you." He was overjoyed.

❖❖❖ ▧▨ ❖❖❖

theres petrol

theres petrol in msasa theyve
just phoned me wont you phone
jane sue and tracy and lets
all queue together but its
five in the morning oh well

my mazda is on a quarter what
if i queue and they run out
before they get to me its a
risk i have to take im desperate

we re there and the queue is l o o o n g
its early and we re tired the petrol
isnt here yet but they said it
had come no i think they said it
would be coming oh well

oh god i need the loo better
walk up the line to the garage ill
count the cars on the way back to
see what kind of chance we have

theres more than one hundred i wonder
how much fuel is coming its getting
so hot have you girls brought any
water any biscuits any chocolate any coffee

its here thank god we ll push the cars
from position to position we ll waste
less that way hey dont push in get
to the back of the queue we ve
been waiting for hours you swine

closer now we re nearly there
ten more cars to go im
sweating like a pig pushing
this car is no joke we re
there fill it up please
thank you god i
can fetch the
kids from
school
today

with apologies to e e cummings

A COMMERCIAL FARMER'S VIEW

Burn down your cities and leave our farms,
And your cities will spring up again as if by magic;
But destroy our farms and the grass will grow
In the streets of every city in the country.

William Jennings Bryan

Author's note: The Commercial Farmers' Union has not approved the following article. The CFU, as an association which avoids involvement in politics, and which tries to minimise friction with other organisations, would strongly dissociate itself from many of the inferences and conclusions drawn by the author. The author is writing from the perspective of an individual commercial farmer. Some statistics have been taken from information published by the CFU. These are public knowledge.

The Commercial Farmers

 he commercial farmers of Zimbabwe are rated very highly by international standards. A significant percentage of them, more than 60%, it is said by knowledgeable sources, have qualified as farmers at colleges or universities. They graduated from such highly rated South African institutions as Cedara Agricultural College near Pietermaritzburg, Natal, the Agricultural Faculty of the University of Natal, or Potchefstroom University, and a number of institutions overseas. In more recent years they qualified at the respected Gwebi Agricultural College near Harare, or the University of Zimbabwe. Many run multimillion-dollar (in US dollar terms) export businesses, and do so efficiently, successfully and in the teeth of strong international competition.

The current generation of white farmers may be the last Zimbabwe will see. Sons and daughters of farmers generally want to work elsewhere because of prevailing conditions in the country. The future on the land here no longer is attractive to them. The process of indigenisation of land ownership will take place automatically as, by default, more blacks buy the farms that come onto the market. Most white farmers in the country are elderly. They will soon be gone. It is to be hoped that, by that time, their black successors will have been trained to manage the land. The government is doing little at present to ensure that this happens.

Ownership of land in Zimbabwe as at Independence in 1980 and then in February 2000 was divided as follows, according to the CFU publication "Facts on Land & The Present Situation" dated 29 March 2000:

Sector	1980 (%)	2000 (%)
Parks and state forests	16	16
Communal lands	41	41
Freehold tenure	39	30
Small scale commercial	4	4
Resettlement	0	9

As can be seen from the above, the only change in the 20 years was that 9% of the land had been transferred to resettlement areas from freehold tenure. Commercial farmers owned most of the freehold tenure land. There were 2 359 commercial farmers active in Zimbabwe as at 31 December 2000.

Millions of blacks currently live in grossly over-crowded conditions in the communal lands. It is imperative that this situation is redressed as a matter of urgency. The Commercial Farmers' Union (CFU) is eager to assist in the urgently required massive and rational resettlement of competent black farmers on former freehold tenure commercial farming land.

Importance of the Illegally Occupied Farms

An article by a respected Zimbabwean economist in the independent press recently pointed out that the commercial farming sector is the largest employer of labour in Zimbabwe. In February 2000, 250 000 people were employed on the 3 000 commercial farms ZANU PF is trying to confiscate. More than 850 000 of their children went to farm schools. The government pays a grant towards the salaries of teachers in these schools. The farmers meet all other expenses. If the farms are taken over, the workers will lose their jobs and the schools will shut down. These workers are unlikely to find other jobs in Zimbabwe's impoverished economy. Starvation looms for them. They will not be able to pay for alternative schooling for their children, whose lives will be severely handicapped.

More than a million people will have to move from the farms. Most will be homeless, and will flood into the communal areas. The farm workers displaced from the commercial farms seized will greatly outnumber the invaders to be resettled there illegally. The subsistence farming that will generally replace the commercial farming operations is not efficient enough to support the same population. The farm clinics will close and most of the former employees, as well as the newly settled "farmers" will have no health care available to them. Even if food is available in the country, they will have no money to pay for it.

The farm workers to be displaced are paid a total of Z$ 500 million a month. This will no longer be earned. These farmers will no longer be buying inputs worth Z$2 billion dollars a month. Manufacturers and traders who supplied the needs of the farmers and their workers will lose that market. Many businesses will have to shut down or reduce production, and will have to retrench staff. These will include banks, freight companies, insurance companies, wholesalers and retailers, engineering firms and manufacturing companies.

Agriculture has been the second largest foreign currency-earning sector of Zimbabwe's economy, surpassed only by mining. The efficient operation of the commercial farms is essential for the welfare of the country. The new "farmers", most of them untrained and inexperienced in commercial farming, will not be efficient. The resettled farms will lose nearly all their potential for exporting high quality produce and earning the foreign currency necessary to import the fuel, machinery, spares and industrial raw materials needed to keep our transport companies and industries running. This will lead to a further cycle of business failures. The untrained farmers, once on the land, will barely be able to feed themselves and their families, and there is likely to be a shortage of basic food.

Legality of White Farmers' Claim to Land

Zimbabwe's commercial farmers own their land legally in terms of the law of the country. This has been confirmed by recent decisions in the highest courts of the land, where rulings have been made against the actions of Government in attempting to take land from its owners. A few (there are less than a dozen families nation-wide involved here) inherited their land from one of the pioneers who entered the country at the time of Cecil John Rhodes. Another small minority owns farms which had been allocated to them or to their fathers or grandfathers through a concessionary land lease-hire contract, with a conditional option to buy, available to veterans of the Allied armed forces from the Second World War.

The land they were allocated was not usually taken from any previous occupants; it was generally vacant at the time. With the population of the country then standing at around two million people, as opposed to today's 12 or 13 million, there was plenty of unoccupied land available. They had to clear the virgin bush and work the farm successfully for ten years. If they were skilful enough as managers and farmers, and lucky enough to survive the droughts and floods of the unpredictable Zimbabwean climate and the endless cycle of insect pests, they could then apply for an option to purchase their farms. Many failed, and went back home penniless or looked for employment elsewhere in Zimbabwe. Many more farmed their land for ten years, took up the option to buy it, paid the debt off, and then sold the land to other aspiring farmers. They then returned overseas. A few succeeded and remained.

The vast majority of the commercial farmers today occupy land that they or their families bought at the ruling market price. They have not inherited the land from ancestors who were allocated it by the administration of Rhodes or his post-World War Two successors. Most commercial farms have been bought as business enterprises. Sixty percent have changed hands since independence in 1980, and their ownership was registered during the tenure of the ZANU PF government. Purchasers of farms that were bought after Independence had to obtain a "Certificate of No Interest" from the government, as the government had first option to buy all farms sold. It defies logic for the government to claim now that these farms were acquired in some illegal or underhand manner, and that the owners have no legal right to them.

Many of today's farm owners were attracted to the open-air rural life, and obtained their farming degree or diploma at the tertiary education centre of their choice, or the one they could afford. They worked as employees on farms for years, or often decades, to get the necessary experience and finance, and eventually managed to buy their own

124

farms. They then battled for further decades to pay off their primary bank loans, and they continue to struggle to service the working capital loans they take out annually to pay for each season's operations. Bad weather, crop blights of one kind or another, parasite infestation, livestock diseases or, most heinous of all from the early nineteen nineties on, spiralling interest rates, ruined many competent farmers. Many (or most) now live in an agonising cycle of debt and more debt.

Land Reform

The members of the Commercial Farmers' Union (CFU) are practical people. They are aware that the racial imbalance of land ownership in their country, as determined by Cecil John Rhodes' henchmen and their successors, is not fair or acceptable. As far back as 1991 the CFU proposed, at a special conference on the land issue, a managed land resettlement programme, based on allocation of land to trained black farmers, the land being willingly provided by commercial farmers who wished to sell at the market value.

The CFU produced a pamphlet "Proposals For Land Reform For Zimbabwe, 1991". The summary of the proposals states:

Prior to and since Zimbabwe's Independence the Commercial Farmers' Union has held consistent fundamental views on land reform:

(1) It understands and accepts the need for land reform.
(2) Such reform should, however, be implemented in a manner that ensures land is used on a sustainably productive basis, particularly as agricultural land in production plays a key role in Zimbabwe's economy.
(3) There is much that can be achieved in improving facilities and services resulting in increased productivity in communal areas and also by the acquisition of derelict and under-utilised land before considering the acquisition of productive land for resettlement.
(4) It is concerned that, while resettlement may seemingly ease the problem of overcrowding in communal areas, it creates another in the loss of employment, homes and associated facilities for the resultant displaced farm workers and their families.

The summary further notes that the CFU and its members have participated in plans for settlement and development, including research and training for stockmen, small-scale coffee-growing and tobacco production. It noted that, since Independence, *"the majority of resettlement schemes to date have led to a serious loss of productivity, denudation of resources, insufficient income and even food aid being required for settlers."*

It also stated that *"Government has stipulated and the CFU fully supports that in future, farmers selected for resettlement must be not only experienced and competent, but receive additional training."* How one wishes that government had remembered this stipulation, and abided by it.

The summary concludes: *"Fundamental to the success of the proposals and the resettlement programme will be the CFU's and the individual farmers' continued willingness to assist in any way possible."*

In the conclusion to the proposals it is stated: *"The most important single issue facing Zimbabweans of the future will depend on how the land question is managed today. To this end a national livestock and crop policy is essential."*

The importance of the training of small-scale farmers was also emphasised, and the CFU undertook to work with government *"to map out a land strategy that will encourage farmers and those who wish Zimbabwe to develop and prosper, to work together."*

The willingness of the CFU to co-operate with government in land resettlement is apparent in this important document.

In the normal course of events, as many as eight commercial farms a week are advertised for sale in a single newspaper. It would be easy for government, with its right of first refusal, to acquire these for resettlement. Foreign donors, throughout the 1990s, had agreed to help pay for the resettlement process, including full compensation to the farmers. They honoured this agreement until they found that the government was abusing it, taking some of these farms as gifts, selling or leasing them at unrealistically low prices to its favoured few, and not allocating them to the people who should have benefited from the re-allocation - the land-hungry black farmers.

The Harare Agreement of 1998 was drawn up by and agreed to by the ZANU PF government, the CFU and a number of foreign donors. It was a more comprehensive plan than the 1991 proposal of the CFU.

The foreign donors would fund the purchase of land from commercial farmers, ensuring a huge flow of foreign currency into Zimbabwe, as a substantial amount of the payments would have remained to circulate in the economy. The government publicly endorsed the Agreement and agreed to implement it. The objectives of the land reform effort, it was agreed, were to be the alleviation of poverty and the provision of land for black farmers who were capable of farming it efficiently.

Though the party felt that it could hardly be seen to reject this offer of free assistance, and therefore accepted it, a progressive, peaceful and managed land reform programme did not appeal to ZANU PF. No political benefit would accrue from it to the ruling party. It would not be able to take all the credit for supplying the land to the beneficiaries. It would not be able unilaterally to designate which farms would be reallocated or to whom, depriving it of its most powerful weapon and perquisite - patronage for the party faithful, the tribal allies, and the relatives.

The allotment would, instead, be done on merit, monitored by the participating donors and agencies. It would be obvious to all that the land being made available was being paid for by foreign donors, in large part the former colonial power, Britain. There was no direct benefit for the party mandarins in this accord. It would also have been a gradual process, lacking the impact that ZANU PF desperately needed of an issue that might salvage its political fortunes. Land ownership was an emotive issue - the Party would exploit it to the full. It wanted swift and dramatic action.

The commercial farmers would have assisted in the management of the proposed phased programme, and would have helped with training and logistical support for the black farmers who would benefit from it. This posed a problem politically for ZANU PF, whose main campaign issue, its posturing as protector of the poor blacks against the British colonialists and their white settlers, might lose some of its appeal to the electorate. This managed hand-over would see that land would gradually be allocated to land-hungry black farmers without crippling the agricultural production so vital to the country.

The first action required from the government by the Harare Agreement was that it should set up a technical committee of qualified people to draw up a programme for the implementation of the Agreement. The committee would have been broadly based, and composed of representatives of government and of the donors, commerce and industry, academics and the agricultural unions. There would have been a balanced representation. The government has never bothered to set this up. It did not suit its agenda. This demonstrates its lack of commitment to the Agreement, and to viable land reform.

The technical committee was to have opened bank accounts, which would have been subject to careful control by professional accounting firms. Payments from the accounts would have been strictly monitored, so there would also have been little opportunity for "graft". The ruling party took no steps to set up the committee or to carry out the programme. Its implementation would have seen billions of dollars flooding into the country to finance the organised and efficient setting up of black farmers in viable agricultural businesses. The fact that it was not adopted has been disastrous for the country, and particularly for those blacks with farming skills who could have benefited from the re-allocation and become owners of their own productive farms.

The government had initially gazetted around 1470 farms for compulsory acquisition in 1997. Many of these were challenged in court. In terms of its own regulations, these designations fell away after it omitted to follow them up within a specified time.

The legal route was, in the end, superseded by the illegal invasions of farms from March 2000. On 2 June 2000, the government designated 804 farms indiscriminately for resettlement, ignoring totally the criteria set by it previously.

The CFU had always attempted to foster good relations with the government and to liase with it regularly. For ten years until 1999, the Minister of Agriculture, Mr Kumbirai Kangai, whose pragmatic attitude had been appreciated by the farmers, had attended the annual CFU congress. Mr Joseph Made, the new Minister, did not attend the congress held in 2000, though he was invited. The invitation, it is said by CFU sources, was hand-delivered to his office. Mr Made did not respond, did not attend, and denied having received it.

Land Already Bought For Resettlement

A substantial portion, 3,5 million hectares of the land bought for resettlement from commercial farmers with funds supplied by donors has been leased at uneconomically low rates to ZANU PF leaders. The leases stated that the farms would be offered for sale to the lessees after five or ten years, conditional upon their having demonstrated that they could farm properly. Despite this, some were offered for purchase after only one year, and have been bought. Most of the land is lying fallow or being grossly mismanaged. Some has been allocated to unqualified and inexperienced people who attempted to farm it, but failed, or just neglected it. The bulk of the farmland has deteriorated very badly, as proper farming procedures have not been followed. Since the land has been misused, the donors have withdrawn support.

The CFU accepts that rational land redistribution, without destroying the productive capacity of the land, is essential. Productivity must be the keyword. According to the experts, to transfer five million hectares of land, as is envisaged by the government's fast track programme, while maintaining productivity, should take 20 years if it is undertaken properly, with the resources currently available. This time frame could be modified by the level of investment in training facilities, which depends on the donor community.

Commercial farmers would endorse enthusiastically the press statement released by the National Chairman of the Land Reform and Resettlement Committee of Ministers and Minister Without Portfolio in the Office of the President and Cabinet, The Honourable JW Msika MP. On 6 February 1999 Mr Msika, Vice President of the Republic of Zimbabwe, said in Harare, that *"The Government of Zimbabwe continues to implement the second phase of the Land Reform and Resettlement Programme with the determination to resolve the land issue IN AN ORDERLY AND PEACEFUL MANNER (author's capitals). .... Government intends to acquire a total of five million hectares for resettlement purposes. The target(s) include:*

1. *Derelict farms*
2. *Under-utilised farms*
3. *Farms belonging to absentee landlords*
4. *In certain cases farms adjacent to communal areas*
5. *Owners of multiple farms."*

It is unfortunate that the Government did not adhere to these criteria.

The Donors

Zimbabweans must accept that, since the donors invest in a programme of this nature voluntarily, they have a say in how it is implemented. They are under no compulsion to help and do not feel obliged to do so. We Zimbabweans are not entitled - we have no legal or enforceable right - to demand that they assist. They do not suffer from some awful feeling of guilt that they are bound to expiate (though certain of us may find it hard to accept this) by throwing money at us, and could easily divert the funds to some other impoverished beneficiary country.

There are those in Africa who tend to think that the people of the Western World should feel guilty about the fact that their ancestors enslaved Africans and took them to America and other places. They think that the Western World owes them compensation. Most Westerners believe that the descendants of the slaves born in the West had better opportunities to develop themselves than they would ever have had if they had lived in Africa.

The Western World banned slavery more than a hundred years ago. However, it still flourishes in many countries in West and North Africa, but not with any assistance from the West, which now disapproves of the concept thoroughly. Westerners refuse to feel guilty about their erstwhile involvement in the slave trade, and believe that the main and initial slave traders were African rulers who enslaved and sold their own people to foreigners.

People generally have a tendency to believe that which suits them best. We should all, however, in our own interests, make an effort to understand what others consider to be the truth, especially if those others have the whip hand, or control the funds we so desperately need, as in this instance. We might see things differently but, if we want them to help us, common sense dictates that we should at least be polite to them.

Those who donate or advance funds to Zimbabwe are not all starry-eyed do-gooders. Their main motivation for providing aid and loans is simply that it is better for them to have a healthy economy here than yet another third world basket case. They would rather make money trading with us than fund famine relief for starving Zimbabweans. Some give commercial loans with the intention of making a profit.

130   *Voices of Zimbabwe*

There are also genuine charitable donations, but they are hard to justify to the more pragmatic of their voters. Fortunately for us, there are organisations which feel that they have an obligation to assist other human beings in danger of starvation, however self-inflicted that danger may be. They will therefore offer this assistance with varying degrees of reluctance or enthusiasm, depending on their view of our society and its leadership, and on how much we are prepared to conform to their ideals of good governance.

The donor community had suggested that transferring 60 farms per annum would be the ideal. The government now wants to process 3 000 in three years. It is not possible to achieve this without severely damaging the farms' productivity. The capacity of the training and infrastructure-building facilities should dictate the pace. While these can be expanded, there will be limitations. The government's "plan" is totally unrealistic. In fact, the government, in a state of panic, inspired by its unexpected defeat in the constitutional referendum of February 2000, rushed into the fast-track land reform programme without having prepared any plan at all.

The Supreme Court has highlighted this omission in a judgement (Judgement No. SC 132/2000 issued on 21 December 2000) rejecting the ruling party's actions on the land issue. The Court concluded that there was at that time "no programme of land reform". The party has now come up with a plan, which will have to be approved by the Supreme Court. It will be easy to discredit it. It is neither sensible nor workable, and, if implemented, would destroy Zimbabwe's agricultural base, and most of the rest of the economy, since the different sectors are inter-linked. Incredible though it may seem, it is evident that ZANU PF is prepared to destroy the economy in a desperate attempt to remain in power. It dare not lose the election - it has too much to hide that might be revealed by another party in power. It therefore has to bribe voters with the promise of land; it has nothing else to run on. The ruling party can hardly rely on its record over the past 21 years to impress the electorate.

The government's US$1,9 billion programme, recently presented by Mr Joseph Made, the Minister of Agriculture, calls for a ten-year plan. Land acquisition would occur in the first three years, and the development of the infrastructure would take a further seven. The plan requires productive farmers to be removed and their replacements moved in before any of their infrastructural needs are in place. Even if the government plan went according to its expectations, which is unlikely in view of past experience, settlers would occupy the land for years before the roads, schools or clinics are built.

The government has shown itself unable to meet most of the targets it has set. Zimbabweans will recall the ambitious promises - one could not call them programmes - "Health For All By The Year 2000" and "Housing For All By The Year 2000"? They were monumental failures, largely because no serious attempt was made to implement them, and also because the required funds were either not budgeted for or were spent on projects more dear to the ruling party's heart.

The government can supply little technical support. Agritex, the previously efficient Government Agricultural Extension Service which should provide technical expertise, lacks the resources and staff to be an effective force, now. It has been hit by retrenchments demanded in the government's economic reform programmes and a general lack of resources.

The government's plan calls for land to be allocated without full ownership being transferred. There will therefore be no title deeds. The land acquired will be transferred into the "state land" category and then either leased to a farmer or granted to him under customary law by a chief. Government could, at some future time, move the new settlers off the land at its whim. Could it be that it wants the resettled farmers to be dependent on the party, and not masters of their own destiny? Consequently they will be unable to pledge the asset of their land to banks for financial backing as is the case with today's commercial farmers. They will not, therefore, have the security necessary to secure loans. Some will, no doubt, scream "Racism!" when the loans are not forthcoming, especially when elections are on the horizon, but banks are obliged by law and common sense to be circumspect with their depositors' funds.

The CFU was aware of the potential for trouble over the land resettlement issue prior to Independence 21 years ago. It has always been in favour of resolving the issue in a manner that will not disrupt the economy or its own production. The CFU is aware that redistribution is necessary and inevitable, and wants to achieve this in a systematic way. It is committed to on-going dialogue with the government to effect the

132

necessary changes. At the CFU congress in March 2001 it was again emphasised that a confrontational approach to government was not the right approach and that dialogue was essential.

Simply putting untrained people onto farms and letting them just get on with it does not work. The lesson has been learnt from large schemes such as those in Mtoko and Murewa, where farming co-operatives were established. All failed. A number of schemes were set up after independence in which ex-combatants were installed in farming co-operatives. Most of the participating members no longer live there. They were not properly trained, and most failed. A few horticultural co-ops near Harare did succeed, after entering into contracts with private sector vegetable wholesalers.

The Master Farmers

Zimbabwe is lucky to have a highly effective programme in place to train Master Farmers. Set up by the old Rhodesian government, it is still working. Those training to become Master Farmers are tested practically during their course, and must run a farm successfully. They can be trained on their own plot of land or can be attached to estates, and work under supervision. They can also be communal farmers. Applicants are selected on merit. Trainees are instructed by Agritex and by the private sector. They are taught farming techniques and management skills, including accounting methods. Both the government and the private sector fund the project. The Master Farmers' programme has proved its worth at successful resettlement projects in Gokwe, Copper Queen, Mount Darwin, Chesa and Vuti, among others. This is an example of a government programme that has worked. These schemes are called purchase areas, as the land is available for purchase, with full title being granted to proven farmers.

These is no set time for the Master Farmers' course. The farmer has to prove his abilities which are measured by his success on the ground. Training is open to any communal land resident and each is monitored carefully as he puts his training into practice.

On completion of the course, the farmer is issued with Agritex's Master Farmer Certificate.

The qualified Master Farmer is then moved to a leased farm. He has an option to buy if he proves, over a period of five years, that he is a competent farmer. If the required standard is not reached in five years, then the farmer is reviewed again after a further five years. When the farm is paid for, he is granted title deeds.

The qualification is highly respected and the Master Farmers have demonstrated that they can succeed and become an important asset to the nation. They have also proved that farming expertise in Zimbabwe is not the preserve of white commercial farmers.

There is a large pool of successful and potentially successful farmers in the communal lands who could benefit substantially from a properly managed land redistribution programme. They are anxious for the opportunity to demonstrate their abilities and to improve their lives dramatically. It is important that they are given the chance to do so and the CFU is willing to help them make the most of this.

A major cause of failure for small-scale farmers is poor financial management. To a large degree, this skill can be learned, but it is also a matter of personal character or discipline. The Master Farmers have shown that they have the necessary qualities in abundance. An expanded form of this scheme could enable new farmers to take over resettlement land for their own benefit and that of the country.

Farm Invasions

The farm invasions commenced within three days of the "No" vote on the government-backed constitutional referendum in February 2001. They are euphemistically defined in government documents crafted after the event and apparently designed to give them a stamp of respectability as "The Fast-Track Land Redistribution Programme". Alleged war veterans (many 10 or 15 years too young to be actual war veterans) suddenly invaded hundreds of commercial farms. They disrupted production and drove many farmers and their employees off the land.

The Party had freed the country from colonial rule two decades before - its main if not only claim to fame. It would now give the commercial farmers' land to the masses. This would serve to buy their votes in the elections! The sole qualification for allocation of land under the programme was that the recipient was loyal to ZANU PF. Supporters of the opposition party were expressly banned. Farming experience or competence did not count. No consideration was given to the fact that the farm invaders would displace more commercial farm workers than they could hope to settle on the farms. It did not matter that most of the farms would become non-productive, and that a great deal more poverty and misery than wealth would be created. Those were not the important issues. Retention of power for the party hierarchy was the only factor that counted.

The farm invasions were a blueprint for economic disaster, as must have been well-known to their architects. The lure of land for nothing might buy a victory in the election - and buy power for the party for another few years but it is a strategy for short-term survival. However, it was the best and only plan the party could come up with.

Despite the extent of the invasions and their continuance after more than a year, there has been considerable restraint shown by landowners and, indeed, by the invaders. Most of the latter have not been armed with firearms, which has helped to minimise casualties. Professional hit squads, and not the farm invaders, are believed to be responsible for the murders of most of the farmers who have been killed. The culprits have not been brought to Court, so the truth is not fully documented. Those few entrusted with arms seem to come and go. Many farmers have been disarmed, and some have only handguns left. Most had an array of weapons - mainly hunting rifles and pistols. These have largely been taken from them by government agencies, one of the more sinister developments that has taken place. What can the motive be? Why render the farmers helpless?

Unfortunately, as it becomes increasingly unpopular and more desperate, the government has issued threats to arm more of the war veterans on the farms.

Tobacco Farming in Zimbabwe

Tobacco is the richest, most important export crop grown in Zimbabwe. It is, however, grown best on poor, sandy soil, preferably on a slope so that water, from rain or irrigation, runs off readily. Tobacco grown on nutritious soil, with the qualities required by other crops is not favoured by the consumers because of its taste. The farmers feed their tobacco the nutrients it requires directly and artificially, by fertiliser application and top dressing. The land of most tobacco farmers is not, therefore, suitable for peasant farming. It appears that this is not realised by most of the farm invaders, as many "rich" tobacco farms have been invaded. The invaders have planted some crops, mainly maize, the staple food, on them. This is not using the land to best advantage, and the crops have not grown well. It is evident that many of the farm invaders do not have the intention or ability to fertilise, grow, cure and sell tobacco, or any commercial farm produce.

The year 2001's early tobacco crop, grown from May to November 2000 and then cured, is less in quantity, but better in quality than last year's harvest. This is the first of two annual crops, and is grown under irrigation and intensively cared for. It seems that it has largely escaped the attention of the farm invaders. The dual-cropping system is an example of the efficiency of Zimbabwe's commercial farmers. With the crops being staggered and grown on different lands, the processing barns can cater for twice the acreage they would manage if only one crop was reaped and cured in a year. This halves the cost of the very expensive curing infrastructure required.

Law and Order

Zimbabwe's media coverage world-wide, and in all but the ludicrously biased government media, depicts a society without effective law and order.

The Supreme Court of Zimbabwe has confirmed the situation. It declared: (reference Part V, Sec. 3, 2nd paragraph S.C. 132/2000) "The rule of law in the commercial farming areas has been overthrown." Further, it stated in Part V, Sec. 8, 3rd paragraph of the same ruling "Wicked things have been done, and continue to be done." Yet again, the courageous judges of this Court ruled, in Part V, Section 6 of this judgement, that "A network of organisations, operating with complete disregard for the law, has been allowed to take over from Government" and that "the settling of people on farms has been entirely haphazard and unlawful".

In Section 6, page 22 and in Section 8, page 28, respectively, of this important judgement the Court declared of the government: "It has then failed to obey its own law" and "The reality is that the Government is unwilling to carry out a sustainable programme of land reform in terms of its own law."

The government and the Commissioner of Police have been ordered by the Supreme Court to evict the war veterans from the farms they have illegally invaded. They have refused to do so. Prominent politicians have stated openly that the Courts will not prevent them from seizing the farms as they wish.

One war veteran has been dealt with properly by the Courts and has been sentenced to death for murdering a policeman investigating a stock theft. The policeman, who had tracked the missing animals to the veterans' camp, was shot in the head. The sentence has not as yet been carried out and, if previous performance is anything to go by, the murderer may well receive a presidential pardon. Presumably this murder, witnessed by many, was considered to be going a little too far, even for a war veteran. The police force was not happy about it, and a show of legality was thought to be advisable.

Most other murders and stock thefts have not been effectively investigated, and the farm invaders seem to have virtual carte blanche to help themselves to whatever livestock or farm produce they want. Stock and other thefts are often investigated half-heartedly, and only a few isolated prosecutions have taken place. It appears that these have been staged so that it cannot be claimed that the government never upholds the law.

"War veterans" or other ZANU PF supporters are known to have murdered more than 30 people (others are missing, presumed dead) from March 2000 to February 2001. Thousands of vicious assaults and other crimes are attributed to them, and even to the police, army and other government bodies. Ruling party politicians, it is reported in the independent and international press, exhort their followers to kill political opponents. Senior government officials are reported to have stated plainly their intention of killing people wholesale if the presidential election does not go in their favour. They claim that they will start a full-scale war under those circumstances. No action is taken against them, because the government has no respect for the rule of law.

War veterans, we read in the press, have been enlisted in the police and have been promoted over competent officers, even though many of them are illiterate and totally incapable of performing the tasks of even the most junior police officer efficiently. Known murderers who have killed people for daring to support an opposition political party are roaming free, continuing to participate in and to take a leading part in further atrocities. They blatantly intimidate the witnesses to their earlier crimes. It appears that the government has no desire or intention to allow the police to enforce the law of the land in the farming areas (and, more recently, in the cities) as regards people claiming to be war veterans.

Since tourists in general are too frightened to visit Zimbabwe, our once flourishing tourist industry has been largely ruined. It is not inconceivable that foreign tobacco buyers will feel the same, which would be a disaster for the tobacco farming industry, and for the country.

Zimbabwe is not the only source of tobacco in the world. Other producers could increase their production to cater for the demand unmet by Zimbabwean tobacco, or totally new suppliers could emerge. Those buyers who do come will pay as little as they can for the crop on offer. If there are fewer of them to bid for the crop, the prices will drop dramatically. Farmers were occasionally pressured by war veterans to sell their crops early, at low prices. This would have had an extremely adverse effect on the prices gained, if generally practised. Pressure of this nature could be exerted again and the buyers would be delighted to buy at artificially lower costs. The foreign exchange earned by our tobacco farmers is vital for the economy, and the farmers need to be able to negotiate the best selling price they can.

If war veterans invade the tobacco auction floors, the buyers will leave immediately.

Zimbabwe is the only country in the world that has important tobacco auction floors, aside from a small floor in Malawi. In the other tobacco-producing countries like Brazil, tobacco is bought while standing in the fields, if it was not contracted and pre-bought before planting. Only in Zimbabwe is a significant crop hand-picked, carefully graded and certified prior to sale, and only here are buyers able to choose exactly the grade and even the specific bale they want, and to check it physically. In this way they can be sure of the quality they are buying, which means that the farmers can command higher prices - if all goes well. Zimbabwe simply cannot afford invasions of the tobacco floors.

CFU Activities

The CFU represents the majority of the commercial farmers of Zimbabwe, most of whom are white. The members have given the executive a mandate to enter into dialogue with the government on their behalf.

The CFU is the only industry, apart from mining, that provides education for its employees. It also runs its own highly effective Aids Control Programme which is a model for the country and for the developing world. Farmers' wives, who have volunteered to work as Co-ordinators, distribute HIV/AIDS literature, videos and condoms, using their own and their farms' transport. The 30 co-ordinators in the project lecture farm employees and, on request, inhabitants of communal and resettlement areas on the pandemic of AIDS. They also instruct Peer Trainers who are active in the local communities.

Working in tandem with Ministry of Health operatives, the CFU AIDS Control Programme is the most effective of its kind in the country. It has managed the almost impossible task of actually changing the attitude of the bulk of its target population segment towards unprotected and promiscuous sexual activity. Its Project Manager is a member of the National Aids Council board, and has represented Zimbabwe at international seminars on HIV/AIDS. There are 800 000 AIDS orphans in Zimbabwe at present, and 25,8% of the adult population is infected with the HIV virus. The AIDS problem is therefore massive in Zimbabwe, which has the second highest rate of infection in the world, and the CFU is providing invaluable help to combat the pandemic.

Their involvement in education and health is a measure of the social responsibility displayed by the CFU members. With the exodus of the farmers, this vital work will be discontinued.

The War Veterans

There is a limited pool of war veterans, but they are very mobile. They can get from place to place very quickly, ferried in government transport. The squatters on the farms are not, in the main, war veterans. They are generally hired to stay there and are paid and fed by the government. **The national army, the police and the District Development Fund**

(DDF), a government department, organise and supply them with food and transport when necessary. There are said to be fewer than 1 000 real war veterans involved. There are 20 000 to 50 000 people, many claiming to be war veterans, who occupy the farms.

The war veterans' operations have brought other sectors of the economy closer to the CFU. They are aware that if the farms collapse, the rest of the economy will follow. In particular, the Confederation of Zimbabwe Industries, (CZI), the Zimbabwe Institute of Bankers and the Zimbabwe National Chamber of Commerce (ZNCC), the Zimbabwe Tobacco Association and the Chamber of Mines have been very supportive. Bankruptcies and unemployment have increased drastically since the farm invasions began.

The country is heading for an economic meltdown. Now the towns are being brought into the equation in a more direct way. Commencing in April 2001, war veterans have invaded city boardrooms and assaulted managers and directors doing their best to keep their businesses alive in an economy ravaged by the government. In particular, they set themselves up as arbitrators in industrial matters, especially in labour disputes, adopting the role of benefactors of the poor and oppressed. Little police action has been taken against them. In the short time that they have been active in the towns, they have already cost the country a significant volume of prospective investments and lost the economy hundreds or even, potentially, thousands of jobs.

"War veterans" loyal to ZANU PF are being appointed and promoted in the ruling party and the police and army in an apparent attempt to increase their influence.

If the government sees that it is making more enemies than friends with the land invasion strategy and that more votes are being lost than gained, then it may consider it expedient to stop. It will then no doubt claim that it was not responsible for the whole sorry mess, and look for another populist issue to exploit to win the forthcoming election. Winning votes and staying in power is the name of the game, and the only thing that matters at this stage. The government may end up trying to lay the blame at the feet of the war veterans. The bad workman blames his tools!

The urban invasions of businesses by "war veterans" have in fact turned out to be most unpopular with employed urban workers, who see their jobs disappearing rapidly as some invaded businesses close down.

Financial Considerations

Commercial agriculture is of massive importance to the collapsing Zimbabwean economy. If all or a substantial number of the farmers whose land has been invaded go into liquidation and do not pay off their debts to their financiers, there will be a massive series of bank and finance house failures. This will cause a "run" on the remaining banks and finance houses, resulting in further massive harm, which will cause a "snowball" effect. Savings of thousands of people will be rendered valueless. Near total damage to the economy would result. There would be a massive exodus from Zimbabwe of most of the remaining qualified people, whose managerial skills are irreplaceable.

After this, little will be left behind of our economic structure and our nation will become a virtual wasteland. Unemployment, already at a chronic 60% level, will continue to escalate; chaos and starvation for those without a privileged position will result. It is most unfortunate that those who have the power to influence events are more concerned about the consequences to themselves of their losing power than they are about the welfare of the majority in the country.

Prognosis

Under current conditions (as at July 2001), according to an authoritative source, most of the current commercial farms will not be in existence as functional business units in 2002. The damage to the country arising from this will be colossal.

The present situation for farmers in Zimbabwe is likely to get worse in the short term in the run-up to the presidential elections due to be held by early 2002, as illegitimate pressure is brought to bear on the electorate by the ruling party.

Zimbabwe needs an efficient farming sector. Seventy-six percent of the 12,5 million people of Zimbabwe, 7,5 million in the communal areas and two million on the commercial farms make a living directly from the land. Under the fast-track land settlement scenario, the farms seized will be in a state of ruin or will have reverted to more or less virgin bush, without the benefit of tree cover, within three years. With no adequate infrastructure being provided as part of the initial resettlement exercise, and without sensible allocation of land to people capable of making proper use of it, no donors will be prepared to assist. Degradation of the land will therefore be swift. If the commercial farms are destroyed, as seems likely, the rest of the crumbling economy will not be able to earn enough foreign currency to sustain our people on imported food.

Zimbabwe will then become a nation of beggars, dependent on handouts from the developed nations, not least of these our former colonisers. With an abrasive and xenophobic government in charge, such handouts will be less generous than those the country might otherwise expect to receive. The prognosis is for a collapse, not only of the farms, but also of the whole nation.

This Bumper Sticker Says it All.

QUEUES

There is a small branch of Beverley Building Society at Hillside Shopping Centre in Bulawayo. One particular searingly hot sunny day, a long queue stretched the length of the room, as it was pay-day.

Margaret was hot, tired and impatient. She had been there for more than half an hour and she was going to be late for her next class if the queue didn't move faster. At last, she found herself one person from the front and watched, vulture -like, as the teller attended to the gentleman ahead of her. Then, she became aware of a young black man with a cap at a jaunty angle, a satchel on his back and well-worn running shoes on his feet. He was filling in a withdrawal form at the nearby counter. As the man in front of her finished his transaction, the young black man stepped into his place ahead of Margaret in the queue.

Margaret was utterly incensed. How dare he? But she was a small grey-haired middle-aged white woman in an all-black queue in Zimbabwe. To speak out or not to speak out - that was the question. "Bugger it," she thought, "I'm not going to put up with this." Leaning forward, she tapped him sharply in school-marm fashion on the shoulder. "Hey, what do you think you are doing? I was here before you. Get to the back of the queue and wait your turn like everyone else."

The youth looked over his shoulder at her arrogantly. "I am a War Vet. I don't have to queue like other people."

For a second, Margaret was totally floored. But rage lent her courage and she began to swell up, about to speak her mind in no uncertain fashion. At this moment, a tall black man in overalls behind her leaned forward and whispered, "What is wrong?"

Margaret turned to him and indicated the young man - "He says he's a war vet."

"War vet, is he?" was the response. "We'll see about that." Next minute, he and another man from the queue stepped forward, grabbed the "war vet" by each arm and frog-marched him to the door and threw him unceremoniously onto the pavement.

Pandemonium broke out. Everyone in the queue danced up and down in delight. Gleeful "high fives" were exchanged and shouts of "Hamba kahle, war vet!" rang through the little banking hall.

Then a head popped round the door. Straightening his cap, the young man braced himself for a courageous and face-saving parting shot.

"Next time, I will go to CABS," he said.

Footnote: CABS is The Central African Building Society

BEYOND THE REAL WORLD

It is in the darkness of their eyes that men lose their way.
Not, as they suppose, in any darkness that shrouds their path.

Black Elk

If you haven't experienced the land invasions first hand,
they're hard to imagine.
Set aside the real world for a moment,
and come with me into a different world:
the journey begins on our farm.

It was a golden morning, like yesterday,
and the mornings before
that have traced my life from childhood.
But this one was different:
the tension in the atmosphere was tangible.
I checked the radio and our telephone line:
both were still working.
My dog moved uneasily beside me,
intuitively sensing something.
I glanced at the hands on the kitchen clock:
they had barely moved.

From the window I could see the road
where it passes our biggest dam,
and the dust, which churned and billowed like smoke...
a vehicle was coming.

At the newly planted maize,
where my husband was fixing an irrigation pipe,
it halted.

The driver climbed out and closed the door behind him.
Even from a distance, the swagger and shape were unmistakable:
it was the local war vet "heavy".
Wasting no time on a greeting, he began his script.
"You must not plant one more seed -
the land you have planted is *yours*;
the land still unplanted is *ours*."
Controlling his anger, as we have been warned to do,
my husband ordered him to leave.
"You will regret this," the war vet said.
"You *will* regret this."

Casting a satisfied eye over his easily acquired lands,
he left.
Silence edged back onto the farm;
an uneasy silence.

Ray, being the man that he is, thought for a while,
then resumed planting.

For two weeks we lived on the edge, waiting,
waiting for the retribution.
Watching, and waiting.
All week they stoned cars and trucks on the district road,
smashing our nephew's windscreen on his way back from town
and threatening him.
Somehow he escaped the mob alive.

Finally, the warning came:
our farm was next on the list for attack.
We alerted our staff,
set the emergency plan in motion,
locked our security gates,
locked all the doors and windows,
and brought the dogs inside.
It was like living out a slow-motion nightmare
without knowing how the nightmare would end.

Three war vets arrived with two policemen in tow.
Their message was clear:
since Ray had not listened to the orders the first time,
the war vets would also take half of our mealie crop
and, if we caused further trouble,
they would take the lot.
At this point Ray lost it - he'd had enough, and so had I.
He told them to go to hell.
They left, and the die was cast.

A group of farmers called a meeting with the police and war vets
to stop the attacks on the district road,
but could get no support.
It was futile.
The farmers regrouped on a neighbouring farm
and the owners phoned us to join them.

Set high on a hill, their house is an excellent vantage point
to view the broad sweep of the valley below.
In the heat of summer, cool breezes drift through the open doors
and the night skies are studded with a myriad of stars.
In the late evening you can hear the spotted eagle owl
and watch bats swoop like shadows across the lawn.

But the shadows we face now are of a different kind.

Before we left our farm, the numbers had built up all day
with war vets milling around our farm store, dancing and chanting.
At about 4.30, the crowd began swarming towards our gate,
waving the ZANU PF flag threateningly.
As we left for the meeting, all eyes were on us,
and the weapon-brandishing paused for a moment.

When the meeting was over, I stalled our departure,
overwhelmed by a deep sense of foreboding;
I knew then it was not safe to leave.
The warning came a few moments later over the radio:
the invaders had stormed our yard.

Fear registers deep in the pit of your stomach,
and there are different kinds of fear.
This was like descending into a wasteland,
or falling down a dark pit.
It was a sensation of hopelessness,
powerlessness.
The world about us was falling apart;
the world beyond had abdicated all responsibility.

My husband and three other farmers leapt into a truck
and raced back down the hill to our farm.
I stood in stunned silence for a moment,
as the vehicle disappeared into the dark night.

Finally, after the longest two hours of our lives,
they returned and told us their story.

When they drove past the line of tall trees
at the bottom of our driveway, they could see nothing.
Somewhere, they knew, the war vets were waiting.
As they stopped the vehicle and climbed out,
dark shadows emerged from the trees
and within seconds they were surrounded.
While groups of the dagga-stoked mob
raced around with huge burning logs,
Ray tried to negotiate with the leaders.

Only when it was agreed that the invaders
could take the land they wanted,
were our husbands allowed to leave.

That night we stayed with our friends on the hill,
but could not sleep.
Looking back, the decision to join the meeting
had saved our lives:
Someone was looking after us.

Next morning,
the news was phoned through from our farm:
shortly after midnight
the war vets had broken through the security fence,
stolen meat from the butchery - and all of the knives.
They had partied all night on our veranda,
thrown garbage into the pool
and left their excreta on the lawn.

We went home briefly that evening
to check on the safety of our workers
and to feed and love our animals.
Our staff had been deeply traumatised
and we did our best to comfort them.
Next morning we drove home again
and started cleaning up.
It took a long time.

On Friday we opened the newspaper
and read the announcement:
our farm had been designated.

TOURISM, A CRUMBLING INDUSTRY

As I looked out on the dawn over this perennial landscape,
I felt I was watching the dawn of the world...

From "The African Elephant" by Boyd Norton

'll sing you a song of the beauty that is Zimbabwe. And I'll tell you a tale of the ruin and destruction that is taking place here. Our wonderful tourist industry is in shreds and tatters. In 1999 we had a thriving industry that brought the country many millions of dollars in foreign currency. Tourism, Agriculture and Mining are our three largest foreign currency earners. In 1999 foreign visitors poured into the country to enjoy our marvellously diverse attractions and facilities. True, we had some problems - fuel shortages existed, but they were not of crisis proportion, as they are today. Hotel groups and tourist operators managed to put contingency plans in motion, and they were able to ensure that their clients did not suffer. Today, the industry is crippled, and we are limping along, barely surviving. All we can do, at the moment, is hope that the situation in the country changes before we are all ruined. If it does not, tourist operators and hotels will have to shut down completely. Our game, if unprotected, will be poached and slaughtered, and Zimbabwe will be left with a few goats and chickens. The teeming herds of buffalo and antelope, the spectacular elephant, the graceful giraffe, the endangered rhino and painted dogs, will be treasures of the past, wistful memories only.

This is happening already, as Zimbabwe, without the rule of law, spirals out of control. Poaching is reaching epidemic proportions. Acts of barbaric and pointless cruelty are being perpetrated daily, as animals are being snared and left to rot and others have their tendons cut or their entrails pulled out. These are the very animals at which tourists gazed in appreciation and delight. These are the very animals that foreign visitors captured on film, as a record of their fascinating holidays in Zimbabwe.

In October 2000, the Research and Development Division of the Zimbabwe Tourism Authority (ZTA) compiled a report based on their Business Confidence Survey conducted in August 2000, two months after the June elections. Their study covered the whole country. They interviewed randomly-visited tourist establishments and their findings were alarming. The situation has continued to deteriorate even further. I would like to summarise what the ZTA said, based on the figures up to August 2000.

Zimbabwe's tourism industry has been one of the fastest-growing economic sectors in the country with an annual average growth rate of 18,5% (tourist arrivals) from 1989 to 1998. Tourism receipts increased by an average annual growth rate of 25% over the same period. In 1998, the industry was estimated to be employing over 180 000 people directly and indirectly. It had been forecast that by the end of the year 2000, the industry would be employing well over 200 000 people directly and indirectly.

The period ending 1999 to the end of August 2000 saw a major drop in business performance. Average occupancy rates plummeted to an average of 20% from the 1999 average of 60%. This is a decline of 67%. Foreign markets were affected the most. The domestic market, to a large extent, and the South African market to a lesser extent, are now sustaining Zimbabwe's tourism industry. About 12% of the employees were retrenched and 66 of the 1412 registered tourist facilities closed. The retrenchment affected all levels of staff, from managers to shop floor workers. Of the operators, who did not retrench, 15% of those interviewed introduced shorter working hours, 24% sent staff on unpaid leave, while the remaining 61% took measures like reducing rates and offering discounts to attract business. (Many more people have been retrenched and many more facilities and tourist-oriented businesses have had to shut down during the months following the completion of this survey.)

Most operators indicated that booking cancellations from the domestic and South African markets were due to fuel shortages. Booking cancellations from the overseas markets were mostly a result of negative publicity in these markets. Those operators, who had always relied on the domestic market, were affected the least. About 90% of the respondents indicated that May/June 2000 were the worst months, with occupancy rates dropping to as low as 10%. This level is not viable in any industry.

The results of the study show that the major causes in the decline in business performance were fuel shortages; political violence during the general elections; the land issue and farm invasions and the perceived breakdown of the rule of law. These factors resulted in adverse publicity in the tourist source markets, creating a very negative perception of Zimbabwe as a destination. The withdrawal of some international airlines (70%) from Harare International Airport, and the poor domestic air service has also created difficulties. Although lack of foreign currency was another contributing factor, most operators indicated that it did not affect their operations to the same degree as the other factors mentioned.

As tourist operators, we welcome the concern and the lead of the ZTA. For us, things are critical. Victoria Falls, for example, is like a ghost town today. People joke about the new game there - Spot the Tourist. In 1999 visitors from far and wide were flocking to see one of the seven natural wonders of the world. The hotels and lodges were full. There was a vibrant nightlife. During the day hordes of adventurous young people would be jostling for bookings to go white-water rafting, canoeing or bungee jumping from the Victoria Falls Bridge spanning the Zambezi. For the more conventional person, we would book charter flights over the Falls and sunset cruises on the Zambezi River above the Falls.

Even backpackers are going to Zambia, instead of to the Zimbabwean side of the Falls. Long-lasting damage to tourism occurred when Mr Sol Kersner was allegedly told by a high-ranking government official that the government wanted a donation of a 31% share of his proposed investment (a huge 5 star hotel that he planned to build) in Victoria Falls town. Mr Kersner's palatial hotel, which he chose to locate on the Zambian side of the Falls in Livingstone is nearing completion.

The ripple effect of the situation impacts adversely on people across the spectrum. Thousands of talented black craftsmen and women, who rely on visitors to buy their artifacts and crafts, are struggling to survive. Markets and road-sides are lined with stone and wood carvings, metal sculptures, pottery, beadwork, woven articles and crochetwork, and there is no one to buy them. It is of interest to note that, of the world's ten leading stone sculptors in 1990, seven were from Zimbabwe.

 Kariba town is empty. The people of the area were subjected to vicious intimidation before, during and after the elections in June 2000. The luxurious houseboats lie idle at their moorings. There are very few who come now to marvel at the fabled sunsets on the lake and to watch the herds of elephant and buffalo on the lake shores.

Great Zimbabwe stands brooding, sprawled across seven and a half square kilometres of valley and hilltop. With very few visitors to explore the ruins and examine the intriguing stonework, the atmosphere inside the Great Enclosure becomes even more eerie. Very few people now climb to the hill complex, the royal residence of Great Zimbabwe. This is the World Heritage Site that is home to the most significant ancient ruins in sub-Saharan Africa. And there are very few people coming to wonder at it.

To the south of Bulawayo, our second city, lie the spectacular Matobo Hills, once the home of the San or Bushmen and a place of deep religious significance to the later Karanga. Mzilikazi, founder of the Ndebele nation, likened the rounded domes of the amatobo, or bald-headed hills, to those of his counsellors. These thousands and thousands of granite kopjes (hills) are fascinating with their rocky crowns: boulders, standing one upon the other, at improbable angles.

This area is the biggest rock art gallery on earth. There are some 3500 individual rock art sites in the Matopos alone. These "bushmen paintings" are to be found elsewhere in the country, too, wherever erosion by sun, wind and water over millions of years has created rock shelters and caves.

Bird watching, or birding, is said to be the world's fastest-growing leisure activity. Zimbabwe is a paradise for birders, as over 600 species have been recorded, from the two metre ostrich to the smallest of the jewel-like sunbirds. There is a great variety of colour and song in the birdlife of this country. The haunting call of the fish eagle flying above the Zambezi is very different from the melodious, liquid call of a summer visitor, the European bee-eater. Birds of prey are represented by 73 species, and, of these, 17 eagles have been recorded. There is a larger concentration of black eagles in the Matobo Hills than of any large eagle species elsewhere in the world.

Zimbabwe has approximately 1200 species of indigenous trees. In contrast, there are only 24 indigenous trees to be found in the United Kingdom. The vegetation ranges from rain forest to desert bush, from montane flora to tropical forest. The unique baobab tree is instantly recognisable by its strange shape and huge trunk that can reach a girth of 28 metres. Those with a diameter of eight metres or more are thought to be over 3000 years old.

Throughout the veld, brightening the brown winter landscape, vividly coloured aloes are to be found. There are approximately 35 aloe species in Zimbabwe, varying from the delicate mountain aloes found in the Chimanimani area to the distinctive Aloe excelsa, rising from granite outcrops in its regal crimson splendour.

There is so much variety in Zimbabwe. Nothing could be more different from the Matopos, for example, than the cool Eastern Highlands of Nyanga, the Vumba and the Chimanimani. Here waterfalls cascade down steep mountain slopes and the fresh, heady smell of pine trees fills the air. There are wonderful golf courses and picturesque hotels. After the tropical heat of the Falls, the cool contrast of the Eastern Highlands is delightfully invigorating.

Throughout Zimbabwe, lodges are to be found that offer the visitor personal hospitality. Many of these in the "bush" areas have been constructed in such a way that they merge with their surroundings. There are tree houses, spacious rondavels (round huts) and thatched cottages. They stand on hillsides overlooking the Zambezi River, on the granite rocks in the Matopos and beside the sparkling trout streams in Nyanga.

As we move from the scenic beauty of the country to the cities, we find different attractions. We would introduce our visitors to Harare's modern shopping centres, to our excellent restaurants and to the city's vigorous night-life. In Bulawayo (a much quieter city than the cosmopolitan capital of Harare) we would visit the railway museum. Steam enthusiasts have come from all over the world to see steam locomotives in action.

Voices of Zimbabwe

Until recently, a steam locomotive would take passengers in luxury coaches from Bulawayo to Victoria Falls. With the decline in tourists visiting the country, this service, sadly, has had to be discontinued. When business improves, it will, no doubt, be reinstated.

We are lucky in this country to have such wonderful, friendly people. The hostile, aggressive, slogan-chanting rabble that appear on television reports, are not in any way representative of the ordinary person. Our people are educated, and almost all speak English. This makes life very easy for most tourists, who can make themselves understood.

Zimbabwe's very diversity is her most important asset. There is so much to do and see. At the moment, however, Zimbabwe is portrayed by the international media in a dreadful light. News bulletins focus on violence, war veterans, random murders and mismanagement. Travel agents overseas discourage their clients from coming to Zimbabwe, because they feel that they cannot guarantee their safety. No medical insurance or baggage insurance is available to a German tourist whose destination is Zimbabwe and the Americans are following suit.

Overseas tourists book a year in advance. The few bookings that we have had for 2001 are hunters' bookings, and those that were made for the viewing of the total solar eclipse on 21 June 2001. There is virtually nothing else from the international market.

It will take us, in the tourist industry, a minimum of 12 months to get back on our feet. It will be difficult, but it can be done. We cannot do it alone, however. Until the government provides an environment in which the tourism sector can survive, we will be without our overseas visitors. Tourists will not come here until law and order has been restored. It is as simple as that. We will have to prove to the world that Zimbabwe is stable, not a country that has stumbled into a state of anarchy. Only then will the tourists come back to us. Only then can our industry be revived. Only then will the tourism industry be able to make its contribution to the country's economy. Only then will it be able to provide work for our people.

❧ ❖ ❧

PERSPECTIVES

Only this century..., with the growing appreciation of non-Western artistic traditions, has African art, and above all African sculpture, come to be recognised as a major cultural phenomenon in its own right.

Duncan Clarke (African Art)

is face is finely chiselled, as if, in a moment of quiet contemplation, he turned his tools on himself, etching depth and character.

These sculptures are exceptional. Each is a work of art to be explored from every angle; each reflects a different dimension as the light changes. In shadow, his expression is thoughtful, echoing the mood of the carving on the roughly hewn table before us.

"Yes," he says sadly, "the lack of visitors is affecting our business. Before, the tourists would come regularly to this place. Some would buy what we had to offer, others would commission something special. Those who ordered from us would sometimes provide photographs so that we could bring memories to life, or create unique pieces for a wife, a husband or a girlfriend. Sometimes the pieces would be religious, sometimes landscapes with the animals of Africa, sometimes they would ask for festive scenes.

"Today the tourists do not come. They are afraid. They do not understand what is happening here. We continue to carve, but we must also find other ways of making money. And when we do carve, we have to work hard at becoming better - and being different. People do not want to buy the same things."

We ask if he comes to work every day, as we would like to visit his make-shift studio again. "The cost of transport is high," he explains, "so it is not always possible. We cut back on expenses where we can, so that there is enough money for food for our families. Our lives have changed. The craftspeople of Zimbabwe are suffering. The price of mealie meal has risen by over 700% within the past few years, but we cannot put our sculptures up by the same amount. Nobody would buy them. Even buying a loaf of bread today is expensive."

"The government buys land and it buys cars; we have even heard that it buys ships. Why would they want to buy ships?" He tells us that America and England gave the country a lot of money after Independence, and that the money was squandered. "Why would people in the government need so much money? The time must come when you have enough."

"They have forgotten that we are all the same. They have forgotten the people. Whether we are rich or poor, we are all the same. When we have a celebration, the rich and the poor come together. Whether you wear fine clothes or torn clothes, you are welcome. We believe in dignity and respect for all."

"We must learn to support each other. And to care for each other. When we have learnt enough about a craft - or the work we do - we must pass on the knowledge to the next person. In this way we can all survive."

"Today the hospitals are full of people suffering from stress. To create here is like climbing a high mountain. We stay because we must stay with the children. We cannot leave them, even if we have been offered jobs in other countries. We feel pain for ourselves, but we feel more pain for the children."

"In Zimbabwe we have become too passive. We are not taking a stand. In the Cote d'Ivoire, when the people had finally had enough, they all went out into the streets. The soldiers could not shoot the entire nation. And so there was change. We do not want to be political, but we need change."

The afternoon slides towards evening and the light drains slowly from the African sky. In the lengthening shadows, the sculptures before us take on the growing darkness of a country that was once described as "the Jewel of Africa".

▌◄⇨▐ ▌✖▐ ▌◄⇨▐

SPEAKING OUT

*Things get better when enough people decide
that they should get better. Things change
when ordinary people come together
in a common purpose.*

Kofi Annan, Secretary-General of the United Nations

aria Stevens, a Swedish national, came to Zimbabwe after Independence 20 years ago to help the black people of the country.

"I joined an aid organisation which had done some good work in Mozambique and believed I could make a contribution to their Zimbabwean programme," she explained, curling up on a couch in one of the sparsely decorated rooms of her new home in Harare.

Travelling overland from Kenya gave Maria a perspective of Africa she had not anticipated and changed her view on aid as a solution to the continent's problems. Despite this, she chose not to renege on her commitments and took up a post in a tribal trust area as planned. When her involvement in the project was complete, she spent three months travelling in South Africa and Botswana. Back in Sweden on holiday with her family, Maria created "a theatre" of her time in Africa to present a balanced perspective of the situation.

While working in Zimbabwe, Maria met her future husband, David Stevens. The attraction was immediate, intensifying into a deep love which spanned their 20 years together. Side by side, they transformed Arizona, a run-down tobacco farm in the Virginia area east of Harare, into a productive operation. In addition to cultivating tobacco and maize, they introduced cattle and ostriches.

David was a talented, dedicated and stable farmer with unracialistic views that complemented Maria's liberal approach. As a result, they maintained good relationships with their farm workers and the rural people who lived in the communal land bordering their farm. These neighbours were welcome to collect firewood on their property and utilise water from the rivers that flowed through the farm - provided they respected David's environmental controls. "As the farm increased

156   *Voices of Zimbabwe*

in value, so we improved the living standards of our workers and then our own," said Maria. "It was a conscious choice we made."

The wide-open spaces and magnificent colours of Africa captured Maria's imagination and she thrived on farm life. "After the bush war 20 years ago, we were all so hopeful for the country's future. But last year changed our lives for ever."

In April, soon after the land invasions began, David was abducted from the farm by a group of "war vets" and taken to the local police station. The farming community was alerted immediately and five farmers raced to his assistance, only to find that he had been taken by his abductors to their headquarters, where he was beaten, tortured, forced to drink diesel and then shot in the head and back. Later his body was thrown on top of two of the farmers who had themselves been abducted from the police station and severely beaten. David was one of the first people to die in what was to become a bloody election battle fomented by the ruling party.

Maria was left with their four children: Marc, their 16 year-old son, Brenda, who was 14 at the time, and the one-year-old twins, Warren and Sebastian. Devastated by the tragedy, they returned to Sweden for a time to recover. For many people, the logical choice would have been to remain in the safety and comfort that Sweden afforded. But Sweden was no longer home. "Although I don't like what is happening here, I have lived more of my life in Zimbabwe: this is now my home," said Maria.

In her view, the tragedy of the current situation is that the black people have not realised - or understood - the level of energy which the white people have put into the country. "We should be living in a symbiotic relationship. Instead, the white man has become the ox who walks around the water wheel and gets so beaten and abused that he sinks deeper and deeper into the quagmire. If the government had looked after us, instead of trying to destroy us, there would be food and jobs for the population and we would have been able to fix the failing infrastructure, in particular the roads. Africa has missed our energy completely.

"In Europe and Scandinavia the approach is different. There they promote and reward brightness and hard work. Here the knights are stifled - Africa breeds a 'no going forward' type of character. The country needs pioneers - people who are courageous and are prepared to put in the extra effort required. It is too easy to quench the spirit of the indigenous people."

"I believe that the Shonas need to be empowered so that they understand that they can trust us. But you cannot empower anyone until he feels he has done a decent day's work, or until he's fed his children. In Africa it should be easier to survive. Here you plant a crop and it grows. In Sweden and Europe you have to plan more. Like the squirrels, you have to collect for the long winter months. But there *is* a dry season here - why is there still no planning?"

Maria believes that, until Zimbabweans live in a society which promotes ownership of property and people are given title to their land, there will be no respect for the land. "People living here for generations on allotments have a 'hired' mentality which fails to promote a sense of responsibility. So we have over-grazing by their cattle and goats, and trees are chopped down with no thought for the future. It comes back to integrity. If it is mine, I will look after it and respect it. If it is not mine, I will milk it."

Despite the problems and frustrations of Africa, Maria finds it an exciting continent. "One of the things that first attracted me is that we live constantly on the edge here. However, the government-controlled land invasions have catapulted the country into a total breakdown of law and order and it is this lawlessness which has killed my husband. I blame Mugabe, but I also blame the government and those members of the police who failed to protect him - they were gutless. If I were in a senior position, I would resign. There is no integrity left. The role of the police is to guard the citizens of the country, but they have failed in their duty and people are afraid of them - it is so undignified."

Maria believes that the farmers should have been allowed to make a stand back in February 2000 when the trouble first started. "We should have downed tools until the war vets and squatters left our farms. All the farmers in Zimbabwe, South Africa, Mozambique and Namibia should have stood together; instead we were not allowed to retaliate."

Today Arizona, the tobacco farm that was her home for 12 years, stands empty. "I'll never go back there," Maria said, "it would be too painful. There's nothing left now, it's completely fallow. Our workers are scattered. They had to sell their cattle and live in hiding for four months. They have nothing."

Rebuilding one's future requires courage and determination. Maria has developed a five-year plan for herself and her children, and has enrolled for an international teaching degree so that she can start working before her money runs out.

"I'm not worrying about money - I've made a conscious decision not to do so. Through all of this I've learnt to let go. If you struggle against the changes, you will get nowhere. You have to learn to be open to change, to be strong and also to be humble. Most of what I have in this house has been given to me. When you have accepted that you have lost everything, a new energy will come in. But you have to be open to that energy. You give and the universe gives back. I have made a conscious choice to be happy and positive. If my children want to do something but there is not enough money, I say to them: 'We can't do that, but we can do this,' and they understand."

Maria's daughter, Brenda, has also accepted her new life and the experiences have deepened her spirituality. Initially she remained in Sweden after her mother returned to Zimbabwe, but was unhappy without her family and friends. She also missed the strong family values she had grown up with in the Zimbabwean farming community. Marc, who is currently studying to be a pilot with the Swedish airforce, is still struggling to come to terms with the loss of his father and the farm. The twins have settled well at a school around the corner from their new home and are happy, energetic children.

Fuelled by the pain of the past year, Maria has continued to voice her anger with the current situation in Zimbabwe. "Mugabe's policy is to divide society. By setting people against each other - black against white, women against men, heterosexuals against homosexuals and Christians against traditional healers, he has continued to wield his power. People are guilty by omission - they are too afraid to work together. It's no good saying, 'Get rid of the government and then I'll help.' Zimbabwe has to change itself. If the Shonas don't talk to the Ndebele, or to the Karangas, or if there is friction among the various racial groups, how can we achieve unity?"

"We have to mobilise a force for good - women's groups could be a powerful starting point. When I moved to town, we started a women's pressure group. Women are more spiritual than men and we should use our spirituality. We may not be able to change the political state of the country, but we can change the emotional state. We can pick up the pieces and help to rebuild Zimbabwe. "Since David's death, I have had support from many people, including strong Christian support. People from all walks of life have said: 'Let me pray for you.' Christianity has come through as being both humble and beautiful."

"Each of us must make a stand in our surroundings and operate with integrity." Referring to the work of Dr Stephen Covey, which focuses strongly on personal values and integrity, Maria said: "Integrity is what one's own conscience allows one to do. No conscience, no integrity. How can Mugabe attend the Human Rights Millennium Conference when he is waging a war on his own people?"

Since Maria holds President Mugabe personally responsible for David's death, she attempted to institute a civil damages claim against him last June, but was unsuccessful. Even the then attorney-general would not support her. Finally she was invited to institute the claim in America. The case, which is currently pending, has been instituted on behalf of Maria and four other Zimbabweans who have lost family members and property. According to protocol, the State Department has recommended that the courts grant Mugabe immunity as a head of state. It is now up to the American Courts to decide whether or not he has immunity.

"We have to speak out," said Maria, with conviction. "We have to hope that justice will prevail - and we have to believe that there is a God."

❚◄⇦►❚✖❚◄⇦►❚

To know what is right and not to do it
is the worst cowardice.

Confucius, Chinese philosopher
c 551-478BC

THE HUNTING PARTIES

Surely the Holy One is not deaf.
He hears the delicate anklets that ring
on the feet of an insect as it walks.

Kabir

ver week-ends, members of the armed forces come down on hunting parties. Armed with .303 rifles, they wreak havoc on our property. Day and night you hear shots, followed by the piercing screams of wounded game. Sometimes the animals sound so close you can almost smell the blood.

Before these people took over our farm we had more than 60 zebras, 40 kudu and about 300 impala. Until they arrived, our guards had managed to protect the game from poachers. But our shotguns are no match for their .303s and, in any case, the guards are too frightened to shoot.

Our maize used to grow in rows as straight as a gun barrel, stretching far into the distance. This year, like many other farmers, we have planted less than half of our normal crop. Apart from the instability of the situation, any farm which has been taken over is no longer eligible for bank loans or overdraft facilities, so the farmers are hamstrung.

Those workers who have been with us for more than 10 years were given 4,4 hectare plots for cropping and their cattle were allocated land to graze. The workers cleared and fenced the plots and we bought the left-over wood to fire our tobacco barns.

When the squatters and war vets moved in, they forced our workers off their land. Then one day the forces arrived and demanded to be shown around the farm. "We can take anything we want," they said. "And we can take it today." I would prefer not to report what else they said. It requires a great deal of courage for a farmer to accept this.

Before the war vets were thrown off the land by the forces, they had stripped all the internal paddock fences. They had also taken the roof off the new broiler shed - the chickens could have fed many people in the area - and sold the sheeting in a nearby communal reserve. Our irrigation pipes, which cost a few thousand dollars each, have been stolen and converted into pots. We cannot get access to our silage pits or to the boreholes. If we remove anything, our lives are at risk.

Before the land invasions, we had hundreds of guinea fowl, pheasants and francolins on the farm. Today there are snares everywhere. They use string or nylon for the birds and small animals, and stolen wire for the big game. A few months ago we found a zebra caught by a snare attached to a log. The wire had bitten deep into its leg and the animal was in horrific pain. We had no option but to shoot it. The poachers revisit the snares infrequently: the agony of a dying animal is of no consequence.

The environmental impact of the land invasions is criminal. Destroy the balance of nature and, ultimately, you will destroy yourself. Today the monkeys and baboons are taking over because the predators have been shot out and there is no food. They too are hungry.

The farm to the south of us is finished. After it was designated a few years back, squatters and poachers ripped up the fences and the government sent in teams to cut down the trees. For two years the trucks rolled in, carting wood to line ruling party pockets. The reservoirs and boreholes are wrecked and the dipping tank is broken. No one lives there now. After a heavy rain-storm, water roars across the veld, causing sheet erosion. You would not want to go there again.

We stay here because we have nowhere to go - we are financial prisoners. In this area, thousands of acres were offered to the government on a willing seller, willing buyer basis. But the government wouldn't buy the land - it was easier just to take it. The invaders are lucky that the rains are late. If the rainy season had finished at the usual time, their crops - which average less than an acre per person - would have failed, and they would have no food.

This farm was our future, and our son's heritage. We encouraged him to study further and set up home overseas, but Africa called him back: the call of Africa is strong. Today we stand to lose everything. And so do our workers. They are devastated. We are all playing a waiting game - it's a question of whose nerve gives first. And, in the end, we are all losers.

:◄⇨►: ⊠ :◄⇨►:

LOSS

The power of the Holocaust is that it demands we confront ourselves in the very ways we generally avoid - forcing a burden of understanding that should provoke dread - a tiny glimmer of inspiration as well, but primarily dread. Even as it tells the hideous and unprecedented story of what Nazis did to Jews and others, it also tells a tale of caution about what human beings did, and can do, to other human beings. It shines a pitiless light on bystanders as well as perpetrators and collaborators. It teaches us that indifference is not neutral; silence always aids the perpetrators.

"The Holocaust and the New Century - The Imperative to Remember"
Alexander Kimel - a Holocaust Survivor - United States Holocaust
Memorial Museum

 unday 4 June began quite normally for me. I had breakfast with my family fairly early, and then went out to join my friends. An MDC rally was being held in our area and we were all going there to help, as we were members of the MDC youth. It was exciting being a part of the huge crowds that gathered to listen to their candidates speaking. The election was only three weeks away and tension, fear and excitement were steadily intensifying. Stories of beatings and intimidation however, were reaching us daily, and we had decided to form a security network. We would move about in groups if we could, or in pairs if this was not possible, but never alone. It was too risky to be isolated. We no longer wore our MDC T-shirts, as we stood out like beacons, and we certainly didn't want to draw attention to ourselves at this crucial time.

We could hear members of the youth on their loud hailers calling the people to the rally. Crowds were hurrying towards the stadium, talking and laughing. The stands were filling quickly. Rap music started and the atmosphere became festive. Our rallies were always good fun. It was great to be involved and to feel that you could play an important part.

We watched the build-up for a while. This rally would certainly be successful if the crowd was anything to go by. So far there hadn't been a problem with the electricity supply. At an evening rally a few weeks before, the power had been disrupted, just as the event was about to begin. Fortunately, our team had installed a back-up generator, in case the opposition should decide to sabotage us again. Our candidates were able to communicate without a problem on that occasion, but if we hadn't anticipated a dirty trick like that, our meeting would have been a total disaster.

Just before our candidate was due to arrive, two young boys ran up to my partner, Amos and myself. "There's a group of war veterans coming this way," they whispered. "One of them has a gun, and I think they are bringing others here as well." Amos and I decided to investigate, so that we could alert the rest of the security team if we needed to.

We went cautiously in the direction the boys had indicated. Sure enough, three men were standing together near a butchery, and one of them was carrying an AK rifle. Amos and I watched them for a few moments. Then a shrill voice shouted, "Look, look - those two boys over there across the road are MDC. I've seen them wearing the T-shirts and carrying red cards. They are MDC." Within seconds, we were grabbed and our arms were pinned behind our backs. The girl, who had alerted the war veterans, was looking very pleased with herself, little bitch.

Our only chance was to deny everything. "We're not MDC members, we're going to a football match. We need to go quickly - the match will be starting and we want to support our team." We couldn't have been very convincing, in spite of our grovelling and protesting. They didn't believe us for a moment.

Three more men joined them. Five of them were older men and one was about 20 years old. - the same age as Amos and me. One of the older men was obviously in charge. He had a pistol and, pointing this at us, he instructed the others to drag us over to a pick-up truck parked behind the butchery. They flung us into the back of the truck and climbed in. Their commander drove the truck. It was rather like movies we had seen, when the get-away truck's screeching tyres leave rubber burns on the road. But we weren't watching - we were a part of the movie, and we were terrified. We had heard plenty of stories about what war veterans did to people who were not ZANU PF.

Suddenly the truck stopped. The commander went into a house and came out again, moments later, with two twists of mbanje. He threw the "grass" to his men and they lit up and began to smoke. Their conversation became louder and louder, as we travelled along. Every so often, they would look at us and laugh, but they didn't speak to us.

We soon found that our destination was a deserted rubbish dump. The truck stopped near a foul-smelling mound of plastic packets and bottles, tins, bones, rotting vegetables, discarded car parts and bits of glass. The stench was bad enough, but what was worse, was the realization that Amos and I were completely alone, kilometres from town, with no-one to help us.

They pulled us out of the truck. By now, we were trembling uncontrollably. We didn't know whether to beg for mercy or remain silent. Our training as security personnel had not equipped us for this type of situation. They made us take off our belts and shoes and throw them onto the rubbish dump. The mbanje had taken effect by now. Their eyes were glaring strangely and their voices were even louder and sounded more aggressive.

And then they began to beat us. At first they punched and kicked us, shouting encouragement to one another and laughing crazily. We tried to shield our faces. We begged them not to do this. It was awful. We were completely helpless. We didn't stand a chance against six men.

Their commander then told them to stop. Amos and I were lying among the rubbish, bruised and battered. The men went to the truck and took out an axe and several logs of wood about as thick as a man's arm. We had seen them in the truck before, but only now did we realize what they were to be used for. They started with Amos. They hit him a few times with the logs. He was bleeding and crying. Then one of them grabbed the axe and swung it at his head. Miraculously, the axe head flew off its handle. Amos took to his heels and ran for his life.

They let him go. They still had me. They hit me with the logs and opened deep gashes on my face. The blood was pouring from my head and soaking my shirt. Through a haze of red, I saw a card fall from the commander's pocket, as he raised his arm to hit me again. It was a CIO card. The leader of this band of war veterans was attached to the President's Office. The CIO receives its orders directly from the president himself. We all know this.

What chance did I have? I felt despair overwhelm me. The CIO commander leered at me and struck me hard, knocking me flat on my back. He forced my legs apart. "Come, Elias," he said to the "war vet", who was my age. "Castrate this MDC fool. Let's show him what happens to people who try to cause trouble." Elias came forward eagerly and raised his log. He smashed it down between my legs. The pain was indescribable and I blacked out.

When I came to, I could hardly move. I was alone - they had gone. Did they think I was dead or dying? Aching all over, I managed to drag myself away from the rubbish dump and down the road. I was sobbing, desperately afraid that they would return. I crawled on and on, until I came to a small settlement, where a group of very poor people were living.

They were horrified at the sight of me. I was covered in blood and dirt and I couldn't stop shaking from the shock of my experience. One kind villager went to call the police, but he came back after an hour or so. The police couldn't come, they said, as they had no transport. By this time, I was on the verge of collapse. Another man went to call an ambulance. Again, I must have fainted.

When I regained consciousness, competent hands were lifting me into the ambulance and I was given an injection that helped to take the pain away. It was such a relief to be safe. I spent the night in hospital and the next day I was taken to see a private doctor. He was kind and understanding. He told me that he would have to operate and remove one testicle, as it had been badly crushed and there was internal bleeding.

Last year I was a young man of twenty, carefree and bursting with life, energy and idealism. This year I am a young man, nearly twenty-one, but I feel very different. When the weather changes, when it is cold or if it rains, I feel wrenching pain gripping my lower abdomen. It makes me double up in agony and I have to take painkillers. I try not to complain too much, as everyone has problems. What worries me most is a gnawing anxiety that will not go away. "Will I be able to have children? Have they robbed me of what every man wants more than anything else?"

The doctor isn't sure. And I feel nervous now about girls. I haven't been out with a girl since this happened to me. Would a girl understand my horror and my fear? Would a girl be caring and patient with me? Would she sit and stroke my face gently, as we sit under a tree together and say that she loves me, no matter what? I don't know, and I am too scared to take the chance. I would rather have no one, than someone who would laugh at and humiliate me.

So I will forget girls for the moment, concentrate on my studies and hope for change. I will hope for a brighter future for myself and for my country. I will pray for a leader, who cares about his people. I will pray for a leader who does not castrate his own kind. I will pray for a brighter tomorrow. I will pray.

❙◆❖◆❙◆❬✖❭◆❙◆❖◆❙

QUEUES

Zimbabweans complain 24 hours a day - how boring we have become! We seem to be attempting to out-do one another with stories of our experiences, determined to have queued for longer than the next person!

The best queue I have ever joined was at least 200 metres long. It was a cold, overcast morning with rain expected. The conditions made not the slightest difference to the 500 or 600 people waiting there with me. There was a truly festive atmosphere with strangers becoming friends, as people shared their deck chairs and flasks of coffee and chatted animatedly about their hopes for the future.

Within a short time, an enterprising food outlet was taking orders for bacon and egg rolls, cokes, hot coffee and magazines. Not once in the five hours of waiting did I hear one person complain. A first for Zimbabweans! For the first time in 20 years we were a united force of people, black, white, coloured, Indian, Greek - in fact a mixture of the cultures of the country, all with a common purpose. We had come to vote in the election on 24 June 2000. We recorded our X on our ballot papers and returned home with a feeling of hope, knowing that we HAD made a difference.

THE RAP

This is the rap that you can't beat,
This is the story from the street,
People don't want you 'round no mo',
That's one thing you can be sho'.

They know you trying to keep yo' station,
Claimin' only you can lead the nation
Mtukudzi said it, he meant no harm -
Time you rested back on the farm.

However they do it, can't be worse,
You, for the nation, yo' become a curse;
So wake up old man, before you fall,
It's the other side that's on the ball.

You had yo' chance, for twenty year,
Pity you hashed it, shed no tear -
Money you got stashed away,
Keep you going fo' many a day.

Let the country heal, let's be friends,
Make yo' peace before it ends,
Move over nice, let it all go,
We may forgive you, you never know.

Rasta

NB: Oliver Mtukudzi is a famous Zimbabwean folk singer. He wrote
a song about an elderly man who was not prepared to retire.

‖•✥•‖⊠‖•✥•‖

Cricket?

It civilises people and creates good gentlemen.
I want everyone to play cricket in Zimbabwe
I want ours to be a nation of gentlemen.

His Excellency, The President of Zimbabwe
Cde R G Mugabe, Patron of The Zimbabwe Cricket Union

QUI TACET CONSENTIRE VIDETUR

He, who keeps silent, apparently approves.

In 1945, Pastor Martin Niemoller, looking back over the events of the Second World War in Germany, confessed:

The Nazis came first for the Communists - I did not speak up because I was not a Communist. Then they came for the Jews - and I did not speak up because I was not a Jew. Then they came for the Trade Unionists - and I did not speak up because I was not a Trade Unionist. Then they came for the Catholics - and because I was a Protestant, I did not speak up. Then they came for me. By that time there was no one to speak up for anyone.

he Son of God was born, an ordinary person, to a carpenter and his wife who lived in a small village. Jesus, the Messiah, would have had an ordinary childhood with lessons on the Holy Scriptures. He must have helped Joseph and learned His father's trade. He must have had friends, played games and run errands for His mother. When He became a teacher, it was to ordinary people that He spoke. He understood their concerns (however mundane) and He empathised with their problems. The intention of His ministry was to direct His followers to observe what was important. He summed up the essence of living a moral and honourable life as follows:

You must love the Lord your God with all your heart, with all your soul and with all your mind. This is the greatest and the first commandment. The second resembles it: You must love your neighbour as yourself. On these two commandments hang the whole Law, and the prophets also.

I came out to Zimbabwe as a young priest just over two years ago. My mother was horrified when she heard that I was to be sent to this trouble spot. "Liam," she said, "I shall pray to Our Blessed Mother every day for your safety. But please be sensible and take care of yourself, too." I said nothing at the time to her about the troubles in Ireland. Unknown or unfamiliar problems always seem more frightening than those to which we have become accustomed. I settled down in my large urban parish, rather relieved that I had not been posted to a rural area. At least this way I could learn something of the history of the country and study the languages, before being sent to a remote mission station.

My superior is an elderly man who came out to this country more than fifty years ago. He is close to retirement, and finds it quite wearying having to share the parish house with a youngster, who is fresh out of the seminary. Father Edmond is not very talkative. He loves watching football on television in the evenings. His answer to most of my questions is, "Read, my boy. This house is full of books by different authors on all sorts of interesting and varied subjects. Browse through these, and you'll find your answers."

So I have followed his advice, and I have devoured all his books about Zimbabwe. There are, surprisingly enough, a great number. Those I have read include: "The Struggle for Zimbabwe", "The Great Betrayal", "Mukiwa", "The Valiant Years", "Sometimes When it Rains" and, most recently, "African Tears". All fascinating. All with very different attitudes and different points of view. Of course, I have also read Nelson Mandela's autobiography," Long Walk to Freedom".

And I have talked to the people. I've talked to everyone who will talk to me about the past, the present and the future of Zimbabwe, a country I am growing to love. I talk especially to the ordinary people, because it is they who are suffering most. And I am becoming aware of an inescapable fact. History is repeating itself. What happened in the past is happening again. And it is happening to the ordinary people. And if the ordinary people don't stand up and speak out, their silence will be taken as acquiescence, as consent.

This, therefore, is why I am writing this. It is my job as a priest, as a follower of Christ, to teach and to guide. Many have said that religion and politics are separate concepts. This is not so. If a religious man does not speak out against an evil system, then it can only mean, either that he condones what is taking place, or that he is afraid and does not love his neighbour as himself. Christ is very clear about who one's neighbour is. This person is the Samaritan, the least likely individual, not the obvious friend or the person next door. One's neighbour is the man or woman in the street, the hungry child, and the sad and lonely grandmother who does not know where her next meal is coming from. One's neighbour is the person with AIDS, the man who has been beaten, the woman who has been terrorised and the child who has witnessed unspeakable horrors.

The ordinary person is suffering terribly in today's Zimbabwe. Inflation is rampant, food costs a fortune, fuel is scarce and, therefore, it is becoming increasingly difficult to get to work. School fees are becoming unaffordable, health care is minimal and housing at a premium. The ordinary person is afraid for his safety and for that of his family.

In April 2000, Archbishop Pius Ncube in his Prayer of Hope for Zimbabwe, spoke out bravely about *"the disturbing events taking place in our country now"*. He said:

We make this communication, calling on our leaders to engage in constructive policies and all citizens to avoid violence and to contribute positively to the welfare of this country and all its peoples. As Church we stand for justice and the well-being of everybody. We do not take sides with any political party. We strongly deplore the lawless invasion of the farms; sometimes by villagers who are being forced against their will to settle on the farms. We see anarchy growing in the country...Destitution grows and misery increases. The decline of the economy is largely due to corruption and nepotism in the government...

Twice the High Court orders concerning land invasion have been ignored by government and the police, and yet they claim to abide by the rule of law. There is importation of violence from one district to another where groups come to harass, beat and sometimes even kill. Whereas after the war, arms had been very well collected by the government, surprisingly many civilians and war veterans are being given guns to increase violence. To compound the situation, the police have at times not come to the assistance of those who have legitimately requested help. We all acknowledge that people need land, yet it must be distributed in a legal and orderly way. On the other hand 270 farms meant for resettlement were sold at bargain prices to government officials...

Twenty years ago the then Prime Minister, Mr R G Mugabe, on the first Independence Day made a particularly encouraging speech on reconciliation: "As we become a new people we are called to be constructive, progressive and forever forward-looking, for we cannot afford to be men of yesterday, back-looking, retrogressive and destructive. Our new nation requires of every one of us to be a new man, with a new mind, a new heart and a new spirit. If yesterday I fought you as an enemy, today you have become a friend and ally with the same national interest, loyalty, rights and duties as myself. If yesterday you hated me, today you cannot avoid the love that binds you to me and me to you. If we look to the past, let us do so for the lesson the past has taught us, namely that oppression and racism are iniquities that must never again find scope in our political and social system. It could never be a correct justification that because the whites oppressed us yesterday when they had power, the blacks must oppress them today because they have power. An evil remains an evil whether practised by white against black or by black against white." (Reported in The Chronicle 18 April 1980).

We call on people to have hope and courage. Rulers have come and gone. "Jesus Christ is the same yesterday and today and forever." Heb.13:8...Let us all cultivate a culture of tolerance and respect each other, even those with a different point of view. "Love your enemies and pray for those who persecute you." Mat.5:44.

As Catholic priests, religious and faithful in the Archdiocese of Bulawayo, we shall pray and fast for peace until it prevails. Since God loves us and wants us to have peace, by His power we shall attain our goal...Trusting in God we shall overcome all adversity, for Christ is stronger than all other forces: "With God all things are possible." Mat.19:26.

The President and civil servants are there to serve and uplift every individual person and the nation according to the spirit of Christ, "whoever would be great among you, must be your servant...the son of man came not to be served, but to serve." Mat.20:27.

We appeal to the government to bring about justice, order and peace in our country."

Archbishop Ncube spoke out confidently and bravely about the situation in Zimbabwe. He appealed for peace and justice. He organised marches every week through the City of Bulawayo. He endorsed the report of The Catholic Commission for Justice and Peace "Breaking the Silence" which records that during the 1980s, the Gukurahundi machine (the Fifth Brigade) killed more than 20 000 people, assaulted thousands more and systematically attempted to starve a large proportion of the Ndebele-speaking population.

The worst reaction of an embattled people is weak-kneed apathy. It is certainly easier to do nothing. Passivity and negativity are infectious, however, and very dangerous. They strip a person of dignity and self-respect. They reduce him to a snivelling wreck. As an example of this type of "reasonable behaviour" I shall quote in full a letter written by someone sitting safely in Adelaide, Australia, cautioning us here in Zimbabwe to do nothing in case things get worse. This sort of approach is the emasculating work of Satan.

Letter to The Daily News Saturday, 7 April 2001
Postpone Elections to Avoid Bloodshed

We read the declarations made by President Mugabe against the main opposition MDC that they will never rule our beloved country. This might sound weird, but I think it's a wise idea not to have the elections at all and let these people rule without further bloodshed. Who really would want to sacrifice his or her life for the change of governance? We as a nation are not bold enough to be like the Yugoslavs. Last year's parliamentary election cost us quite a number of our beloved ones and from the look of things that number might double if not treble in the bloodiest upcoming elections. To think that the elections are going to change the leadership is daydreaming. Whether we like it or not the truth still remains that at the end of the day Mugabe will be celebrating. It is very difficult to uproot a gum tree that has been growing for the past 20 years because its roots are as widespread as the distance between here and Egypt. The saddest part of the whole thing though, is that we put in structures for a democratic election and then smear the whole process with vote rigging, which may not happen at the ballot box but elsewhere. If we campaign for this strategy then we may save our brothers' and sisters' lives because it might be you and me who are victims in this election.

Brighton M, Adelaide University, Australia

Frightening, isn't it? This is the sort of counsel that delivers people up to those who seek to terrorise and dehumanise them.

There are other priests and ministers of religion who have spoken out. Two of these men are the Rev Tim Neill of the Anglican Church and the Rev Paul Andrianatos of the Presbyterian Church. The Rev Paul Andrianatos has had to leave the country, as his work permit was not renewed. Such persons have shown great courage in the face of threats and attempted intimidation. Organisations such as The Catholic Bishops' Conference and The Zimbabwe Council of Churches need to speak with a strong and authoritative voice. They must strike out against evil and wickedness. They must set an example to the people of Zimbabwe, and refuse to tolerate criminal and inhumane actions. To date, their voices have not risen above a whisper.

I commented earlier that history is repeating itself. This is, perhaps, the most frightening aspect of all. Among Father Edmond's books and articles, I found a report from the Rhodesian Catholic Commission for Justice and Peace entitled "Civil War in Rhodesia". It is dated 1 October 1976. The authors comment as follows:

The prime purpose of this report is to inform, not to accuse. "It is not so much the hatreds, the fears, the brutalities which are the social evils of our country - it is the ignorance, and with it the acceptance of the evil. (Father Trevor Huddleston, writing in 1956 about the situation in South Africa.)

Civil war is the obvious outcome of a history of conflict in Rhodesia. Both sides pursue their aspirations in the name of justice and peace. While the politicians push their strident rhetoric, now for black majority rule, now for white power, the focus of the fight, the people who live in the country, experience increased violence and a desperate hopelessness...Sympathies have markedly polarised. The Government insists on total commitment of the people to wipe out the insurgents. It uses every means at its disposal to convince us that what it calls "terrorists" are a communist force, invaders from outside the country, people who are fighting against what is valuable and just in the life-style we know here. But it is common knowledge that the many hundreds who invade this country are citizens of this country, that they are fighting for the right of self-determination for their fellow-blacks and for a share in the wealth which would enable them to live their lives in conditions of basic physical health and social decency.

The report sets out to show the sufferings of blacks at the hands of the government forces. It asserts that the RF Government of the day used every means of propaganda at its disposal to *instil in its people a conviction that their cause is righteous and just. Deviation of any kind or a faltering faith is regarded as the first rumblings of treason.* It goes on to explain: *A soldier can, in good faith, shoot and kill any person whom he thinks supports terrorism. He has the Indemnity and Compensation Act to protect him and the man he shoots has to prove the soldier's bad faith. The result is that rural Africans live under a virtual martial law...*

As is the case today, some spoke out then, but there were not enough of them. Christians have a duty to foster respect for the dignity of their fellow human beings. Apathy and self-interest cannot be tolerated. The Rt Rev Donal Lamont, Catholic Bishop of Umtali (Mutare today) had been a thorn in the flesh of the Rhodesian Front Government for years, as he spoke out against their policies time and again. After initially being sentenced to ten years in prison (a sentence he did not serve), he was deprived of his Rhodesian citizenship and later deported. In 1976, before this happened, he wrote an Open Letter to the Government of Rhodesia, condemning many of their actions.

As a Catholic Bishop I cannot be silent while civil discontent, racial tension and violence are so much in evidence and daily on the increase. There is a serious danger of bloody confrontation between the races within Rhodesia itself, of the political involvement of other countries, and the consequent escalation of the conflict throughout the whole of the sub-continent. Already along the full length of my diocese a state of war exists...

Conscience compels me to state that your administration, by its clearly racist and oppressive policies and by its stubborn refusal to change, is largely responsible for the injustices which have provoked the present disorder and it must in that measure be considered guilty of whatever misery and bloodshed may follow...You may rule with the consent of a small and selfish electorate, but you rule without the consent of the nation, which is the test of all legitimacy..

Neither can you deny that the world community of nations rejects your claim to legality. Your administration is an outcast from and stands condemned by the civilised world...

No wonder the oppressed people, made marginal to society in their own country, have welcomed and continue to welcome those they call "freedom fighters" and whom you call "terrorists". This is readily understandable. It is understandable too that such a force should have arisen and that it should daily be on the increase. Your oppression has called it into existence and given the young men and women who belong to it an attractive cause to espouse. They feel themselves compelled in conscience to fight for the elimination of all the discrimination, which has degraded their people and made them second-class citizens in the land of their birth.

While I say this, I must make it absolutely clear that, as in the past, I deplore and denounce with all the power which I have to command, all acts of violence which may have been perpetrated by these or by any other individuals or groups. The Church can never condone such violence, no more than it can turn a blind eye to its causes. At the same time I must repeat - no matter what the consequences for myself - that the institutional violence sanctioned by your administration and made respectable by Acts of Parliament, is itself the root cause of the physical violence which Rhodesia has experienced during the past ten years...

In spite of their limited vision and of their consequent denial of integral development to all the people of Rhodesia, the efforts of previous governments had indeed brought many of the benefits of Christianity and of Western civilisation to this country. You, however, by your total insensitivity to the rights of the human person and by your inability to read the signs of the times, have undone much of what had previously been accomplished. Yet you refuse to recognise your sorry condition and appear satisfied to continue your oppressive policies even though they should bring ruin to Rhodesia... If intensification of racial hatred, widespread urban guerrilla activity, increased destruction of property and fearful loss of life are to be avoided; if the whole sub-continent of Africa is not to be engulfed in a cruel war, you must without delay change your present tragic course of action...Pope Paul VI, when addressing the United Nations on the subject of Racial Discrimination, said: "As long as the rights of all the peoples, among them the right of self-determination and independence, are not duly recognised and honoured, there cannot be true and lasting peace, even though the abusive power of arms may for a time prevail over the reactions of those opposed...All men must participate in the life of the nation. Power, responsibility and the decision-making cannot be the monopoly of one group or race segment of the people".

It is up to you to give the lead. The fate of Rhodesia and its people is in your hands.

Does this sound familiar? Who will rid me of this troublesome priest? On 25 February 1977, The Rhodesia Herald reported the Minister of Justice and Law and Order, Mr Hilary Squires, as saying: "If he (Lamont) can be deported, the country will be a better place...it will deprive him of the...spectacular martyrdom of imprisonment which he has ardently desired for some time."

My Brothers and Sisters in Christ, history is repeating itself. We cannot afford one more moment of man's inhumanity to man. The people of this poor strife-torn country have had enough. Violence is contrary to Christ's supreme law of love. *"...There are three things that last: faith, hope and love; and the greatest of these is love."* Let us practise love by caring for one another, by respecting one another and by attempting to be less self-engrossed. Let us try to emulate Christ, our Saviour, who shoulders our burdens and who loved us enough to lay down His life for each one of us.

¦ ⟨⟩ ¦ ✕ ¦ ⟨⟩ ¦

SUBSEQUENTLY

On Sunday, 13 May 2001, a pastoral letter "Tolerance and Hope", signed by nine Catholic bishops, was read from the pulpit of every Catholic Church in Zimbabwe. It was the long-awaited condemnation by the Zimbabwe Catholic Bishops' Conference of the lawless situation prevailing in the country.

The pastoral letter emphasised the dignity of all human persons: *"...society with all its various organisations must recognise and uphold this dignity. No government or political party can appropriate it..."* The bishops said that holders of political power tended to abuse fellow human beings to achieve their own political ends.

A person is only useful as long as he is a means to their political ambitions.

A human being is reduced to a thing that one uses and, in fact, abuses. A case in point is the way political figures and political parties have used our unemployed youths during election times. Violence, intimidation and threats are the tools of failed politicians. We must point out to them that they are engaging in unjust activity.

The bishops said that the people had the right to take part in political activities and that the government had an obligation to ensure that members of society were free to express their political views without fear of being victimised.

Frustration of this basic right of the person leads to turmoil in society. It impedes the harmonious development of the person and of society as a whole. In fact in a society such as ours, which is multi-cultural and multi-racial, we will always differ in opinions, and therefore we call upon every citizen to exercise a very high degree of tolerance.

The lack of this tolerance is clearly evidenced by the violence that continues to grip our country. It is a shame that we who claim to be modern resort to violence in order to advance our political ideas. We have witnessed with sadness the loss of human life and the destruction of property due to differences in political views and opinions. We Zimbabweans fought for justice, peace, democracy and economic well-being of all our people. Each Zimbabwean has a right to security of life and property and no politician has a right to deprive any person of this right. Public officers are supposed to serve the common good... However, we note with sadness that in many cases public officers come to be associated with self-enrichment and corruption. There is need for transparency and accountability in public office...

The bishops went on to discuss *"the activities of war veterans in both urban and rural areas".* They said that this behaviour was not *"solving problems in the proper manner"* and that *"it was the duty of government to ensure that the nation is not held to ransom by a few..."* They voiced their concern about the lawlessness prevalent in the country.

We urge the government to allow the law enforcement agents to perform their duties without interference so that there is a sense of security in the country. Let us remind each other of the fact that no one group of persons liberated this country alone. The great majority of Zimbabweans, because of their love of freedom and sense of justice, liberated it through their sacrifices.

The bishops then tackled the thorny question of land redistribution. *The one pressing issue which must be settled urgently, in fact it should have been settled long ago, is the question of land. We acknowledge that there is an urgent need of economic reform to redress the imbalances that exist in our society today, where we have 75% of our population living under the poverty-datum-line. Unfortunately, the distribution of land has been marred by violence, deaths and intimidation. The programme of land distribution should target the people who are really in need of it. We should be careful not to create more injustices in the process of addressing legitimate concerns. It is also important that the farm labourers are catered for in the exercise. Priority should be given to the setting up of infrastructure and providing resources. Small-scale farmers have proved that they can contribute meaningfully to the economy of the country.*

The bishops stressed the desirability of national dialogue. They discussed the need for the media *"to serve society as a whole, not just the narrow interests of the ruling party and government of the day or of the business sector alone..."* They voiced their concern about the deteriorating health services and the horrifying HIV/AIDS pandemic.

Their message ended with a call for unity of purpose and vision. *Let our common enemy be poverty, disease and ignorance, not fellow citizens. Let us unite our efforts to defeat those enemies and we shall earn our rightful place in the family of nations...As a nation we are one body with many parts, therefore whatever one part does affects the whole.*

GLORIA OLDS' FUNERAL

Those who do not understand must be beaten until they do understand.

Moven Mahachi, Minister of Defence

 hey came from the farms. They came from the small-holdings. They came from the towns and villages. And they came from the cities. They came in Landrovers, in farm pick-ups, and in cars. Some came by plane; others had travelled long distances on foot. They came to pay tribute to a 72-year-old woman, a loved and respected farmer from the Nyamandhlovu area of Matabeleland, who had been shot down in a hail of bullets from AK 47 rifles. Her name was Gloria Olds.

It was a hot summer afternoon and St Andrews Presbyterian Church in Bulawayo's Hillside suburb was packed to capacity. Seated in the front pew beside the flower-strewn coffin was Mrs Olds' son, David, with his own young son Ryan, on his knee. Next to them were his wife Laura, their daughter Mandy, and other members of their family.

Strategically placed at the front of the church, the television cameraman and press photographers had the task of capturing the pain of a family bereaved a second time for audiences around the world.

When everyone was seated, the Reverend Paul Andrianatos began the service with a reading:

Come unto me all who are weary and I will give you rest... I am with you always to the very end... neither death nor life... nor danger... nor sword... neither angels nor demons... nor present, nor future... will be able to separate us from the love of God.

"We are saddened to be parted from this love. And there are many questions at this time. Let us set aside our fears and open our hearts to Your love. Let Your spirit speak to ours so that we can be sure that You are alive..."

After singing the first hymn, the congregation fell silent. The minister continued:

"We are here today to give thanks for the life of Gloria Elizabeth Olds, a mother, grandmother, sister, colleague and friend. Gloria leaves behind her son David, who is married to Laura, and their two children, Mandy and Ryan. Gloria also leaves behind her other grandchildren, Martine and Angus, the children of Cathy and Martin, her son who was murdered less than a year ago. At the time of her death, Gloria was still grief-stricken over Martin's death.

Gloria's other child, Elizabeth, died in a motorcar accident in 1978. After Elizabeth's funeral, the parents, Alf and Gloria, and the brothers, Martin and David, stood at the door of the chapel consoling others. Gloria's husband, Alf, died three and a half years ago, from emphysema. He was at home at the time, so that he and Gloria could be together.

In Gloria, we have a loving wife, mother and grandmother. Gloria also leaves behind three sisters - Shirley, Tessa and Marie. Gloria was the eldest of the four girls. Owing to the nature of her father's work, Gloria had the responsibility of taking care of her younger sisters. While they were growing up her parents lived in the bush, erecting telephone and electricity lines.

Gloria was also a strong person... I believe that she had to be in order to survive. This strong-willed, no fuss, independent woman was also compassionate. She was a person who loved and cared for her family and others. I now quote from a letter written to a Bulawayo newspaper shortly after her son Martin's death by Sister Janice McLaughlin, an ex-matron at George Silundika School.

MARTIN OLDS' MURDER, TRAGIC END OF NATIONAL HERO

The 20th anniversary of independence has been irreparably marred by the political violence that has claimed the lives of so many innocent people in recent weeks... Their murders are a crime and a tragedy, and benefit no one.

I wish to pay tribute to Martin Olds, the commercial farmer who was murdered at his farm in Nyamandhlovu on 18 April. He was a neighbour of George Silundika School, which was set up shortly after independence by the Zimbabwe Foundation for Education with Protection (ZIMFEP) to provide education to former refugees and ex-combatants.

The late Martin Olds, his wife and parents helped the school in many ways, when others, both black and white, wanted nothing to do with it. ... Mr Olds Snr lent the school a water pump that his son, Martin, installed and maintained for the next three years.

Mrs Olds collected books from farmers' wives to help start the school library. She and her husband used to bring gifts to the 200 orphans at the school and donated meat for open days. She helped to start a women's club...and managed to obtain a sewing machine for the group as well as stoves for baking.

Mr Olds worked closely with the first headmaster, Matthew Mtobi, to ensure that the school survived during the early years after Independence when students and staff were still living in tents and some officials in the Ministry of Education wanted to disperse them and close the school.

While I do not know all the details of his death, it is a tragic irony that a white farmer who accepted the hand of reconciliation, and went out of his way to embrace change, should be the target of politically motivated violence.

I mourn him and the sad loss George Silundika School has suffered. My deepest condolences go to his wife and children, and to all those Zimbabweans who believe that the land issue and political differences can be resolved through dialogue and negotiation rather than by confrontation and violence.

Sister Janice McLaughlin, Silveira House, Harare

Returning to Mrs Olds' contribution to the community, The Rev Paul Andrianatos said, "Many a black child was brought to Gloria because of illness, hunger or poverty. The children would always leave fed, clothed and cared for. Gloria got on well with the local blacks and spoke the language fluently.

Her compassion and care extended beyond her family and friends. It also reached beyond people, for it extended to animals. Joy Smith's collie was knocked over by a motorcar and its two front legs were broken. When the breaks healed, he still could not walk, so Gloria took him in and taught him to walk again. It took six months, but she succeeded. Someone once commented that they loved Alf's and Gloria's home as everything in it moved, including the odd animal orphan being reared. Gloria loved her dogs and they loved her. Three of her dogs lost their lives in the attack and died at her side. They were Blondie, Duke and Panarotti or Rotti (a stray Rotweiller she took in from the SPCA)."

On Sunday morning, March 4, Gloria got up as she had for the past 50 years and, after an early morning cup of tea, went to the gates of the fence around her house to open them for the day's business. It was a crisp morning - clear after weeks of wet weather, and three of her dogs accompanied her. As she unlocked the gates, she was cut down by a hail of AK47 rifle bullets, fifteen of which actually hit her. Then the attackers turned their weapons on the three dogs that had tried to defend her, before escaping with her vehicle.

Since it was Sunday, her son, David, came out to the farm from Bulawayo to see her and to check that the farm was in good order. He arrived just after 9 and found his mother dead, with the three dead dogs at her side. Absolutely distraught, David armed himself and for the next five hours sat with his mother and would not allow anyone to approach. Eventually local farmers who had known David since he was a child on the farm, aided by their minister, the Rev Paul Andrianatos, persuaded David to allow them to take his mother's body to the local mortuary. Even after that, David remained in the house and would not allow anyone near the property.

It was the second killing on their farm. The first had been less than a year previously, when David's brother, Martin had been shot dead outside his home by a group of over 100 ZANU PF thugs, aided by both the police and the army.

It is the image of a grown man sitting in the sun next to his mother's body, unable to accept what had happened, and angry with everyone, that will remain. He was especially angry with those who had failed to do their duty: to protect ordinary citizens going about their daily work.

What went on in David's head as he sat with his mother and mourned both her death and that of his brother? How could he come to terms with the fact that he might have known the killers? And that this should have happened after all his family had done over the years to help the local community - to provide assistance to victims of the liberation war and the people in the nearby communal farming areas? Year after year his family had ploughed back every cent into the land they owned.

They had struggled to build a life and to pay for schooling... They had struggled daily with the elements - drought and flood, disease and despair during the fifteen years of civil war when every move had to be planned like a military exercise. There were the awful funeral services as the community buried their best, killed in 'the line of duty'. And now this, a senseless, needless killing of an old, defenseless woman outside the house that had been her home for a lifetime...

After his tribute to Gloria Olds, the Rev Paul Andrianatos turned to the reading: Samuel 1 and 2:

Now the Philistines fought against Israel. The Israelites fell before them, and many fell slain on Mount Gilboa. The Philistines pressed hard after Saul and his sons, and they killed his sons... Then David and all the men with him took their clothes and tore them. They mourned and wept and fasted until evening for Saul and his son Jonathan, and for the army of the Lord and the house of Israel, because they had fallen by the sword.

Following on from the reading, the minister said:

"When a loved one is taken away, especially in such a brutal and cowardly way, we have a right to express our grief. We have the right to show anger. We have the right to privacy. On Sunday, after David had come across the body of his mother, he had the right to be alone with his mother... a right no one should be denied. He had the right to privacy from the press, and even from the police and farmers. He had the right to be angry with me and with God. A right that the Psalmist, David, often invoked...

A 72-year-old woman has the right to dignity in death, and so it was fitting that Gloria's body be covered and removed, so that she would not become a spectacle for others.

These cowards with AK 47 rifles were able to steal Gloria's life, but they were not able to steal her dignity - a dignity secured by her son, David...

Let us stand in honour of Gloria Olds. Let us stand in silence, thinking about all that she did and all that she was. Let us stand..."

The minister paused for a few moments and then continued:

"Love at this time is very important, especially the love of a family. They might have taken away the life of Gloria, but they cannot take away the love she had for her family, nor can they take away the good memories.

I say to all the farmers here, they may take away your land, but they can never take away the love your family has for you - love that is more important than any land... Let us now pray for families and family love..."

After the prayer, the Reverend Paul Andrianatos read out an editorial from The Bulawayo Chronicle:

IN THIS, THERE IS NO HONOUR

The anguish of members of the Olds family of Nyamandlovu, who lost their second member to a violent shooting incident inside the space of 11 months on Sunday, is shared by responsible citizens.

Seventy-two year-old Mrs Gloria Olds had doggedly remained on the family farm, despite the brutal slaying of her son, Martin, last April. Her reward was to be killed in a hail of bullets, together with three of her family dogs.

In truth, barbarism knows no bounds.

Even in a war scenario - which, to our knowledge, does not apply here - the murder of an old woman in so callous a manner is bereft of honour, and leaves civilised society cold.

The Zimbabwe Republic Police has reported no arrests so far in other farm slayings ..."

Setting aside the hard-hitting editorial, the minister said: "Today is a sad day. It is a sad day when one has to say farewell to a loved one - a mother, grandmother and sister. It is even a sadder day when that person does not die peacefully in her sleep, but is shot down in cold blood. It is a sad day when one cannot live peacefully on one's property.

It was a sad day for the police and law and order. When the police were informed, they said that they could not come because they had no transport. No police roadblocks were set up and it was left to the farmers to try to track down the missing vehicle. I commend the farmers for the time and effort they put in. Two planes were sent up and many farmers used their own vehicles to track down the perpetrators.

It is a sad day when Mbeki only acts against Mugabe because of external pressure. It is a sad day when a ZANU PF official says, "We are willing to let this country go to ruin so that we can stay in power."

It is a sad day when leaders no longer care about the welfare of their people, when they no longer have compassion. It is a sad day when leaders tolerate and, in some cases, encourage lawlessness. It is a sad day when men need semi-automatic weapons to murder a 72-year-old woman. They are not men, they are ... scum. They are cowards. For them I have bad news, for the Bible says, *"Cursed is the man who kills his neighbour secretly."* Deut.27:24. In connection with law and order, the Bible says, *"Cursed is the man who withholds justice from the alien, the fatherless and the widow."* Deut.27:19.

The Reverend Paul Andrianatos paused once again, and the silence was tangible.

"I will now pray for blessings and curses:

Father God, I thank You for those persons who have committed their lives to law and order. I thank You for those persons who are willing to work in the police force. Lord, I pray for Your blessing upon those policemen and women who uphold and administer the law fairly. Lord, for those who do not, I pray for Your curse to be upon them.

For those judges and magistrates who administer justice fairly, I pray for Your blessing and for Your strength to carry out their duties. For those officials who implement the laws, bless them, O Lord. For those officials and cabinet ministers who do not, and who ignore and act against just laws, I pray for Your curse.

For those persons responsible for murder, especially the murder of Gloria Olds, I pray that they be cursed, and that they be aware, from this moment, that they are cursed.

I pray for the leaders of this country. I pray that we may have leaders who are honest, sincere and have compassion for the people. For them I pray a blessing. For those leaders who are not, I pray for change, but if they are not willing to change, I pray that they be removed or cursed.

For those who mourn, Lord, I pray for blessing. I pray that they may be comforted and strengthened, that they may know Your peace at this time. I pray this in the name of Jesus Christ. Amen."

The congregation sat in stunned silence. In today's Zimbabwe, few people would dare to be so outspoken, and to invoke Old Testament vengeance publicly.

The Reverend Paul began once more:

"(But) God is a God of love, a God of second chances. He is a God of forgiveness.

Those who have been cursed can have that curse removed and be forgiven. In order for that, they need to confess what they have done. They need to repent and change their ways. They also need to face the consequences of their sin, whether that be a jail sentence, a death sentence, or something else, it now lies in their hands.

Blessed are the dead who die in the Lord from now on. Yes, says the Spirit, they will rest from their labour, for their deeds will follow them..."

After the committal, closing hymn and benediction, the congregation stood once again in silence, a final tribute to a remarkable woman who had given everything she had to the country she loved, and to their outspoken minister, who had served them so well and so courageously, especially during the shattering twelve months of government-initiated violence.

As they turned to leave, the Reverend Paul Andrianatos delivered his parting shot: "For the convenience of those press members present, there are copies of the funeral service at the back of the church. The cost is Z$30. For those members of the CIO (Central Intelligence Organisation) who are present and require a copy, the price is the same: Z$30."

▌•⟨⟩•▐▐◼◻◼▐▐•⟨⟩•▌

The void left by Gloria Olds' death will be impossible for her family members and friends to fill. They will remember her sitting together with them in the home that she loved so much, with her old black cat, as old as her granddaughter, Martine, curled up on her lap.

They will remember the message sent by Martine and Angus, Martin's greatly loved daughter and son, from their new home in England:

Our darling, darling gogo (granny), such a strong lady, who was so proud of her two strong sons. Whilst evil may try to destroy our family, nothing can ever destroy our precious memories. When we were small, we stuck on the cupboard in your bedroom luminous stars and moons. In your last letter to us, you mentioned how they still shone when the lights went out and that made you happy as you thought of us. Gogo, now when we look up at the night sky, we will see you as the other bright star shining next to our dad's. We love you bigger than the sky.

Martine and Angus.

The Rev Paul Andrianatos had his residence permit rescinded after he had preached at Martin Olds' funeral. As a result, he had to leave Zimbabwe two days after Gloria Olds' funeral.

The Editor of The Chronicle newspaper was replaced.

Sunday 22 April 2001 - newspaper report:
Barely two months after suspected ruling party militants fatally shot a 72-year-old white farmer, Mrs Gloria Olds of Nyamandlovu, the government announced plans to confiscate her family's land.

A seizure notice signed by Agriculture Minister Joseph Made issued on Friday said that the 2 400 ha Silverstreams cattle ranch of Gloria Olds was among a new batch of 142 farms in western Zimbabwe being nationalised.

Olds was the eighth white farmer killed in a year of violence linked to the illegal occupation of largely white-owned land. On 18 April last year, Olds' son Martin, 42, was shot dead.

SUBSEQUENTLY

- ☒ Border Gezi, Minister of Youth Development, Gender and Employment Creation died in a car accident on Saturday 28 April 2001.

- ☒ Moven Mahachi, Minister of Defence (quoted at the beginning of the article), died in a car accident on Saturday 26 May 2001.

- ☒ Chenjerai "Hitler" Hunzvi, leader of the war veterans, died on Monday 4 June 2001. The official cause of death was given as cerebral malaria. Hospital sources reported that the drugs he was given were those normally prescribed for the treatment of AIDS. President Mugabe praised him for his "extraordinary energy" in rallying support for the ruling party. He was buried at Heroes' Acre near Harare.

- ☒ By July 2001 three of the Olds' family farms had been designated.

Those who have no hope of political victory reach for the gun.

Ken Owen, retired Editor of South Africa's Sunday Times

❚◆❖◆❚▓❚◆❖◆❚

NIGHTS OF LONG DARKNESS

Part 1: Inside the homestead

In the stillness of the long night,
the sense of fear is insidious
You can feel it creeping silently
around the trees beyond the security fence,
sense it crawling under the wire mesh
and crossing the long shadows of the lawn,
before wrapping itself around the house.

You can taste this fear in your dry mouth,
feel it seeping through your sleepless body,
sapping its fragile strength.
Down the security-darkened passage
it glides stealthily on naked feet
towards the children's room where they lie,
tossing in the restless confusion of their dreams.

Part 2. Outside on the veld

It is early morning and long shafts of sunlight
slide between the scattered trees, warming our backs.
The grass is winter-dry now and rustles as we move;
in places it is shoulder-high.

This morning, like yesterday, and many mornings before,
we keep close together,
feeding on the tufts that crunch beneath us,
watching, waiting,
uneasy.

Something has changed on our savannah home
and we do not understand.
The sun still climbs the sky until, at midday
it is so hot that we must seek cool glades of shade,
and at night the moon still softens the dry veld,
creating shadows without edges
as we glide effortlessly in its wake.

But something has changed.
Nights that were silent save for the call of owls
or a solitary nightjar
carry different sounds, sounds that bring fear,
and death to the savannah...
often lingering death,
and we bleed through the long darkness
from our wounds.

Strands of silver, that were strung along places in the veld
have become coiled and spring shut like jaws.
They lie in wait beneath bushes, latch onto logs,
or hide high in the branches of the trees we feed on.
The death they bring is slow,
and the pain is unspeakable.

With winter comes the threat of fire to the veld.
Before, small fires that stretched out in long strips
contained the runaway fires
that swept far into the distance,
destroying everything in their wake.
Today these fires rage unchecked,
and the flames leap long-tongued into the sky.
Afterwards there is only blackened stubble,
and the grey, powdery remains of our savannah
covers the hot ground with despair.

It is not only the creatures of the ground
who lose the places where they shelter and feed.
Trees being torn from the earth and carted away
are the homes of birds whose myriad calls
welcome the freshness of dawn
or warn us of dangers we have yet to sense.
The tall trees are also home to defenceless creatures
like the tiny nagaapie
whose soft round eyes grow wide with fear
as his home crashes down and the rain of stones begins.
I have seen his lifeless body
and the blood that colours the earth beside him
dark red.
The rivers that flow through our lives now
are rivers of blood.

We huddle in confusion and the terror returns
as sounds like sharp thunderbolts
close in upon us......
There is no place in the long darkness to hide.

BUILDING HOPE

We ourselves feel that what we are doing
is just a drop in the ocean.
But if that drop were not in the ocean,
I think the ocean would be less
because of that missing drop.
I do not agree with the big way of doing things.
To us, what matters is the individual.

Mother Theresa

I t was new year's eve, 2001. The night was velvety and still; pale moonlight etched the massive granite outcrops of the Matobo Hills in eerie silver. Across the lawn, music drifted like smoke, recalling memories. And she danced. Danced as if there was a tomorrow; as if there would always be a tomorrow; as if the dawn would always come...

"We must pull together in our time of darkness... Let there be light at the end of the tunnel..." In the early morning quiet of her Midlands ranch, Jenny's fingers move easily over the keyboard, sending messages of hope and encouragement across the troubled land. Stored in her computer, or carefully filed for future use, are prayers, sayings, memoirs, extracts of letters from friends, jokes or anything positive to inspire people and help them through the dark days.

"Just over a year ago, when the trouble in Zimbabwe first started, we looked to the Commercial Farmers' Union for direction," said Jenny. "However, as the months went by and the pressures grew, I realised that they were in an increasingly difficult position and that each of us needed to take responsibility and make some form of contribution."

As a result of her growing concern, Jenny began compiling files of motivational material and discovered the Zalome e-mail address. Called Bridge to the World, this innovative e-mail service supplies beautifully illustrated daily prayers on a subscription basis internationally. Since the material is ideal for sending to people in need, Jenny applied to become a member.

"I enjoyed the messages of hope so much that I would take out relevant and meaningful sections and send them on to friends," Jenny said. "The feedback was amazing - they proved to be exactly what people needed. Since humour plays an important role in relieving tension, I also circulated any good jokes I heard or received through the e-mail."

Gradually the concept grew and she began collecting quotations and thoughts of famous philosophers or influential leaders such as Winston Churchill. A presentation to the Commercial Farmers' Union (CFU) by Mike Lipkin, one of South Africa's best-known motivators, got her going on an even more positive note and she often uses quotes from one of his latest books, "Still Mind, Strong Heart".

"Basically, the prayers are my strength and, in turn they strengthen others. They must be short and to the point, so that they have impact." Jenny also has on file extracts of letters from friends expressing thoughts or feelings which will in turn help others, and a collection of inspirational material from her AIDS work.

"Living under these conditions, there are always good and bad days. On a bad day you can receive something which absolutely lifts your spirits, puts you on a high and in turn will influence others. So, whenever I am at my computer, which is usually a few times a week, I go through my files and send out whatever I feel is needed at that particular time. These e-mails are circulated widely and then passed on to anyone whom the recipients feel would benefit."

In Jenny's view, the value of the e-mail under the current conditions has been inestimable. "The e-mail keeps you in contact with the entire world and it is very satisfying when travel is restricted. Communication of this nature is amazing and helps you to feel less detached from the rest of humanity."

Many people report that the material sent out is valuable for family interaction. "A good piece can become a point of discussion and help family members to connect with each other. In times of immense pressure, it is easy for individuals to retreat into their shells and for meaningful communication to be stifled."

One of Jenny's favourite pieces is about wild geese, and how they fly in a 'V' formation, each taking it in turn to lead the flock and then dropping behind when its energy begins to fail, so that another can take over. In this way the flock is estimated to achieve a 70% increase in efficiency. Jenny's piece ends with the following words: *It is a reward, a challenge and a privilege to be a contributing member of the team.*

"Everyone just loves the story," said Jenny. "By circulating it, we are attempting to restore a feeling of security at a time when the hierarchy here is seeking to create division. As a result of their strategies, many people have in fact become divided and, in some instances loyalties are no longer what they used to be. The message of the geese is to encourage us to stay in formation with those who are heading in the direction that we want to go."

This poem, Requiem, circulated on 14 March 2001, summed up the feelings of many:

Some of us have gone, some of us are going, and the rest of us are praying we don't have to go:

Requiem - by a recent ex-Zimbabwean

I'm at home this last time, a requiem,
To pack up and tell friends goodbye.
I'm sure that my new life's a good thing,
So why do I just want to cry?
I can make far more money in Europe
Buy things I have ne'er before seen,
But money's just money, gadgets junk,
My heart lives back here, where it's green...
(It's) a land where the people are friendly,
Where you're met with a hand and a grin,
Where the doors to the houses are open,
And "whenever you're 'round, just pull in".
Where the people are friendly and caring,
Where they all stick together, make a plan,
Where they do what they can for each other,
And will help anyone, if they can...."

For others, leaving has never been an option, as this letter indicates:

Life for us in Zimbabwe is almost beyond description, yet I feel sure that one day we will look back and long for these times again. It is this incredible battle of good against evil in every way imaginable. It is a fight against fear, and against those who say there is no hope, against those who won't help and those who spread despondency. It is a fight against a belief that the enemy is huge and is winning, and that races hate each other, but the enemy is a cornered rat and is injured and bleeding, and races don't want to hate each other.

People are wonderful in Zimbabwe and I am so unbelievably privileged to be part of a group working with such joy at changing the country, not only for our immediate future, but for life beyond that. I am proud to be part of a group of people determined to change our relationships between races, between churches and with people we may not understand, yet to whom we say 'Hey, it's OK, we're not the same - we are allowed to be different.' What a wonderful future we will have if we continue to believe in the warmth, love of laughter and the sheer joy of living which makes up the soul of a huge majority of Zimbabweans. And if we can use that to rebuild the brokenness suffered by so, so, so many...wow what a place this will be!! I will not give up."

This e-mail was headed **"Special People"**:

People come into your life for a reason, a season or a lifetime. When people come into your life for a reason, it is usually to meet a need you have expressed outwardly or inwardly. They have come to assist you through a difficulty, to provide you with guidance and support...They may seem like a godsend, and they are...

When people come into your life for a season, it is because your turn has come to share, grow or learn.   They may bring you an experience of peace, or make you laugh. They may teach you something you have never done...

Lifetime relationships teach you lifetime lessons; those things you must build upon in order to have a solid emotional foundation. Your job is to accept the lesson...and put what you have learned to use in all other relationships and areas of your life...

Wry humour is sent to raise a smile when one's e-mail is opened:

Zimbabwe, a Heavenly Country?

Did you know we live in Heaven in Zimbabwe?
We heaven got petrol
We heaven got deesil
We heaven got lectriciti
We heaven got wota (water)
We heaven got wek (work)
We heaven got Usi dorras (US dollars)
We heaven got socah tunament (soccer tournament)
We heaven got cure for eds (AIDS)

We heaven got honest guvment
We heaven got gudu sevis (good service)
We heaven got gudu menahs (manners)
We heaven got roads without hols
We heaven got jells with locks (jails)
We heaven got a bright fucha.

On 13 March 2001, Jenny circulated a piece from Zalome's "Bridge to the World", called "The Broken Shell":

This shell (a broken scallop shell) has had to fight so hard to keep from being totally crushed by the pounding surf. Just as I have had to. Yet it is still out on the beautiful sandy shore. Just as I am. If our world were only filled with perfect shells, we would never learn from adversity. From pain. From sorrow. We would miss some of life's most important lessons along the way...

Broken shells mean lots of tears. Lots of pain. Lots of struggle. But broken shells are also valuable tools to teach faith, courage and strength. Broken shells inspire others and demonstrate the will to go on in a way that no perfect shell could ever do. Broken shells are shells that have been tested, and tried, and hurt - yet they don't quit. They continue to be...

A wave crashes, sending tiny sand crabs scurrying for safety, and I am reminded that even the smallest creatures depend on each other. Especially in our brokenness, we need the Lord - and we need each other...

For Cathy Buckle, author of the deeply moving book, "African Tears - The Zimbabwe Land Invasions", the e-mail was often her only lifeline on their occupied farm.

All the months through the invasions there was a crippling shortage of diesel, so every kilometre was carefully guarded and we seldom went out. The e-mails kept me going, every day there were dozens and dozens of them. They came from all over - a lot from people in the towns always offering help, anything they could do (and there was never anything they could do). They came from ex-Zimbabweans who had left the country, from strangers, from all over the world until there were so many that it was almost a full-time job just answering them. The support of other farmers was tremendous, phone calls, messages, visits - all the time and they never let up, checking on us every day, sometimes twice a day...

Through the news, the satellite TV, the Internet reports and the independent press we knew that we were not alone, that there was a world out there watching, telling it, caring...

Cathy also writes of the strength she draws from nature:

When I am at a low ebb, I often get up very, very early in the morning to wait for, and then watch the dawn. Just hearing the dawn chorus, seeing the silhouettes emerge from the darkness, and watching that magnificent red ball rising from the horizon gives incredible depth, and strength to face another day of it. Witnessing that goodness every mornng gives me something to hold onto.

"Tensions continue to remain very high at present," said Jenny, "and farmers are really at the lowest ebb I have ever known them. This is due to the fuel crisis, the security crisis and all the financial problems related to running an operation properly...it is very wearing and while they must try to remain strong, it has gone on for so long."

Under these conditions, many would give up hope without the support of caring people such as Jenny. The fact that their own ranch has also been designated makes her courage all the more remarkable. "Our designation is like being sentenced, and all taken from under your feet," said Jenny. "Nevertheless we must be strong and resilient." Her philosophy is summed up in the words of Fyodor Dostoyevsky in "The Brothers Karamazov":

...Love every leaf, every ray of God's light. Love the animals, love the plants, love everything. If you love everything, you will perceive the divine mystery in things. Once you perceive it, you will begin to comprehend it better every day. And you will come at last to love the whole world with an all-embracing love.

A MESSAGE FROM MIKE LIPKIN

There will come a time when you believe everything is finished. That will be the beginning.

Louis L'Amour

 o matter who you are, or where you've come from, there will come a time in your life when you believe you've hit a dead end. You will lose hope and may even reach a point of desperation, feeling as if life is an endless exercise in futility. That's when the real learning takes place. That's when your character is re-formed. That's when the renewal begins. Today's rock bottom is merely tomorrow's launching pad. It's the end of your past and the beginning of your future.

Over the past few years, I have worked in many countries, including Australia, Canada, the USA, India, Dubai, Egypt, Nigeria, Ghana, Kenya, South Africa and Zimbabwe. In each country I have learnt something different. I learnt about humility in India, warmth in Ghana, partnership in Dubai, energy in America, courtesy and generosity in Canada, forgiveness in South Africa and resilience in Zimbabwe.

Resilience is about courage. It's about picking yourself up yet again, learning from the lessons which life is presenting, and moving on. The more situations an individual experiences, the more he learns, especially if the situations are intense. The courage of Zimbabweans is truly awesome and they have much to teach the international community in this regard. The fact that they are also such resilient and innovative people is due in part to their historical and cultural complexity, but also to the periods of isolation when the country was cut off by the rest of the world.

Today no country can afford to be alienated. We are all citizens of a global community and the need to connect with people world-wide grows daily. This is important not only for business purposes, but also for emotional and spiritual stimulation. We've become so interdependent that isolation, even for a short period when the e-mail is down, can cause stress and disorientation. In a fragmented world, we crave the cohesion and logic of like-minded souls.

Zimbabweans are especially innovative, using the e-mail as a way of supporting and uplifting people during periods of grief, fear, isolation and even siege. Messages of courage and hope play a vital role in boosting morale during this turbulent time. Unlike many other countries, where traditional institutions like religion and the family are on the decline, Zimbabweans have deepened their commitment to both, and are achieving significant spiritual growth.

Zimbabweans are also reassessing their values. The intensified focus on values in the new millennium requires us all to hold ourselves to a higher standard. We are all accountable. Ethically, professionally, socially and experientially, we are being called to "ramp up" our performance. Just being acceptable isn't acceptable any more. The behaviour of leaders, companies and individuals alike is being scrutinised for its impact on the communities they serve. We have to walk the talk daily.

The tides of change sweeping the world focus increasingly on self-growth, fulfilment, self-expression and celebration of diversity. The new leaders will be those who can become a microcosm of the world around them, who are committed to ending conflict and promoting creative innovation.

If we accept that harmony, not conflict, is the natural order of things, then it's up to each of us to play a role in this regard. If we stay silent when we should speak up, or refuse to support someone in trouble because we are afraid for ourselves, we have let ourselves down. As the Chinese say, "A person who bows for too long cannot stand up."

It was reported recently that the Zimbabwe Council of Churches, which has been criticised for being too docile, had the courage to voice its concerns to key government officials regarding the country's leadership. It said that the nation as a whole was crying out for principled and prophetic leadership.

Every day we read, see and hear stories of horror, savagery, crime and catastrophe. It is easy to give in to fear, to let it dominate our thinking and control our behaviour. The real message of fear is that something is about to happen that we need to prepare for. When we underestimate our ability to handle it, fear turns into worry, anxiety or even panic. Think about the huge challenges that you have overcome in your life. Then think about the acts of courage and the sheer guts that got you to where you are now.

When we are in a crisis, we often forget what we are capable of doing. Evaluate your current challenge in the context of what you have already achieved and you will discover that there is very little you cannot cope with. Remember the universal truth: God does not give us anything we cannot handle.

If you feel fear, do not show it. No matter what the situation, master it from the outside. People can sense when somebody is in the grip of fear and will immediately use it to their advantage.

One of the power-tools which I discuss in my latest book, "Your Personal Best - Life Tools", explores The Equilibrium Paradox. For example, I am courageous *because* I am scared. We need to remember that there is a natural equilibrium and harmony in all things. What seems like a massive loss today will help us succeed tomorrow. How many times have you allowed a loss or defeat to weigh you down or hold you back? How many times has this loss or defeat turned out to be a benefit for you? We need to move beyond faith. We have to learn to trust.

We must also learn to trust each other - and to be worthy of that trust. The moment you say to yourself, "I'm not sure I can trust this person," it's over. As Robert Bolt wrote in his play, "A Man For All Seasons", "Trust is like water that you hold in your hands. If you open your hands just a tiny bit, some of the water doesn't run out, all the water runs out."

To build trust, you have to invest in your relationships constantly. Help other people, whether or not they can return the favour. Connect them to appropriate opportunities whenever you can. Since we are all connected, their success is ultimately your success.

Recently I delivered a seminar to a group of farmers in Zimbabwe who grow runner beans for Sainsburys' Supermarkets in the UK. The beans are grown in long rows and at the head of each row is a beehive. I was told that the bees are needed to cross-pollinate the plants. Without the bees, there would be no beans. Isn't that what you and I do? Aren't we all just cross pollinators of each other's potential, irrespective of where we live?

If we accept ourselves as being global citizens, then we have to accept responsibility on a global basis. What happens in the neighbourhoods called India, Ireland or Indonesia has a massive, almost immediate impact on the neighbourhoods of Argentina, Australia and America.

Underpinning all cultures are the new global rules which promote respect for the individual in terms of self-actualisation, dignity, interdependence, self-expression, absolute integrity and freedom. Those neighbourhoods and individuals who do not play by the rules will suffer. Those that do will thrive.

If the world accepts responsibility for its citizens, then its citizens include the people of Zimbabwe. Many Zimbabweans have told me that they feel abandoned at this critical and painful time in their history and are in desperate need of international support. Among the most pressing problems are the violence and the looming food shortages which result from the land invasions.

There is an ancient tale of two men talking, one from heaven and one from hell. The man from hell lamented: "This is indeed a wretched place. I feel unbearable hunger all the time." The man from heaven asked, "You mean there is no food in hell?" The man from hell looked at him with his emaciated face and replied, "Oh there's food, lots of it. We sit at banqueting tables heaped with the most sumptuous food your eyes could behold. But we are made to eat with spoons as long as our arms. No matter how hard we try, it is impossible to get the food into our mouths. That's the most unbearable part of hell: I am starving in the middle of a feast."

"In heaven we have similar conditions, except that our spoons are as long as both of our arms together," the other man said, "yet we eat very well."

"But that's impossible," the man from hell replied. "If we cannot feed ourselves with spoons only as long as one arm, how can you feed yourselves with spoons as long as both of your arms together?"

"Ah, but that's the point, my friend," the man from heaven said with a smile, "we don't feed ourselves, we feed each other."

Abundance comes from making a real contribution to others. How many times have you done nothing because you believed you had very little to contribute? And how did you feel about yourself when you did nothing to resolve the problems infecting your community or country? Do something. Every action, however small, is a cause in motion. You can never know the cumulative effect of your personal actions. When the momentum builds up, great things will happen.

Remember the Ethiopian proverb: "When spiders unite, they can tie up a lion."

The tides of change are impacting on people in every corner of the globe, but in Zimbabwe they are magnified by the problems which the country faces currently. Zimbabweans are called to be innovative, honourable and courageous. They are called to unite for their common good. They are called to create a new country where human values are promoted and respected. Your story can inspire the world. I believe it will.

There is a tide in the affairs of men,
Which, taken at the flood, leads on to fortune;
Omitted, all the voyage of their life
Is bound in shallows and in miseries.
On such a full sea are we now afloat;
And we must take the current when it serves,
Or lose our ventures.

From "Julius Caesar" by William Shakespeare

When All Else Fails.

SALUTE TO THE INDEPENDENT PRESS

Power consists to a large extent in deciding what stories will be told.

Carolyn Heilbrun, American social critic, 1988

If you watch ZTV (Zimbabwe Television), listen to ZBC (Zimbabwe Broadcasting Corporation) and read The Herald (Harare) and The Chronicle (Bulawayo), you will be asked to believe the following:

- ☒ That all Whites hate Blacks
- ☒ That all Blacks hate Whites
- ☒ That President Mugabe is much loved and revered
- ☒ That the most important issue in Zimbabwe today is to eradicate Gays
- ☒ That everyone wants the white-owned commercial farms handed over to landless blacks regardless of the consequences for the economy
- ☒ That ZANU PF rules supreme
- ☒ That President Mugabe cares as much for the welfare of his people as he did when he came to power in 1980 (perhaps more)
- ☒ That corruption and unemployment are going to be stamped out by the AAG (Affirmative Action Group)
- ☒ That the MDC (Movement for Democratic Change) has very little support
- ☒ That the MDC was responsible for the violence that was unleashed during the June 2000 elections, and in the by-elections that followed
- ☒ That Zimbabwe's foreign currency problems are the fault of Indian businessmen, who are solely responsible for the running of all private bureaux de change even if they are called "Solomon's"
- ☒ That Jonathan Moyo, the ZANU PF Minister of State for Information and Publicity is concerned about justice for all, freedom of speech and honest governance
- ☒ That the police do not respond to appeals for assistance only because they have transport problems
- ☒ That Britain is planning a second wave of colonisation.

We owe an immense debt of gratitude to our courageous Independent Press. This body includes two weekly newspapers The Financial Gazette and The Zimbabwe Independent, a daily newspaper The Daily News and a Sunday newspaper, The Standard. Without their impartial coverage and reporting, the citizens of Zimbabwe would be starved of the truth. We would be floundering even deeper in the mire of propaganda and lies. We wouldn't have a clue as to what is really happening here.

The offices of The Daily News were damaged last year on Saturday 22 April 2000, when a bomb was hurled at their premises in Harare's city centre. The powerful bomb exploded in an art gallery on the ground floor. The art gallery was situated directly below the office of the Editor-in-Chief, Geoff Nyarota. The only arrest ever made was that of an innocent South African journalist who had rushed to the scene when he heard the explosion. More recently, on Sunday 28 January 2001, The Daily News printing factory in Southerton, Harare was bombed in the early hours of the morning. Extensive damage was caused to the Z$100 million printing press and to the building. Fortunately, none of the security guards was hurt. One guard reported speaking to the occupants of a cream-coloured Mazda at about 1 am. He was able to furnish the registration number of this vehicle. To date no one has been arrested. Only days before the bombing occurred, Information Minister Jonathan Moyo had publicly declared his long-held ambition to silence this newspaper.

The staff of The Daily News refused to be intimidated or deterred, and without losing even one day, managed with the help of other newspapers to get their own publication printed and out on the streets of the cities and towns throughout the country. This was a wonderful achievement that was a huge boost to morale nation-wide.

The Zimbabwean Union of Journalists and other key media representative organisations resolved to hold a peaceful demonstration on 3 February 2001 to protest against violence directed at the media. ZUJ Secretary General Basildon Peta said in a protest note, "The media fraternity in Zimbabwe is under siege and now is the time for journalists from both the public and private sector to come together and fight for their endangered profession." This demonstration was stopped by the police.

In The Daily News of 19 April 2001 the editor comments as follows:

The period following the bombing of The Daily News printing press at the end of January has witnessed an escalation in the orchestration of verbal attacks on the newspaper.

While the identity of the bombers is still unknown and will probably remain a mystery, judging by the complete lack of progress in police investigations, renewed verbal attacks on The Daily News have been launched mostly from the Department of Information and Publicity in the President's Office. They have been disseminated through The Daily News' main rival, The Herald, and through the Zimbabwe Broadcasting Corporation.

The theme of the attacks has been to dismiss The Daily News as a worthless publication which is sponsored by the British government in that government's allegedly on-going campaign to discredit and eventually unseat the ZANU PF government of President Mugabe.

The strategy has been to discredit The Daily News as a reliable source of information by dismissing as false stories that appear in its news columns. While the rebuttal of Daily News stories has become a full-time occupation for Jonathan Moyo, the Minister of Information, it seems to provide him with an opportunity to appear on television almost every night and thus assuage what seems to be an insatiable love for publicity. Moyo is the man who spearheaded the anti-Daily News campaign even before the bombing of its printing press...

...The government routinely accuses Western governments, the opposition political parties and the privately-owned press of creating Zimbabwe's current economic and other problems...

Far from discrediting the image of The Daily News, as they seem hell-bent on doing, people such as Moyo, Chenjerai Hunzvi and Joseph Chinotimba need to be informed that there is something inherently good, in the eyes of the public, about the qualities of any newspaper which is constantly targeted for criticism by officials of a government or ruling party whose popularity is clearly on the wane...

Among the verbal attacks referred to above are the attempts to charge journalists with criminal defamation. In one such instance, the State, with President Mugabe as the complainant, is charging Geoff Nyarota and reporters Julius Zava and Sandra Nyaira with this offence in connection with the newspaper's disclosures in November 2000 of alleged payoffs for a contract to build Harare's new Z$4,4 billion international airport. On 17 April 2001, High Court Judge Moses Chinhengo dismissed with costs an attempt by Jonathan Moyo to bar The Zimbabwe Independent newspaper from reporting the details of the much-publicised allegations of fraud by him at the Ford Foundation in Kenya.

In March 1999, after the kidnapping, detention and torture of two Standard journalists, Mark Chavunduka and Ray Choto, for their reporting of an alleged coup, President Mugabe told a rally that "we are going to arrest all these lying journalists".

More recently, Zimbabwe's Information Ministry deported Joseph Winter of the British Broadcasting Corporation and Uruguayan freelancer, Mercedes Sayagues, who writes for South Africa's Mail and Guardian newspaper.

The Government will brook no departure from editorial policy from within its own ranks, either. On 6 March 2001 the editorial in The Chronicle stated:

The anguish of members of the Olds family of Nyamandhlovu, who lost their second member to a violent shooting incident inside the space of 11 months on Sunday, is shared by responsible citizens. Seventy-two-year-old Mrs Gloria Olds had doggedly remained on the family farm despite the brutal slaying of her son, Martin, last April. Her reward was to be killed in a hail of bullets, together with three of her family dogs. In truth, barbarism knows no bounds...

The Zimbabwe Republic Police, which has reported no arrests so far in six other farm slayings - including that of the late Martin Olds - must now redouble its efforts to apprehend the perpetrators of these murderous acts, so that peace-loving Zimbabweans can get on with their productive lives. The statistics of victims of violent crime have continued to mount, and so have the fears of citizens. They look to the state through the police, for protection.

The judiciary, too, can play a role in creating a more secure environment by showing greater circumspection when granting bail to suspects accused of violent crimes.

The writer then went on to quote the words of Christ: *They that live by the sword shall perish by the sword.* The editor of The Chronicle was replaced, as such condemnation of someone who murdered a white person or an opponent of ZANU PF is not part of Zimbabwe Newspapers' policy.

The editorial in The Chronicle of 21 March 2001, is more in line with the fare Zimpapers is required to serve. The editor is in awe of the marvellous work being done by the police:

The police force is certainly proving its mettle in its mandate of ensuring that law and order is maintained in our country...In a country where criminals have become very daring and will stop at nothing, shooting their victims as if they were quarry - it is a relief to know that the police are making commendable progress in ensuring that such criminals are brought to book...It is now apparent that there is a dangerous culture of violence sweeping the country. This culture is unZimbabwean and has probably been imported from neighbouring countries. *A breed of criminals has emerged which will stop at nothing, and police and innocent members of the public alike, have indiscriminately become the criminals' victims...*

Chido Makunike, writing in The Standard of 8-14 April is less enamoured of the police.

Whenever I come across a police road block, and see the officers checking engine and chassis numbers in a search for stolen vehicles and asking for identification particulars, I have mixed feelings.

On the one hand they are performing a valuable service at a time car theft has sky-rocketed. I know that some stolen vehicles have been recovered and notorious criminals have been apprehended through these efforts. Yet there is a part of me that asks by what authority the police spend their time and resources on this, when on a much deeper level law and order is so imperilled for so many Zimbabweans. The fact of the matter is that the police simply don't feature much at all in considerations of how secure one is walking through the city centre, driving one's car, or even sleeping in one's home. The kind of law and order that the police will aggressively seek to maintain is to turn out in full riot gear at the scene of a political demonstration, but they seem to have become largely irrelevant to a citizen's overall sense of security. How do you restore this, when it takes a long time to build this sense in the first place?

On Wednesday 4 April 2001 parliament passed legislation giving sweeping control over broadcasting to President Mugabe. The new law gives the ZANU PF government the authority to withdraw licences from independent broadcasters. Strict rules have been set out prohibiting broadcasters from criticising the ruling party prior to the presidential polls. Only local companies may invest in the country's broadcasting industry. All licensed broadcasters are now required to give the government one hour per week to publicise ruling party policies. Only one other national licence may be granted. (There is room for at least 35 stations in any given geographical area).

The Daily News of 7 April 2001 published an editorial captioned:

New Broadcasting Act Reflects Rabid Paranoia:

Government's decision to fast-track passage of the Broadcasting Services Bill into an Act of Parliament, against anguished protests from other stakeholders and, worse still, against the recommendations and learned advice of the Parliamentary Legal Committee, is most regrettable...Before it was passed into law, the Eddison Zvobgo-chaired legal committee advised the government in plain language, that no less than eight sections of the Bill, now an Act, were "unconstitutional on the grounds of inconsistency with Section 20 of the Constitution of Zimbabwe". Section 20 protects the citizen's rights to freedom of expression.

Part of the committee's report read: "The imposition of government views on every broadcaster is an unconstitutional infringement on the right to freedom of expression." This was obviously a reference to the Act's numerous restrictive clauses, in particular those dealing with the programming content as they stipulate that every television licensee must ensure that at least 75% of what they air is Zimbabwean.

Among The Chronicle's remarks on 5 April regarding the new Broadcasting Act are the following:

The Minister of State for Information and Publicity, Professor Jonathan Moyo, said the local content clause should stimulate Zimbabweans to take excessive control of their broadcasting systems for self-expression and self-exploration without being displaced by foreign programming that presently dominated broadcasting...

The Bill establishes a broadcasting fund that will, among other things, provide grants to encourage the growth of the Zimbabwean creative arts to enable the film and music industry to supply material to meet the local content obligations...

...Cde Chinamasa said MDC members cared very little about the country and were prepared to mortgage their country to the highest bidder. "It's this clause (clause 6) which captures the vision of what we want to see in this country. We want to see a government and leadership that is elected by the people of Zimbabwe and not imposed by the superpowers," he said. "What the government is saying is that we will cut off the flow of funds to local puppets. We want to empower our local politicians in the opposition to be themselves and represent the people of Zimbabwe and not foreign interests. As we are cutting the flow of funds, we are also providing funds," said Cde Chinamasa.

The Herald and The Chronicle were outraged by Peter Tatchell's attempting to arrest President Mugabe while he was visiting Belgium. The Chronicle, angrily affronted on the President's behalf, proclaimed:

So those blasted souls of Europe, the men who marry one another, think they can successfully propagate the ideology of their inverted sex to Zimbabweans, or to Africa as a whole, as British homosexuals led by Peter Tatchell seem to do? Referring to Tatchell as *the gay gangster* the writer reminded his readers of Tatchell's earlier attempt to arrest the President in London: *...he does not appear to act solely on his own behalf, or that of Outrage; his* *outrage seems to have the approval of the British establishment which has a bone to chew (sic) with Zimbabwe over the land reform scheme...*

The message for Tatchell from us is that there is no way that homosexuals in Britain or elsewhere can hope to act as policemen over Zimbabwe and succeed. They should be content to marry themselves in their native land and leave us to mind our own affairs. Homosexual imperialism has no room here.

Zimbabwe Newspapers 1980 (Ltd) Group is currently the worst performing company on the Zimbabwe Stock Exchange. It used to be one of the top ten performers. One of the reasons the public has been reluctant to invest in Zimpapers is that its management has continued to change. Zimpapers has witnessed a change of face in its board and editorial direction as well as in senior management. Tommy Sithole former Editor-in-Chief of The Herald and company chairman, also recently resigned and was replaced by prominent businessman and banker, Enoch Kamushinda.

One of the serious problems the Zimpapers Group is facing is the withdrawal of advertisers. Since the Group prints only Government-sanctioned news and information, much of the business sector in Zimbabwe has chosen to advertise in the independent media instead. Most literate people feel that events should be reported accurately and impartially. They consider that opposition political parties should be allowed to advertise on radio and on television. It is totally unfair that only the ruling party can use the air waves. It is for this reason that they have chosen to boycott the State-owned newspapers. Not only have people stopped advertising in these newspapers. They have stopped buying them, as well. Subscriptions have been cancelled or they have not been renewed.

The circulation of the government newspapers has dropped to an all-time low, while that of the Independent Press has increased dramatically.

The Independent Press deserves to be successful. It has shown courage and integrity in the face of numerous dangers and obstacles. Ladies and gentlemen of the Independent Press, the people of Zimbabwe salute you.

§←⇔→§✕§←⇔→§

AND THEIR EYES ARE BURNING

O what is that sound which so thrills the ear
Down in the valley drumming, drumming?
Only the scarlet soldiers, dear,
The soldiers coming.

O why have they left the road down there,
Why are they suddenly wheeling, wheeling?
Perhaps a change in their orders, dear.
Why are you kneeling?

O it's broken the lock and splintered the door,
O it's the gate where they're turning, turning;
Their boots are heavy on the floor
And their eyes are burning.

From "O What is That Sound" by W H Auden

The following is fiction:

 had a dream. It was a very bad dream. It is the same dream I have most nights. Nearly a year has passed and still it haunts me. I wake up as usual screaming. Joseph is lying beside me and he is jolted alert. "Be quiet, you fool," he says to me. "I'm trying to sleep. Every night you wake me up with this woman's noise." I am relieved to hear his voice. At least his grumbling is a part of tonight. I lie awake for a while, looking at the stars above me. Although we are out in the open and it is cold, it is not too bad. We have plenty of old sacks and thick plastic packets to keep us warm. We are huddled in the doorway of a shop. The inside of the shop is lit up at night. Loaves of bread are stacked on the shelves. When I look at them my stomach feels hollow. I imagine what it would be like to cram hot, fresh bread into my mouth. I try to ignore the fluttering and cramping sensations that result from this picture.

After a while I fall asleep. And my dream begins again. I am lying in a ditch outside a row of houses. I have been sniffing glue and I am feeling very strange. One of the older boys gave some to Joseph and me to test. I don't think I am going to try this again, I can't seem to keep my balance. Suddenly I hear a lot of noise. It sounds like people shouting. I slowly kneel and raise my head above the ditch. I see a group of men dragging something. Then I realise what they are pushing and shoving is a man. He is bleeding, I think. There is certainly blood on the men's clothing. I shake my head to try to clear it. Am I imagining this? I sluggishly rest my arms on the edge of the ditch.

One of the men notices me. He is attracted by the sudden movement. He turns toward me and bares his teeth. His eyes are wide and staring. He looks at me. I look at him. I have never seen eyes like this. It is as if they are burning. He leans over and, raising his boot, kicks me as hard as he can in the face.

I am freezing cold. My face feels as if it is on fire. My mouth tastes of blood the way it did that time I had a fight with Ndaba when he knocked me down. I run my tongue over my teeth. One of the front teeth is broken, I think. I thought I was sick before. Now I feel a hundred times worse.

Fortunately, Joseph comes to look for me. He and several other boys take me to Mpilo Hospital where the nurses treat me quite kindly. It is days before I can speak without my mouth hurting, and it seems ages before I can eat normally.

But it is not the pain that I have nightmares about. It is that man's burning eyes that seem to come at me out of the night when I am asleep. And I see again the helpless bundle they are dragging. What happened to him? Where did they take him? What did they do with him? Is he still alive?

ı◂⇨▸ı▨ı◂⇨▸ı

This is fact:

On 19 June 2000, Patrick Nabanyama, a polling agent for the MDC in Nketa, Bulawayo, was abducted from his home, following death threats by war veterans. His kidnapping occurred at 4 o'clock in the afternoon in full view of several people, including some family members. This happened just before the elections, which took place on 24 and 25 June. He has not been seen since. Nine war veterans have been charged and are on remand, out of custody. One of these men has also been implicated in the murder of Mrs Gloria Olds.

Every Friday, for a year, there was a demonstration on the steps of the Small City Hall in Bulawayo from 1.00 to 1.30 pm to protest against the government's flagrant violation of the basic principles of law and order, not only for Patrick, but for all citizens of Zimbabwe.

$$\blacksquare \cdot \Leftrightarrow \cdot \blacksquare \bowtie \blacksquare \cdot \Leftrightarrow \cdot \blacksquare$$

On Saturday 7 July 2001, just over a year since Patrick was abducted, a memorial service was held in his memory. It seldom rains in Bulawayo in winter, but on this Saturday the streets of Bulawayo were wet. A large number of people of all racial and religious groups, carrying flowers, marched from St. Mary's Catholic Cathedral through the city centre to the Presbyterian Church.

The speakers paid tribute to Patrick, a man who had believed in democracy and in the need for change in Zimbabwe. Mr David Coltart, the MP for Bulawayo South Constituency, spoke of the culture of impunity that was prevalent in Zimbabwe. He said that justice was of paramount importance in any society. Patrick Nabanyama's abductors were well known in Nketa, and had threatened Mrs Nabanyama recently. People lived in fear, as the law no longer protected them. One thing evildoers could be sure of was the fact that God would hold them accountable for what they had done. Mr Coltart quoted from the Book of Amos 5:24: *"...Let justice roll on like a river, righteousness like a never failing stream..."*

Archbishop Pius Ncube spoke of human dignity, a God-given right. He exhorted the congregation to show respect and concern for others. Mrs Shari Eppel from Amani Trust, a human rights organisation, emphasised the need for families to be able to mourn their dead. There were few worse crimes than torture of another human being or "disappearing" someone. Such acts left relatives in a psychological limbo. People of every culture needed to bury their dead.

The people of Bulawayo pray that there will be an end to such crimes. We pray for justice and peace. We pray that God will comfort Mrs Nabanyama and her family and give them strength and courage.

$$\blacksquare \cdot \Leftrightarrow \cdot \blacksquare \bowtie \blacksquare \cdot \Leftrightarrow \cdot \blacksquare$$

LAW AND ORDER.

And dead is all the innocence of anger and surprise.

From "Lepanto" by G K Chesterton

See No Evil

 he independent press in Zimbabwe daily exposes new examples of government venality. In honestly run countries these reports would be considered scandalous. In Zimbabwe today they are merely a sign that business is going on as usual. In truth, we are so inundated with horror stories that they no longer shock us, and, as Chesterton said, "dead is all the innocence of anger and surprise". How we long to see our country governed by honest men so that we might be shocked, angered and surprised to hear that they were robbing us blind.

An article in an independent Zimbabwean newspaper, published on 27 April 2001, noted that the International Bar Association had that week released a "damning" report on the decline of the rule of law in Zimbabwe. It highlighted "the selective prosecution of cases based on political allegiance". This was, it said, "evident from the handling of politically-motivated crimes by the police". The report stated that there was a "culture of impunity" taking root in Zimbabwe, in which criminals felt that they could get away with any offence as long as the political party they associated themselves with was in power.

The police, the report stated, claimed to have no evidence against known murderers, though sympathisers of the deceased victims claimed to have supplied "mountains" of evidence. The identities of these accused are common knowledge in many cases, witnesses are available, the facts are well known and they have been widely reported. This claim of a lack of evidence is not at all plausible, and the police are obviously not attempting to carry out their duties in a remotely honest or competent manner. The murderers are out on bail and continuing to commit further crimes for the ruling party. It is apparent that ruling party supporters can commit any and all criminal offences with impunity, as long as they are seen to be doing so in the interests of the party.

The party has always had little regard for the rule of law. It has used intimidation as a weapon in all the elections it has fought since Independence, but until the year 2000 it was never in serious danger of losing one. Now it is. The situation is therefore desperate for the party and the gloves are off.

In Zimbabwe today a person can walk up to a kiosk selling food and order a beef roll. He can then claim that he is a war veteran and that he therefore does not have to pay. He won't pay. He will not have to because the police will not take any action against him for theft or extortion. This criminal may not even be a war veteran, the mere fact that he claims to be one and behaves in an aggressive and larcenous manner gives him adequate protection in the eyes of the "law" in Zimbabwe. This situation might seem impossible in most countries of the world, but it is the least of our troubles in present-day Zimbabwe.

This same individual can massacre protected game in a sanctuary, and be exempt from prosecution because he claims to be a war veteran. Wholesale poaching by land grabbers is decimating the wildlife in protected game parks across Zimbabwe. The viewing of wildlife is an important asset, because of the foreign currency it can earn from tourists, and a vital part of our national heritage, is being destroyed. An invader on a farm can steal, assault, abduct, rape or even kill the lawful occupants. He can help himself to their assets. He can butcher their livestock for food or steal animals and take them away. He can unlawfully prevent the farmer and his employees from working, to the extent that crops rot in the fields and can never be brought to market. He will not be prosecuted for these crimes.

He can perform almost any illegal act as long as he does it in collusion with a band of others like himself, claiming as his only justification or defence that he is a ruling party supporter and a war veteran. He might be a decade or two too young actually to be a veteran of Zimbabwe's liberation war, but the police will, generally, take no effective action against him. It is virtually certain that he will never be brought to trial under a ZANU PF government.

If he is arrested for his criminal offences, he can be secure in the knowledge that the police will fail to find the witnesses who are clamouring to give evidence or they will "lose" the investigation docket. If, by some cruel trick of fate, he is actually found guilty and sentenced, he can expect to receive a presidential pardon.

Opposition party officials are, meanwhile, subjected to arrest, investigation and prosecution for the most trivial of matters - for example, for using the peaceful open hand, palm forward, salute of the MDC (Movement For Democratic Change) party. They are arrested for displaying or even possessing the party's red cards, similar to those used by soccer referees to dismiss delinquent players from the field. They are used to indicate that the government must go. These gestures or symbols are interpreted as being "conduct likely to cause a breach of the peace", under the Miscellaneous Offences Act, or, worse, as a serious political offence under the draconian Law and Order Maintenance Act, inherited from the colonial era.

Opposition party supporters who are attacked by ruling party thugs or "cadres", as ZANU PF proudly describes them, are likely to be charged with assault if the police can catch them. This applies whether they successfully defend themselves of whether they get beaten up.

The Judiciary

The foundation of the law in any society is a competent and honest judiciary, and Zimbabwe had been fortunate in this regard. The country has maintained a highly honourable and respected corps of judges through its transitions from a colony to a white minority rebel state, and finally to a state based on majority rule. The ruling party, however, has found that the judiciary does not suit its programmes because it had always administered the law in the traditional ethical way, without fear or favour.

When the Courts started to rule against the government's transparently illegal stance on the land issue, the party decided that changes had to be made. Judges found themselves under threat of violence, and the deliberations of the Courts have periodically been interrupted by riotous mobs of war veterans. The police have not intervened to control them. Specific threats have been made against individual judges by some of the highest-ranking members of government, in an attempt to force them to resign. There is a very real danger that sitting judges will continue to be forced from office, and that more ruling party loyalists with no regard for the rule of law will be appointed to replace them.

The Presidential Elections

Constitutionally, the Presidential Election must be held by the end of

March 2002. Even if a state of emergency is declared, this could legally postpone the election for only ten months. The ruling party is desperately trying to build up stronger party structures before the elections. The election is decided on the total number of votes cast for a candidate, irrespective of constituency boundaries. If the same voting pattern applies to the presidential elections as to the parliamentary ones in June 2000, ZANU PF will lose since more people voted for the opposition than for the ruling party. ZANU PF narrowly won more seats only because the opposition was divided, and prevented by vicious intimidation from campaigning effectively in most rural areas in the country. Many of the votes cast for ZANU PF then, were for individual candidates who were popular in the areas in which they stood. President Mugabe would not personally pick up most of those votes. A substitute ZANU PF candidate is unlikely to do much better than Mr Mugabe would, although he might pick up more votes in his own home area.

The ruling party shamelessly and universally uses the employees and resources of the state for electioneering. The government simply refused to pay to the opposition the millions of dollars it was entitled to by law in the year 2000. It blatantly stole that money and used it for its own purposes. The party has ignored orders from the highest Courts in the land, and its most senior leaders have defiantly and publicly stated that it will not allow those Courts to prevent it from doing as it wishes.

Soldiers and policemen in uniform have embarked on punitive raids in rural and urban areas where the opposition won the vote in the June 2000 parliamentary elections, and have beaten up unarmed and innocent residents just because they or their neighbours may have voted for the opposition.

The ruling party knows that the majority of the voters in Zimbabwe are now well aware that it has largely destroyed a healthy economy for its own selfish ends, with its massive corruption and its hostility towards honest business people. It has created an economic environment that has driven investors, local and foreign, away, and deprived the population of the millions of jobs that would have been created had the government been even moderately honest and competent. It realises that it is held in such low regard that it cannot possibly win an election fairly or legally. To lose would be a disaster for the inner circle of the Party. For many, it would mean exchanging a life of unearned luxury for a well-deserved prison cell, so they must ensure that they win - by fair means or foul. The "fair" route is not a practical option. Only the "foul" is left open to them.

The party is using an overwhelming combination of bribery and intimidation, tempered by a little homicide when that route is considered necessary. It is pursuing this course energetically. It is an organisation of desperate people. For the sake of the impoverished masses of Zimbabwe, it must not be allowed to succeed.

Bribes take the form of cash handouts and a favoured position in the queue for plots of resettlement land illegally seized from commercial farmers. These are openly given only to those who profess loyalty to the Party.

Terror on the Land

For a year from February 2000, the worst excesses of the Party were confined mainly to the rural areas. Illegal settlers who claimed to be war veterans invaded commercial farms, insisting that the land was theirs. They terrorised the farm owners and their workers, and routinely assaulted and humiliated them, forcing them to proclaim their loyalty to ZANU PF, often for the benefit of the television cameras of the state-controlled Zimbabwe Broadcasting Corporation. They also swarmed across the communal lands, and by harassing, intimidating, beating and even murdering their representatives, made it impossible for the main opposition party to campaign effectively there for the parliamentary elections in June 2000. This assault was largely successful, as the ruling party managed to scrape through with a small minority in parliament. The campaign for the Presidential Election in 2002 carried on from where the campaign for the parliamentary elections of June 2000 left off. The pressure has been maintained on the farms and the communal areas to date, as the party is now fighting for survival.

For this reason, senior members of ZANU PF have publicly stated that there will be civil war if they lose the election. This does not seem to be bravado, or a mindless threat. It appears to be part of a calculated campaign of intimidation of the electorate. The government wants people to be afraid of the consequences of an opposition victory. The thinking appears to be that many may then vote for ZANU PF as the lesser of two evils - a continuation of corrupt rule and degradation of the economy as before, but without wholesale slaughter.

The Terror Comes to Town

Urban residents had escaped most of the intimidation of the electorate up to April 2001. It had seemed to many of them to be occurring on a distant planet, a surreal horror that would never affect them directly. After all, ZANU PF would not dare to harass people in the cities as it had in the bush! If it did, it would expose itself to the full glare of publicity. The international media would report such incidents meticulously. Surely this could not happen! The city dwellers had underestimated the desperation of ZANU PF.

The horror came to town. In April 2001, "war veterans" started to invade business premises in Harare and Bulawayo. Playing the familiar Robin Hood role, posturing as defenders of the poor, they interfered in the management of urban businesses. They invaded offices and factories and abducted and assaulted managers and staff, extorting from them ridiculously high sums as compensation for employees in labour disputes, some of them years old. It did not matter that these disputes had often been finalised legally through the government's own Ministry of Labour. Some executives were held captive at ZANU PF headquarters in Harare. They forced the reinstatement of employees who had been legally retrenched from businesses that were struggling to survive, largely because of the devastation wrought on the economy by ZANU PF. This, of course, is likely to have tragic consequences for the continued operations of the businesses involved, and may cost all their employees their jobs.

An article in The Daily News of 24 May 2001 states: *"The war veterans intervened in 186 companies and in the process more than 500 people have lost their jobs following the closure of nine companies."* Many more jobs will be lost when the full effects of the invasions are felt. Huge investments have been and will be cancelled. Fatal damage will be done to the cash flow of companies which have had massive payments extorted from them. Furthermore, they have been saddled with an excess of unproductive and undisciplined labour which they have been forced to re-hire.

Zimbabwe's Information Minister, Jonathan Moyo was interviewed for an article in the Harare-based Financial Gazette of 10 May 2001. It began: *"President Robert Mugabe will not intervene to end the current wave of invasions of private companies by his supporters..."* Moyo was quoted as saying: *"Instead of seeking President Robert Mugabe's intervention, the Confederation of Zimbabwe Industries (CZI) leadership should seek to meet the workers who have genuine grievances and try to address them."* He added that Mugabe would not step in to end the crisis which, the article stated, *"threatened to kill an already tottering economy".* The government in Zimbabwe encourages mob violence in the settlement of labour disputes.

There is a systematic move to increase the influence of hard-line ZANU PF supporters within the police and army. War veterans are being appointed to these forces and given promotions they do not merit. The efficiency and morale of the forces must inevitably be severely affected by these measures. Politicians, for political ends, are orchestrating the activities of the military and the police. Both the police and the army have a tradition of responsible and honourable service. The new Zimbabwean army, in particular, is highly regarded as a disciplined and effective force in United Nations circles, largely as a result of its tradition and of the training it has received from the British Military Advisory Training Team (BMATT) since 1980, which has only recently been withdrawn. It appears that a deliberate attempt is being made to change the composition and ethos of the police and the army, to make them a tool of the ruling party, the better to intimidate any opposition.

Weep For Zimbabwe

The invasions of businesses have done untold harm to the companies looted in this manner, and to business in the country as a whole. One of the companies invaded by war veterans was in the process of being rescued from insolvency by a group of foreign investors. These "white knights" had been prepared to invest Z$250 million in the company. After the invasion, the investors withdrew their offer. At the time of writing, the whole organisation is likely to collapse. Informed sources say that a number of workers, forcibly and illegally reinstated, may be paid for another month or so, until all the working capital is used up. Thereafter, they, together with the remaining and much larger body of workers still legally employed, will lose their jobs. Another foreign investor who had risked Z$ 200 million has been intimidated to such an extent that he has fled the country, leaving his investment behind. These are only two of many incidents. Who will invest in this madhouse?

The few remaining managerial and professional people under the age of 40, from all cultural groups, and still in the country inevitably feel threatened and could leave. This rapidly evaporating pool is our greatest asset, our hope for the future, and it cannot be replaced. The impoverishment and the de-industrialisation of our nation proceeds on its inexorable course, apparently in accordance with the plans of the Party. Its leaders know that while they are in power they will have the resources to enjoy the privileged lifestyle they have become accustomed to, whatever happens to the economy.

The effect of our current state of chaos on other potential investors will be catastrophic. No sensible person will invest in a country in which this lunacy prevails. Zimbabwe is almost daily being dealt blow after crushing blow by its government. The abject poverty of our people is becoming more and more critical. Even many of the minority who still have jobs find it increasingly difficult to put food on the table for their families.

Cry, the beloved country.

❡ ❖ ❙ ❌ ❙ ❖ ❡

QUEUES

It had been a long and very difficult day at Jabulani Service Station. The streams of vehicles had seemed endless, tempers had frayed, as taxi drivers had attempted to jump the queue, and the garage proprietor had barely been able to scrape up enough money to pay the driver of the tanker.

To add to the frustration, there had been an incident at their kiosk on the edge of the forecourt. A young man had ordered a doughnut and had refused to pay for it. Taking a large bite, he announced, "I am a war vet. I don't have to pay for anything." Serena was so taken aback that they let him go without doing anything.

Then, just before five o'clock, the driver of a chemist's motor scooter planted himself at the front of the queue. The petrol attendants refused to serve him, and Serena came over to support them. Angry words were exchanged. The scooter driver yelled at Serena, "Lady, you're dead!"

Understandably, Serena was annoyed. She phoned the chemist (since his name and telephone number appeared prominently on the motor scooter's delivery box). He was most embarrassed, and sent his driver back to apologise in person. The scooter driver approached Serena and told her that what he had meant was that there were lots of medicines in his delivery box, and if he didn't deliver them, some people would be dead. Good story?

BUSINESSMAN

*If we don't change the direction in which
we are moving, we are likely to end up
exactly where we're headed.*

Chinese Proverb

t is with mixed emotions that a person starts a business, especially in a country like Zimbabwe. Starting a business is always a courageous undertaking under any circumstances. But here, faced with Zimbabwe's impossibly high interest rates (70% in February 2001 and reduced by government mandate to around 40% in March), the unstable dollar and the high taxation rate, it is a daunting prospect. An entrepreneur, therefore, must be fully aware of what he is letting himself in for. He needs to be capable of taking calculated risks, and he has to learn to roll with the punches.

In 1994, seven years ago, I had had enough of working for other people. I found myself in the right place at the right time and took the plunge. It has required hard work and commitment, and, by now, my company should be thriving. I should be well on the way to achieving financial security for my family and myself. But I am very far from attaining this "goal". In Zimbabwe we take two steps forward and a large hand reaches out and shoves us five steps back.

Four years ago, in 1997, the economy was growing and fairly buoyant. ESAP (the Economic Structural Adjustment Programme) had got under way in the early 1990s, and the old system of import licencing, which had been in effect for decades, was abolished. People were to be allowed to import what they liked. The ESAP programme had been drawn up between the International Monetary Fund (IMF), the World Bank and the Government of Zimbabwe. Undertakings had been given by the Government of Zimbabwe that it would adhere to specifically agreed goals and targets. In exchange for its promise to attempt to meet these targets, the government was given financial assistance in the form of loans by the IMF and the World Bank. One of the most important resolutions was the decision to cut down on government spending, which would greatly reduce the size and cost of the civil service. It was also agreed that the government would divest itself of most, if not all, of its parastatals such as the Grain Marketing Board, the Cold Storage Company, the Cotton Marketing Board and the National Railways. The intention was that financial discipline would be exercised to enable more of the nation's resources to be channelled into private investment, thus leading to the stimulation of economic growth. The government's implementation of these reforms would be monitored regularly and, provided that it met certain minimum standards, further financial aid would be given.

The country would then become self-financing, and its exports would increase to such an extent that it would be able to finance its own purchases, and price controls, import licencing and other government restrictions and interference would become a thing of the past. If the scheme worked, market forces would be allowed to set prices for all commodities.

The opening up of the economy *did* help to stimulate economic growth. Up to 1997, there had been marked progress. Then, totally unexpectedly, a massive blow was dealt by the government's decision to pay out an enormous sum of money to some 50 000 war veterans. This group of people had been holding protest marches and demonstrations to demand more recognition for their efforts during the liberation struggle prior to the country's Independence in 1980. They were insisting that each individual, who had been involved, should be paid a gratuity and a monthly pension. The announcement that the government was going to capitulate to their threats of disruption was greeted with dismay by the business and financial community. Zimbabwe did not have the resources to pay out Z$ 2,5 billion in gratuities and Z$100 million a month in pensions. It was difficult to believe that the government had made this decision, especially after the years of "belt tightening " that ESAP had entailed.

Another major blow was the decision to commit Zimbabwean troops to intervention in the Congo. It seems that the only motivation for this reckless adventure was the anticipated enrichment of some individuals high up in government circles through the exploitation of the Congo's diamond mines.

The third disaster occurred in November 1998, when the government stated its intention to seize a large number of commercial farms without compensating the owners. Suddenly property rights were worth nothing. Business confidence plummeted to an all-time low.

Almost immediately, on a "Black Friday" that November, the Zimbabwean dollar collapsed and lost half its value in a matter of days. ESAP might as well never have been put into motion. Years of effort had been undone.

The government had borrowed many millions of US dollars over the years. The country now found itself in a situation where it was impossible to repay these loans. The ESAP programme was withdrawn. The chief and immediate problem, however, was the fact that no plan had been made as to how money would be raised to pay for the huge, on-going expenditure of monthly payments to the war veterans. The government simply pretended that it could be done without damaging the economy. Extra money was just printed to meet the unbudgeted costs. It is remarkable that this action could have been taken by a government that was awash with people with degrees in economics. The financial base of the country was severely damaged, and hyper-inflation resulted.

In February 2000, the government instituted a "fast track" land redistribution programme. This was to replace the programme that had been agreed to by the Zimbabwean Government, the Commercial Farmers' Union and the international donors, who were prepared to finance the purchase of farms for redistribution to landless black people who wished to farm. The government now declared that it was no longer prepared to wait for a legal redistribution of land to be acquired on a willing seller basis (with compensation) from established farmers, or from landowners who were not fully utilising their land. It instead opted for the "fast track system" whereby people who wanted to, were allowed to invade and occupy "designated" farms. These were farms that had been listed by the government as being those which were going to be used to resettle land-hungry blacks.

Thousands of people, claiming to be "war vets", settled on hundreds of commercial farms, many of which had neither been designated nor were in the categories that the government had previously agreed would be taken for resettlement purposes. The invaders interfered extensively with farming operations. They pegged out plots for their own use on productive land, they refused to let the farmers and their workers do necessary work and generally disrupted legitimate and necessary agricultural activities. They made pathetic attempts to plant their own crops on the land they had occupied and embarked on a systematic programme of intimidation of farmers and their employees to force them to support the ruling ZANU PF party in the parliamentary elections to be held on 24 and 25 June 2000.

The prevailing lawless situation was widely reported in the international media, and foreign tourists immediately stopped visiting Zimbabwe. This, overnight, deprived the country of a major source of the precious foreign currency it needed. Tourism had been the fastest-growing major economic sector and had contributed a large percentage of the foreign currency earned.

The mining industry was also in serious trouble. For years mining had been the source of more foreign currency than any other sector of the economy. Thirty different mineral products are commercially mined in Zimbabwe. Of these the most important are gold, asbestos, chrome, nickel and coal. There are also major deposits of platinum and it is believed that a significant deposit of diamonds has recently been discovered near Buchwa.

Large mines are huge employers of labour and provide medical care, quality housing, clean water, electrical power and education for their staff. Zimbabwe has produced a large number of skilled miners, and indigenous people now fill most of the top positions. The mining industry still does need to import skilled technical personnel from time to time, however. A severe problem has occurred where the government has refused to issue work permits to foreign staff, despite having undertaken to allow such persons to work in the country for the benefit of the mining industry. It is alleged that, on occasion, essential foreign technicians have arrived at Harare airport bearing the appropriate written authority from the relevant ministries, only to be turned away and sent home by immigration officials.

The Broken Hill Platinum Company from Australia (BHP) set up an extremely important mining operation in Zimbabwe near Chegutu. They terminated their activities in 2000. The official reason given for ceasing their operations was the friable (unsound) nature of the rock strata being worked on. These physical problems were compounded by the bureaucracy of the Zimbabwe Government. It is unlikely that further substantial mining investments will be made in this country until there are significant changes in the system. For example, the commencement of mining operations at BHP were said to have been held up for a year at a cost of millions of US$, because essential skilled staff were not permitted into the country despite government undertakings that they would be.

Several gold mines in the country have shut down and more are threatening to do so, though the government has recently introduced a guaranteed floor price in US$ terms some $50 above the open market price. This "flat rate", currently US$343 for 80% of the gold sold, will be reviewed every three months. The remaining 20% of the value will continue to be paid at the market price. This initiative will keep higher-grade gold mines open for a while longer.

There are also regulations concerning the utilisation of foreign currency acquired through mining operations. Eighty percent of the foreign currency, normally US$, obtained from mining must be sold to the government at the "official" exchange rate set by the Reserve Bank of Zimbabwe. At the moment, (July 2001) the "parallel" (unofficial) market rate for the US$ (Z$160 to the US$) is close to three times the official rate. Foreign currency is virtually unavailable from official financial institutions. Established businesses are forced, therefore, to scour the marketplace for people holding stocks of US$ (which such players are prepared to sell at the "parallel" rate).

The mines have to pay the parallel rate for imported inputs (such as machinery and spares), a large part of their operating costs. The bulk of their expenditure, therefore, costs more than twice as much as it should in relation to their income. It is virtually impossible for a business to operate when faced with such a handicap. Mining sources say that they would be able to cope if they were able to retain 50% of the foreign exchange they earn. They would then be able to buy the bulk of their imported requirements at a reasonable cost. The new guaranteed higher floor price is a help to the mines. It is not a cure for their ills, but it may help many of them to survive until a normal working environment is restored, in which their operating costs and income are weighed on the same scale.

Another problem of mammoth proportion is the fuel crisis. Hours and hours are wasted queuing for fuel. After all this is over (and everyone prays one day soon it will be), someone will produce figures to show how much time and how many man-hours were wasted in fuel queues. Many businesspeople have had to channel their time and energy into importing fuel for their businesses themselves (if they have had access to foreign currency). Some of them have had to pay a premium to buy fuel from small importers just to keep their businesses running.

The fuel crisis has been particularly significant in my business, as our activities have been disrupted on a daily basis. Our company representatives have had to sit powerless in petrol or diesel queues for hours on end, waiting, waiting, waiting. Sometimes it is all in vain, and they have to come back the following day to start again. Morale is, consequently, at an all-time low. Any form of travel becomes a nightmare, as we do not have the slightest idea when the next delivery of fuel will be available. Our sales staff find it difficult to undertake long trips, as they never know whether they will be able to find fuel to complete them.

The extreme difficulty in purchasing foreign currency even at twice the official exchange rate means that manufacturing and retail organisations have found it very difficult to purchase necessary imported components. It is impossible for accountants to budget for raw material or operating costs in advance. Firm orders placed on suppliers often have to be cancelled or amended as prices increase between the time of placing of the order and the delivery date. Business managers have to spend an inordinate amount of time in constantly recosting their products. It is impossible to plan accurately for the future.

Unemployment is generally reported to be at 60% of the workforce. Despite this, the various National Employment Councils push through ridiculously high wage increases for the employees covered by their associations, ignoring the likelihood of the massive retrenchment that will result from these "awards" and their inflationary effects. In addition to law and order, common sense also needs to be restored to Zimbabwe.

The state of anarchy prevailing in the country has dissuaded local and foreign entrepreneurs from investing in Zimbabwe. Thousands of qualified people, black and white, have emigrated, hoping to settle in a country where they can be adequately rewarded for the application of their skills. South African authorities have reported that there are currently two million Zimbabweans living there, most of them illegal immigrants. They are concerned that this situation will deteriorate further if Zimbabwe's collapse is allowed to continue, and especially if widespread starvation should eventuate - as has been predicted by many experts. It is anticipated that, because of the chaos on the farms, the government will have to import huge quantities of maize and wheat during 2001. This problem has been compounded by an erratic rainy season, which saw widespread drought up to January 2001, and massive flooding in February and March 2001.

The latest development in Zimbabwe's already precarious situation is the invasion by the war vets of urban business premises with the express purpose of harassing employers and "arbitrating" in labour disputes. They have already commenced this operation, and have illegally extorted millions of dollars from a number of businesses. They have also forced managers to re-employ staff who had legally been laid off. The police appear to be utterly biased in favour of the ruling party's thugs, and it is apparent that they will not provide protection for business people.

I have never felt more concerned for the future of our country than I do today. There are very few businesses operating in Zimbabwe at this time (July 2001) that can be confident that they will still be in existence in the year 2002. I feel anger, rage and frustration at the people who are deliberately ruining the economy in the pursuance of unworkable policies, because they are afraid to lose power and face the consequences of their criminal actions over the last twenty years. They are quite prepared to destroy the economy to save their own skins and their own jobs. The ruling party is on an express train hurtling towards disaster and destruction. Its members are afraid to jump off, and they refuse to apply the brakes.

Is there a future here? Yes, I believe there is. Businesses in this country have been operating in crisis mode for the last 45 years, at least since the break-up of the Central African Federation was proposed. We have to focus on clear objectives and not lose track of them. We have to be proactive and innovative, and transform difficulties into opportunities. After all, we are accustomed to making do and coping with problems that are unheard of in developed countries. There are so many lives and jobs at stake. Workers and employers share common interests and concerns. The future of Zimbabwe is in our hands. United, we can secure the future for our children.

∎◄⫘►∎☒∎◄⫘►∎

In the hour of adversity be not without hope,
For crystal rain falls from black clouds.

Persian poem

INVEST IN ZIMBABWE

Invest in Zimbabwe! Our country has got it -
So plough in your cash, with luck you may profit.
Here people were wiser than Idi Amin,
We took 'till last year to copy his sin!

Invest in Zimbabwe! We'll keep our word.
We mean what we say, despite what you've heard,
Though farmers claim that we've let them down.
(They saw Kangai's smile but felt Made's frown!)

Invest in Zimbabwe! If you're from the West,
Our people need work, your products are best.
Forget Party speeches, you're not totally hated -
If you're lucky your assets won't be designated!

Invest in Zimbabwe! Though we're "comrades" to you,
Like Pol Pot and Stalin and all of that crew,
Why that should concern you we don't understand -
We may yet tolerate your Supply and Demand.

Invest in Zimbabwe! Go not to Lusaka.
(Strange, but they're going there, faster and faster.)
We'll fix up all permits at rates you can't better.
Please send the bonsela with your next letter!

Invest in Zimbabwe! We'll have some cash soon,
When government spending comes down from the moon.
When parastatals have fired their last crooks,
Then banks can re-open their lending books!

Invest in Zimbabwe! With ESAP and rains,
Everything's changing, despite growing pains.
We'll soon reach the stage where racism ends,
When the last emergent has picked up his Benz!

Invest in Zimbabwe, if you're from the EU,
We'd love to be wealthy just like you.
So we're trying to recover some of our wealth,
That your fathers secured by violence and stealth.

Invest in Zimbabwe, we've property rights here,
If you vote for the Party you've little to fear.
But if you don't like us, you'd better be quiet,
Or we'll strip all your assets in our next riot.

Invest in Zimbabwe, we've got law and order,
At least as much as south of our border.
We're proud of our war vets - they're misunderstood -
They just like to play at being Robin Hood.

Invest in Zimbabwe, did we offend you?
You'd think we deserved to be back of the queue!
You invest in Serbia and Kosovo to boot,
Where's the next handout? We need some more loot.

Invest in Zimbabwe, we have no collateral,
But we're quite keen on a slice of your capital.
It seems that our own has disappeared overnight -
We cannot imagine what made it take flight.

Invest in Zimbabwe, it's a great place to stay,
But when you employ, watch out what you pay.
If your workers don't like it we'll hold you to ransom.
You'll pay through the nose, high, wide and handsome.

Invest in Zimbabwe! We're keen on fair play -
Have you no sense of humour? Don't go away.
When elections are over we may make some sense,
Then bring in your yen and your dollars and pence!

❙◄⬦►❙⬛❙◄⬦►❙

⬛ Idi Amin was the Ugandan dictator who expelled the ethnic Indian community, which ran most of the businesses, ruining the economy.

⬛ Kumbirai Kangai was Zimbabwe's Minister of Agriculture for ten years. Joseph Made is the current Minister.

⬛ Designated: the government of Zimbabwe has designated or nominated more than 90% of the commercial farming land to be given to poor blacks - and to some not so poor.

⬛ Lusaka: capital of neighbouring Zambia, which has an economy we used to pity. It is now less of an economic disaster area than Zimbabwe.

⬛ Bonsela: a gift, gratuity or bribe.

⬛ Parastatal: a government-owned business, generally badly managed.

⬛ ESAP: the Economic Structural Adjustment Programme, adopted by Zimbabwe in the early 1990s.

⬛ Emergent: an indigenous businessman emerging from poverty.

COMMITMENT

 he plane is full. I am going through more than seven hours of notes from one interview. The people on either side are talking about their holidays, clutching tall, hand-carved giraffes, reading the in-flight magazine and complaining about the quality of airline food. A mother is singing gently to her child; intermittent laughter echoes through the cabin.

In the margin of my note pad, I jot down key words: the first attack; the second attack; war vets beat up farm workers; betrayal; under siege; coping; anarchy; AIDS work; stress seminars; son's thoughts of suicide; support; control; manning the radio; leaving with nothing...

When we touch down, I will be in the country where Nelson Mandela wrought a miracle. Left behind is a country where ZANU PF has wrought destruction. Zimbabwe was once a place many people referred to as "God's own country", a bread-basket of Africa and a land of opportunity. The scale of the devastation is difficult to comprehend. Fear silences the public voices of many - CIO (Central Intelligence Organisation) agents lurk in unexpected places, and a chance remark could send one for immediate interrogation. Privately it's a different story and many people want to speak out. They want to air their views on the threats, intimidation and violent attacks. They want to be counted, but they are also afraid.

Kerry Kay is a person who has worked through pain and loss on many levels and has emerged philosophical, proactive and determined to speak out for those who are unable to speak. She represents the agricultural sector on the National AIDS Council and, as an ex-police sergeant, chaired the Security Liaison Committee between the police and the farmers for three years. She is deeply committed to her role as Project Manager for the Commercial Farmers' Union's AIDS Control Programme, which she took over in 1995.

The walls of her office portray the many AIDS projects underway and the cheerful warmth of the AIDS workers, despite the enormity of their task. Beautifully written in italics are quotations from well-known world figures such as Abraham Lincoln:

> *You cannot strengthen the weak by weakening the strong*
> *You cannot help small men by tearing down big men*
> *You cannot help the poor by destroying the rich*
> *You cannot lift the wage earner by pulling down the wage payer*
> *You cannot keep out of trouble by spending more than your income*
> *You cannot further the brotherhood of man by inciting class hatreds*
> *You cannot establish security on borrowed money*
> *You cannot build character and courage by taking away a man's initiative and independence*
> *You cannot help men permanently by doing for them what they could and should be doing for themselves.*

In Kerry's view, truth will prevail. Her dream is to meet Nelson Mandela.

KERRY KAY'S STORY

We need to be the keepers of our brothers and sisters,
wherever they may be.

Nelson Mandela

Whenever I feel absolutely down or frustrated, I go into the communal area adjoining our farm and sit with one of the special women under a tree. The shade softens the relentless heat and we can relax in silence for a while under the limitless blue dome of the African sky. When we talk, we share family concerns - the progress of the children, the illness of a grandmother, the impact of soaring prices on staple foods. Given time, the conversation will turn to the difficulties of a country wracked by violence, and the relentless advance of the AIDS epidemic.

Sometimes, when we pause in the companionable stillness, we can hear the droning of bees in the wild blossom above us, or the rustle of leaves stirred by a gentle breeze. In the distance we may hear the steady chug of a tractor - a reliable, comforting sound which brings a sense of normality to the abnormal days.

These women have set up their own form of hospice, taking it in turns to give moral and spiritual support to family members, friends or even strangers whose lives are ebbing painfully away. I ask how the three children of a dying mother are faring, and I am taken to her, where she lies, frail and uncomplaining, in a dimly lit hut. We talk together for a while, but the effort for her is great and I feel it is time to go. I take her hand, reassure her that her children will be looked after when the time comes, and prepare to leave. Suddenly there is panic in her eyes and she reaches out towards me weakly. "I do not want to die alone. Please pray for me." I take her hand and pray to the God who has become an integral part of my life through Zimbabwe's daily traumas. My tears strengthen her and, as I close the door behind me, her face reflects acceptance and peace.

The women who come to take over have learnt how to turn ill people to avoid discomfort or bedsores. They have also learnt the importance of fresh air, so that patients are not shut away in the darkness, as was the custom.

Although I always bring something to relieve the escalating hardship of their everyday lives, the women never ask for, or expect anything. Each gift, however small, is accepted with enthusiasm and dignity. A day or two later, when I return to the farm after a long day's work, I may find on my kitchen shelf a couple of eggs in a neatly tied plastic bag, perhaps two or three potatoes, a mealie for each member of the family, or a little hand-crocheted mat.

My father-in-law, Jock Kay, who was Deputy Minister of Agriculture from 1992 to 1994, bought this farm in 1948 - a 5 000 acre expanse of virgin bush. My husband, Iain, was born here and grew up speaking Shona like the local people. His second father was Sydney Tuhna, the cook, and Iain would spend endless hours exploring the bush with Sydney's children. For many years, Sydney dreamt of owning a car. When he retired, Iain's father took great pleasure in giving him the trusty Mercedes he had admired for many years.

Iain is committed to this country, and to continuing with our productive farming operation. He is also committed to helping the rural people become more efficient, productive farmers. Several years ago, he started cattle discussion groups which were held once a month in different resettlement communities. The meetings would take place out in the open under an indigenous tree, with topics such as dehorning, disease control and the construction of a dipping tank on the agenda. Since the government provided no assistance or advice to these farmers, the discussion groups were well supported. To ensure the communal farmers retained their self-respect, a nominal fee would be charged and ploughed back into specific projects.

Iain also set aside eight bulls from our herd and each village could have one on loan for a period of two years to improve the gene pool of their stock. A similar programme was set up for goats. The cattle sired by our bulls were magnificent animals and won many prizes on the local agricultural shows. Four years ago the bulls were sent back - it was too risky for the villagers to retain them. Relationships of this nature threatened the government's hold over the communal people and ZANU PF's displeasure was becoming increasingly apparent.

For these communal farmers there is no land tenure. If they had title to land, and were equipped with better farming skills, they could be self-sufficient. Increasingly, the rural electorate realises it has been betrayed. As a result of government policy, and the rapidly degenerating state of the economy, mere existence today is an on-going struggle.

Throughout Zimbabwe, one basic meal a day is becoming increasingly prevalent in a country which was not only self-sufficient, but a significant food exporter.

This government's current strategy is to force the communal people into submission through fear and to wage an escalating war of terror on farmers and their farm workers. The first time my husband was attacked and beaten up was in a resettlement area where he was helping to hand out opposition party leaflets. The second attack took place on our farm, in front of the children of farm workers, while he was taking measurements for an additional classroom. Resident war vets and squatters, who were psyched up on dagga, beat him with sticks, axe handles and fan belts tied onto sticks. It was like a feeding frenzy. Then they tied his hands with wire and demanded that he show them where the guns were kept in our home. Fortunately our son, David, was alerted and he raced to the scene in a truck. The diversion of his arrival was sufficient for Iain to unshackle himself and dive into the nearby dam. The mob fanned out immediately, hurling sticks and stones each time he came up for air. Single-handedly David managed to drive them away and, in a last act of malice, they set fire to Iain's Honda 125 motorbike. David raced Iain to hospital in Marondera. His father's face was covered in blood and his back was zigzagged with appalling welts. They took a long time to heal.

It is strange how premonitions occur. As Project Manager for the Commercial Farmers' Union's AIDS Control Programme, I had been selected to go to America on the USA Information Service's International Visitors' programme. Initially I had been reticent about travelling at this time because the farm had already been invaded and I sensed that something would happen. Over the past three years we had lost four friends, two of whom had been killed in a plane crash. I could not face another death. However, Iain had encouraged me to accept. It was a wonderful opportunity to represent our country, he said.

The night before I left, I tucked a card under every family member's pillow. On each was a cross, with the words: "Never will I leave you, never forsake you." Heb.13:5. When the war vets tried to kill Iain, he remembers a vision of this cross flashing before him.

My group was just about to leave Atlanta when the news reached us and I flew home immediately. For over a month, Iain's eyes remained expressionless. It was as if the person inside the shell was far away.

When the curtains finally drew back, he still would not talk about it. Men have to come to terms with things in their own time, and we must learn to be patient.

During this period, the support we received was incredible. Offers of help poured in from the district, from friends and strangers countrywide, and from people across the world. Many of the letters we received were deeply touching, especially those from people who were close to us and in permanent danger themselves.

Madam Kay

The .... farm workers are very unhappy because of what has happened to Mr Kay. There are cruel people here on earth. Mr Kay would have been killed. God is there. Our country is very corrupted. War veterans is fighting people ... the uneducated mujibas whom they recruit are playing dirty games... AIDS is also fighting us. S....... is still in bed, he is very serious. This sickness is not understood.

Thank you....

Mr Kay

We are very sorry with what we have heard.... We thank God that you haven't been killed. We are created in different ways, some of us need to be helped in thinking and some are hot-headed for nothing. We know that God is going to punish them somehow.

We hope you are going to recover very soon and we are gong to pray to God to help you.

Thank you....

Two weeks after Iain's second attack, David Stevens, who farmed near us at Virginia, was abducted and severely assaulted, together with the five farmers who raced to his rescue. He was then shot in the back. The mob burnt his entire tobacco crop, including the portion curing in the barns, which would have brought in vital foreign currency. Afterwards, they ransacked the farmhouse, burnt it and then set fire to his workers' village. More than twenty homes were razed to the ground. Since Iain was becoming a thorn in the flesh of the ruling party, threats of a petrol bomb attack on our home began to reach us.

By this time, I was beside myself. We had four children depending on us: our sons, Clive, David, and Bruce, and our adopted daughter,

Lindsay, who had lost her parents tragically in the plane crash the previous year. She could not afford to lose a second dad.

We immediately called over eight farmers from the area to discuss the situation. Iain felt that his presence was fuelling the violence and endangering the lives of others, including our farm workers. He then consulted with the workers and a consensus was reached. We would leave the area temporarily.

It is hard to describe what my home means to me, and what it felt like preparing to abandon it. For 21 years we had lived in a 'shoebox' until, two years ago, we built a beautiful thatched home. I love every bit of the house and cherish every beam, every piece of thatching grass and especially my beautiful kitchen, made big enough for the whole family to gather in while I cook. Leaving was a painful decision.

At a time like this, knowing the enemy and being prepared are among the most effective ways of overcoming fear. I was not a stranger to this type of situation. In 1979, during the bush war, our tiny thatched cottage was attacked. I was alone with David, who was a baby at the time. The firing started about 9 pm. As I carried him quickly from the kitchen to his specially-made armour-plated cot, I had a premonition of the sequence of events about to take place: who would answer the radio, what the person would say, and what I needed to do in the interim. It was an extraordinary experience. I knew instinctively then that I was not alone.

Once David was safe, I crept outside with my automatic shotgun and started firing in the direction from which the tracer bullets were coming. Suddenly the gun jammed and I had to run back inside, light a candle, try to unjam it and then reload. Although the 'reaction stick' was on the way, it would take about half an hour to reach us. When everything went quiet, the fear set in. My mouth went dry and, for over 45 minutes, I could not get one iota of saliva going. It was pitch dark and the only way to be safe was to slip into the dark garden to hide so that I would have a chance of seeing the attackers if they came through the security fence.

In today's situation, our lives are still being threatened but we live vigilantly and keep in radio or phone contact with each other, wherever we are.

The night we were warned that our house would be petrol bombed, we slept in tracksuits and shoes, and had our backpacks ready. Each pack told its own story. Iain's included a torch, Swiss army knives and a Leatherman, and David's a compass and matches. Clive had packed the bandages and ammunition, and I took all our personal papers. To ensure their safety, Iain and I had sent Bruce and Lindsay to friends.

Before we went to bed, we discussed in detail our plans for getting out in an emergency. Since it would probably be dangerous to leave by road, we needed another option. However, when the call came through at 11.30 pm - Dave Stevens had just been shot - they said we must leave immediately by road. We experienced no fear at all in leaving. It is amazing how, when you carry out rehearsed plans, the adrenalin gets going and everyone takes a task and gets on with the job of evacuating. There is comfort in taking intelligent action. In my experience, the worst stress is the anticipation of something happening. Once it has happened, you can move on.

The men who ransacked our home after we had left included two people we had helped to start a security firm. They had sat around our table on a number of occasions drinking tea and asking for advice. Three of the youths sent to kill Iain during the second attack were sons of a farm foreman who had succumbed to AIDS, as had his wife. We had cared for the couple and had made sure that their sons were employed or at school. Betrayal is a difficult concept to comprehend.

The two weeks after we left the farm were the worst of my life. Many black friends advised us not to return home, and I could not come to terms with the loss of our home, our farm and all that life as we knew it meant to us. I remember sitting on a rock on the KwaZulu-Natal south coast, consumed with anger and bitterness. When the anger threatened to overwhelm me, I would counter negative with positive, evil with good. It took long hours of soul-searching to realise that I could not live like this and, for the first time, I admitted to God that I could not cope. Finally I realised that, at this point, the answer was simply to accept what had happened.

While we were away, our neighbours took over the land preparation tasks and, with the help of our workers, planted the tobacco seedbeds for the next crop. When the war vets tried to stop them and put burning grass under a tractor, our workers went ballistic and drove them away. When the crop was finally reaped, it was sent to Harare for grading.

Those who are fomenting the destruction of our country and perpetuating the violence on our farms have no conscience. During the attack on our farm, they killed our dairy cows and broke the leg of Starlight, Bruce's polocrosse horse. Bruce had played polocrosse on Starlight since he was six and she was his soul mate. Starlight had to be put down and Bruce was inconsolable.

The incredible pain you feel for your children is almost suffocating - it's like being inside a wave shattering on a rock. At times like this you struggle to keep yourself going and to buoy up your children. The lesson of adversity, I have found, is to be more philosophical and to turn the difficulty into an opportunity.

In trying to reduce the trauma of our lives for the children, I made a mistake. I told them that we had many wonderful, supportive friends and that home could be anywhere. But the children had lost something very important in their lives and needed time to come to terms with their grief. Lindsay had kept all her special things in a box, and this too had been stolen. The most important item was her parents' St Christopher, found at the scene of the plane crash in which they lost their lives.

Clive had been deeply shocked to see his father so badly beaten up - why would someone want to kill Dad when he is so loved by everyone, Mum? Leaving his home late at night and armed had compounded the situation. Since all his clothes, and those of the rest of the family had been stolen in the attack, he had nothing. His friends were generous and caring, and I phoned him and the other children at their boarding schools every day.

During one phone call, Clive told me that he could not face another class. He needed time out. I sensed it was serious and phoned the school chaplin. The next morning Clive did not attend classes and wrote all day. What emerged was "Desperate", a poem expressing deep-seated pain at the devastation of his home and his country, and the futility of it all. The following day I went to see him, and read the poem. Part of what he wrote follows:

DESPERATE

A certain calmness has returned.
Day to day chores are carried out;
the mind strays little from work
Every so often a thought or two
disturbs the tranquillity of school,
but stays only for a short while.

Seldom is there anything worthwhile;
one just drifts through time,
hoping and being ever patient.
Coping is the hardest goal to achieve.
Never offer a glimpse of sadness
as it will only dissolve what little
happiness there is left to enjoy.

Like adrenalin injected straight into the heart
so the feeling of violence erupts,
the desperate desire to punish.
The ultimate goal is to annihilate
the perpetrators without remorse!
The devil has blown through your life
like a wild fire, consuming what
little good you had ever grown in your heart.
Some may say he and the Lord do not exist.
If this is so, then why do you feel, touch, think,
fight, love, hate, live, die and then live again?

Your home is where your heart is;
and my heart is in ZIMBABWE.
When someone threatens my home,
they threaten my heart,
my existence
I want to exist, therefore I will fight.

"Focus, don't let it disrupt your work,"
the less affected say;
they don't and can't feel what I am feeling,
keep drumming into my head.
Consciously I am alive;
subconsciously I am dying.

I feel alone and isolated from people,
from those around me,
they do not understand my pain
How do I make them understand?
I am cornered and slipping down the
wall and falling to my knees.
I am fighting with myself
And drowning in my own thoughts,
and in so doing losing my loved ones.

Being temperamental, impatient and volatile
inhibits communication.
Trivial matters become monstrosities
and I turn on those who care.
Slowly my courage and strengths
are being consumed and I am
retreating into darkness.
Quitters are losers;
I guess by giving up I am quitting
If so, I have lost.

Clive's poem was circulated internationally by e-mail and through the Internet. The response from people worldwide was incredible and offers of help poured in. Families we had never heard of were prepared to look after our children or animals and we were humbled by their concern. Months later, Clive, a big strapping 'rugger-bugger', took on one of the stress seminars in my overloaded schedule and admitted publicly for the first time that he had been suicidal. Referring to the work of Dr Stephen Covey, which focuses strongly on values, principles and integrity, he pointed out that there were people in Zimbabwe who were compromising their principles for short-term gain. He said this was totally unacceptable. Since then, Clive has spoken at a number of seminars and has helped many young people to cope with the stress of life in today's Zimbabwe.

At this point, my husband was also struggling with the on-going trauma of our lives. Heading up a substantial and successful 5 000 acre farming venture, he was the main provider for his family and our 200-strong workforce, most of whom had dependants themselves. Iain was highly regarded as a farmer and for his work in the communal areas. But overnight he had lost control of his life and could not return to the farm. Furthermore, he had been seriously assaulted on two occasions and had had to borrow money in order to continue paying our workers in full. He was also reliant on our neighbours for overseeing all operations on the farm. "It's like driving downhill flat out and then your brakes fail," he explained. The workers on a farm in northwestern Zimbabwe which has been devastated by the war vets expressed similar feelings regarding the current situation on their farm. "We are like a trailer behind the tractor. We have no brakes, no steering and no acceleration."

Despite the fact that we were without a home of our own at this time, we found many other homes and the wonderful friends who took us in became like an extended family. Through the e-mail our network had grown tremendously and support flowed in with unceasing dependability.

For a while, we lived in a small apartment in Harare. However, on two occasions our neighbours drove me back to the farm, hidden in a truck, so that I could see how the workers were getting on. When they realised who it was, everyone, including the children, would come running to greet us. For a few minutes we would catch up with each other's news and then we'd have to leave, otherwise they'd be hassled by the "war vets" and squatters. When we were gone, the workers would be on their own again. It was very worrying.

The attack on our home had been planned carefully. Using trucks and a trailer, the invaders had sought to disperse their pickings throughout the communal areas. One of the elders, who was offered the goods, refused to take over anything stolen from the Kay's house.

"We will send people to kill this man," the villagers were told. "He is a security risk." When the next wave of attackers arrived, the elder managed to escape by slipping away into the night. Bent on destruction, they burnt his home and his tractor, leaving him with nothing.

Directly the story reached us, I arranged to meet him in a hotel in Harare. I arrived with loads of clothes, and he came in a borrowed suit. We were delighted to see each other, and he immediately wanted to know how Iain was managing. Suddenly he broke down and cried - a difficult thing for a black man to do in front of a white woman.

Later, when we were back on the farm, Iain ploughed 20 acres for him and helped to plant his mealie crop. With assistance from many quarters, a truck was filled with things for his home so that he could rebuild his fragile existence.

The day after our return - we had been away for eight months - a little boy arrived at our door. He explained that his father was dying of AIDS and his mother was already dead. His family had sent him to us to look after.

It was exciting to be back home and to see the workers and our animals. While we were away, our caring, thoughtful neighbours had cleaned up our home and put what goods remained intact into storage. To break the emptiness, there were roses in every room and clothes for the whole family. The kitchen too was stocked - they had even managed to find baking tins!

It was also good to be in control of our lives again. As evil as the men who ransacked our home were, there must somewhere have been a scrap of decency and an appreciation for what we had done for them to make them stop short of arson.

For years I had collected beautiful African artifacts from all over the continent. These had been left. However, they had taken most of our special pieces - my inherited bone china, the crystal glasses, my grandmother's table and my Chanel No 5 perfume - a thirty-year old bottle that had belonged to my mum. Did it matter? Was I just trying to hang onto the long-gone past - to 33 years ago when our parents and grandparents had all died within three years? The silence of the empty rooms spoke volumes.

Surprisingly, the pot plants were still alive and, outside on the compost heap, the nasturtiums were coming into bloom. Just before we had left the farm, Lindsay had planted two lucky bean trees in memory of her mum and dad, and they were also doing well. It is remarkable how nature's resilience puts everything back in perspective.

The second week-end we were back, the war vets started burning our workers' homes. About a hundred marched up to the house, chanting and armed with their standard weapons of "war". A number of our friends were at the local club when we phoned through for reinforcements and their response was immediate. Everyone raced to the farm, including farmers from Wedza, which is over 35 kilometres away. As a result, further bloodshed was averted.

Within a few days, news of this latest violence had resulted in the arrival of truck-loads of goods for our farm workers from as far afield as Masvingo. In cases like this, the people of Zimbabwe have learnt not to feel beholden, as we all need each other. Trouble occurs on a revolving basis and each must support the other.

Throughout all the violence, the police countrywide have done little to protect the farmers and their farm workers, claiming that "their hands are tied". I trained as a policewoman and, as a police reservist, have supported our Police Force for over 31 years. However, their fear for themselves, their families and their jobs is so great that they have failed to protect many of us during these critical times. Yet, when I asked for help to search a couple of communal homes for our goods, they agreed to assist. It was an uncomfortable experience to go into a stranger's home and find one's stolen property.

Later, sitting in the front of the police van with the two black policemen and a suspected thief in the back, I began to feel ill. On three occasions they had to stop the truck, but both men were very sympathetic. "We can understand your stress, Mrs Kay," they said. It is an overwhelmingly traumatic time in our country. Together we are having to deal with loss of life, loss of livelihood and the loss of things we have held sacred. We have also had to accept loss of dignity.

Just before midnight, the police dropped me, filthy and exhausted, at a friend's house. Within minutes, hot water arrived from the boiler, the bath was filled with sweet-smelling bath foam and a fresh set of clothes was laid out on the chair. My dirty clothes were whisked away for laundering. I don't believe that you would get as compassionate a response from a community anywhere else in the world. Zimbabwe is truly an extraordinary country.

It is strange how stolen things have a way of turning up again. Months later, some guards found our trailer, now converted into a Scotch cart, in Rusape. Inside was Dave Stevens' diary. During September, five months after the ransacking of our home, my son's copy of Dr Stephen Covey's book, "The 7 Habits of Highly Effective People", was discovered in the bush. Our family has been profoundly influenced by Dr Covey's work, which focuses on values such as integrity, ethics, trust and principle-centred leadership. We find that interest in his material grows here daily.

Leadership is such an important issue at this time. For two weeks a year the Commercial Farmers' Union holds a programme called "The Leadership Challenge", which discusses principle-centred leadership within the family, community, society and government. It also examines the concept of servant leadership. The role of a servant leader is to serve and protect the people he leads, and to act all times with honesty and integrity, for the common good.

Increasingly, Zimabweans are reading the works of the Dalai Lama, who is revered across all cultures. Our AIDS co-ordinators have recently ordered "God Calling" to help them with the overwhelming challenges they face daily. We have consciously to remind ourselves that there is a greater force than ZANU PF and to learn to be at peace.

Each of us handles the stress of our lives in different ways. One of my coping mechanisms is to ensure that I spend a few hours on my own every day, either reading or praying in a quiet place. The rest of the time I work at a frenetic pace. My advice to people when I speak at stress seminars is to do something positive. Look around and see who needs help more than you, and find a way of helping that person. If you are committed to this country, you must stand up and be involved. Seek out positive people and avoid those who are always negative. Accept that things will get tougher and work out a strategy to minimise the effect.

If you are really down, have the courage to ask for help and accept it. Visit a hospice. Talk to a counsellor. Be honest with your feelings, especially with family members, and encourage them to express theirs. Remember that "fine" can be a dangerous word. You have to interpret what it means. It could mean that the person is not coping, and perhaps even close to suicide, but is afraid to admit it. We have to face the reality that we are living in a very critical time, in an abnormal world, and we have to look after ourselves and each other. Before we returned to our farm, we discussed the risks together, decided that the pros outweighed the cons, and then put our lives into God's hands.

One evening after Iain had been attacked for the second time, I was cooking in my kitchen, feeling deeply distressed, when Clive walked in and sat down to keep me company. After watching me intently for a while, he said: "You are also allowed to cry, Mum. You can't be Superwoman all the time." I realised then that I was not allowing myself, or my children, to be normal.

The support from our urban community has been outstanding. Town and city dwellers send cards, letters and e-mails to the farming community, offer accommodation when we are destitute, supply clothing when the homes of farm workers have been destroyed and set up prayer groups. They also help in other small but important ways, like offering to baby-sit our children when we have to come to town.

To alleviate some of the pressure on farm workers, we've set up a Farm Workers' Assistance Fund through the Commercial Farmers' Union and the National Employment Council for Agricultural Workers. As a result of this initiative, those who have been retrenched but who are still resident on a farm can have their children's school fees paid. We organise for boxes of clothes to be sent to them and provide mealie meal and vegetable seeds. After homes of workers were trashed on what was previously a highly productive farm in the Mazowe area, people collected clothes, blankets, pots and buckets. It is important that they realise we care. My husband talked to them for a long time, and was deeply impressed with their courage and morale. We are in this together, they said - together we will survive.

We are deeply concerned about what will happen over the next few months - inevitably there will be bloodshed. We organised a two-day Medical Air Rescue Service course at our club during April and asked the instructor to replace the snake-bite section with information on dealing with gunshot wounds and the setting up of drips. Everyone who took the course was asked to purchase a MARS kit so that medical support would be spread throughout the area. Our district has been divided into blocks and all routes have been marked on maps.

Countrywide, people are extremely worried about the escalating damage to the environment. Wherever possible, formal and informal planting programmes are underway to counter the devastation of the indigenous tree population. The barren landscape of farms that were designated and then stripped of their protective vegetation mirrors the pain of the men, women and children who face a bleak future. Despite this, a common bond is being forged and the country has grown spiritually over the past year. We are in this predicament together and we have to realise that the decisions we make now are not only for ourselves, but for future generations.

High up in the steeply-pitched roof of our thatched home, the starlings are nesting once again. The lucky-bean trees have grown a few more centimetres and the nasturtiums have almost covered the compost heap. Our workers tell me that Iain has taken on the totem of the Zebra because all of us, black and white, need to support each other. Time will heal. But the scars of these wounds will remain forever.

THE KAY'S CHRISTMAS CARD: 2000

I asked for strength...
And God gave me difficulties to make me strong.
I asked for wisdom...
And God gave me problems to solve.
I asked for prosperity...
And God gave me brain and brawn to work.
I asked for courage...
And God gave me dangers to overcome.
I asked for love...
And God gave me troubled people to help.
I asked for favours...
And God gave me opportunities.
I received nothing I wanted.
I received everything I needed.

SUBSEQUENTLY

During the morning of Friday 6 July 2001, approximately 60 squatters and war veterans invaded Iain Kay's Chipesa farm, wielding axes, sticks and whips. They lit a fire in the grassland close to the paprika crop, and, while David Kay tried to create a fire break, hurled rocks at him and the security manager. The situation was reported to the police, who arrived late that afternoon. Two neighbours, Trevor Steel and Kim Nilson, drove to the farm immediately to support Mr Kay and his son, David. Eventually the four had to barricade themselves in the house. Throughout the night the invaders sang songs and threw rocks onto shed roofs.

The following day, the mob broke through the fence around the yard to attack Mr Kay, who retreated to his office and managed to lock the door. A group captured the security manager, assaulted him in front of the police and then began beating the workers, including a very old man and a number of women. Two workers sustained serious injuries and had to be taken to hospital in an ambulance which was standing by on the next door farm. Workers' homes were searched for MDC membership cards and T-shirts, and the terror campaign continued unabated. Tobacco and seedbeds were destroyed, causing Z$250 000 damage.

That night, the thugs attempted to break into the section of the house where the four farmers and ten workers were now barricaded. Mr Kay managed to keep the mob at bay with a pistol. Chanting of slogans and attempts to "re-educate" the workers continued throughout the night.

Next morning about 40 farm workers were forced into the house and beaten from behind. At 3 pm a team of government and ZANU PF officials arrived. While negotiations continued, a "reaction stick" of 80 farmers waited on the next door farm for a call to storm the homestead and rescue the besieged farmers and workers.

Mr Kay was ordered by the war vets to leave his farm within a month. Although Chipesa has been designated, it is not "fast tracked".

┇•⇌•┇⊠┇•⇌•┇

The Standard: 15-21 July 2001

In a recent interview with Iain Kay reported in The Standard, one of Zimbabwe's independent newspapers, journalist Chido Makunike referred to the first assault on Mr Kay by war veterans and noted:

Whites may earlier have been verbally abused by high government and ruling party officials, but the pressure on them was clearly increased with the campaign over land and ZANU PF's quest for electoral survival.

Whites were (now) no longer physically untouchable. After what was seen by ZANU PF as the outrage of the white community in general, and the white farmers in particular, in throwing their weight behind the MDC, they became fair game for the ruling party's violence, in a way only poor blacks had been before.

Mr Makunike concludes his article with the following comment:

The case for land reform has been strong for ages now, and there is plenty of blame to go around for why it has not been accomplished so far.

As an African conscious of his history, I should be feeling a sense of triumph that a great historical wrong is finally being corrected in my time. Yet, when I look at how botched this great opportunity for the country to make a great leap forward on so many fronts has been, from empowerment to new, more enlightened race relations, I can't help but wonder and grieve at yet another aspect of how Mugabe has brought this country to this present state. He has managed to make us appear bungling, blood-thirsty people sabotaging our own future, rather than the brave, heroic people we were at independence and who are now reclaiming their birthright...

VOICES OF FARM CHILDREN: TOO FRIGHTENED TO CRY

Before we disappeared behind the hills, I turned and looked for what I imagined was the last time at my village. I could see the simple huts and the people going about their chores; the stream where I had splashed and played with the other boys; the maize fields and green pastures where the herds and flocks were lazily grazing... Above all else, my eyes rested on the three simple huts where I had enjoyed my mother's love and protection...

Nelson Mandela: Long Walk to Freedom

In April 2001, The World Conference on Religion and Peace (WCRP) and the United Nations' Children's Fund (UNICEF) convened a small inter-religious consultation of experts on the role of religious communities in addressing the plight of children confronting violent conflict, poverty, HIV/AIDS and discrimination.

The consultation produced the following statement:

Despite the positive gains of the decade, countless and growing numbers of children are subjected to unspeakable violence, poverty, discrimination and preventable diseases. Our failure to protect, provide for, respect and free children denies our humanity, threatens our future, and betrays our beliefs. All of our religious traditions recognise that moral responsibility is proportional to capacity. Today, because of our collective capacity, we can protect and provide for our children, and because we can, we must. Societies will be judged ultimately by the condition of their most innocent dependants and most vulnerable members - their children. Meeting our inescapable moral duty to children is also a key to human fulfilment. Our traditions know, each in their own way, that human satisfaction and joy lies in building communities that respect, nurture and love children...

The nightmare for the farm workers' children is recurring. It wakes them up at night, every night, for weeks and months on end. But, in the morning, when the sun should slip gently over the horizon to exorcise those evil spectres with its warmth, the nightmare continues. Sometimes it is played out in actions and events that eclipse even the most terrifying, ghoulish images that a traumatised brain can conjure up in the darkness when fear is in free-fall.

... Far away, beyond the bend in the gravel road, we can hear soft chanting. Once, long ago, our hearts would have lifted in what would have been a song of celebration. But today there is reason only to fear... the war veterans are coming... The chanting gets louder and louder... They are armed with sticks, machetes, axes and knobkerries... Their songs are revolutionary songs, and they dance, dance wildly as if all the beer that they stole from the farm store beyond the hill has been drunk in one long night of madness... Like army ants they swarm down the road, bent on destroying all that lies before them... They fear nothing... Our parents cannot save us. There is no-one to save us.

Like dogs, we hide in the veld close by, huddled together for comfort, listening to the frightening sounds as they dance and chant around our homes, setting the dry thatching grass alight, so that the flames leap high into the air, and the smoke boils black in the sky. Like locusts they swarm through the houses, knocking over dishes of milk and the pots of mealie meal cooking outside on open fires. The chickens that were outside scatter in fear, but inside the wire enclosure, a young goat, only a few weeks old, cannot escape. Two men armed with knives chase the goat, laughing, until he is cornered. They slit his throat, skin him and cut the meat into pieces. Then they scrape together the coals from one of the cooking fires and carry them in a bucket to the far end of the village, away from the burning huts. When they have found enough beer to drink, they sing and dance wildly as everything we own burns quickly to the ground.

▮◆▷▪▐✕▌▪◁◆▮

The radio tells us that everything is fine in Zimbabwe. That we will be given the land that is ours, that we will all be free. But we have heard stories from places not far from us where farmers have been killed. Where armed gangs have terrorised the farm workers and beaten the men until some of them died; that their corpses were hanged from

Voices of Zimbabwe

the trees. Where others have been burnt with iron heated in the coals until it glowed red-hot, where mothers have been raped or injured in dreadful ways. People have heard their screams from far away, and they too have feared for their lives...

In the day-time they watch us. When my mother is working, they stand sometimes, for many hours, not far away, just watching, watching. She is so afraid that it is hard to work. And at night she is unable to sleep. Their eyes are sometimes wide and red with the dagga that they smoke. Their drums are so loud that we children cannot sleep. And we are afraid of what will happen when we do sleep.

We have seen our fathers forced to attend ZANU PF rallies, where they have to raise their fists and shout "Pamberi! (Forward!)" We have heard of the war veterans who call themselves Satan, Messiah and The Undertaker...

One day, when it was still very hot, we heard the lorries arriving. There were men, women and children, and there were many of them. The faces of the children were blank, as if they had seen so many dreadful things that they could no longer see at all. The men had sticks and knives and they made us sing until late into the night. When we did not sing loud enough, they beat us until we sang louder. Early in the morning, we had to sing their songs again. Then they made us run until we were so tired and weak from no food that we could no longer run. So they gave us food stolen from a farmer on the next-door farm. And then they made us run again. If we voted for the MDC, they said, this would happen a second time, and many more after that...

The farm workers from the ... farm, which lies across the river from us, have abandoned their homes. My grandfather saw them leaving the farm with the clothes, blankets and cooking pots that remained, waiting in long lines on the side of the road for the buses to take them into the communal lands. Perhaps one day soon our turn will come...

A LETTER TO MR MANDELA

Dear Mr Mandela

With each day that passes, the people of Zimbabwe lose hope. We believed that the last parliamentary elections would solve our problems - we had hoped for a new Zimbabwe. But the ZANU PF government only became more angry and stubborn. Today it is like a lion trapped in a corner: it has become very dangerous.

This government, the government of Zimbabwe, has overstayed its welcome. And so has the President. We are afraid that he no longer knows what he is doing - we fear he has become desperate. He orders the army to attack his own people, and they obey. We are afraid of a massacre. We are also afraid that, if things get out of hand in the DRC, the civil war could spill over into Zimbabwe.

The people of Zimbabwe speak with one voice. Despite government's attempts to create divisions, the people of Harare and Bulawayo also speak with one voice. But the people of Harare have suffered more from attacks by the police and the army. In Bulawayo there has been less trouble so far, but the pain of Gukurahundi, when the ZANU PF government forces massacred many thousands of people in Matabeleland, is still fresh in their minds.

We believe that the MDC is genuinely committed to changing things for the better. We also believe that, because the government wants to hold onto power at all costs, there may be a lot more blood before changes are made. The slogan for the MDC is *Make a Change* but, because the government is hungry for power, there may be a lot of blood before these changes are made. Mr Mandela, Zimbabwe cannot afford more blood. We want peaceful change. The people are united - Shona, Matabele, white... We are all one. Those who were not affiliated before, understand the need for change. Today we have the same agenda.

The government says that the MDC wants to bring back the colonial era. This is not true. ZANU PF ministers appear on television saying that the MDC are puppets. This is ridiculous. They tell us that the MDC is given sweets by the whites. Nobody believes them. We know that, from Morgan Tsvangirai's challenge, something good will come. The MDC has done well and has gained much support. It is shaking up this government.

When Mr Tsvangirai went to South Africa, we were relieved. The people outside Zimbabwe would hear us. When Archbishop Pious Ncube went to South Africa, we expected to hear a response. When our former President, Canaan Banana, went to South Africa, we wanted to know what he said to South Africa's Former President. And we wondered, Sir, what you said to him.

We believe that President Mbeki has been too "diplomatic", and we have been disappointed. We were grateful when the Democratic Alliance Leader, Tony Leon, came to Zimbabwe. Our government has tried to paint the wrong picture of Mr Leon. They know he has international influence. The people appreciate the fact that Mr Leon has spoken for them.

We understand, Sir, that you are in a difficult position, but we need you to speak your mind on our situation. The people of Zimbabwe - and the people of the world - need to hear your voice. Our people respect you and believe that you have the solution for us. Many of our homes have Nelson Mandela posters on the walls. Many of our kombis carry South African flags. It is because of you, and what you have done for Africa, that we carry these flags.

At this time, however, we can offer our children - the children of Zimbabwe - no hope. The economic situation here is very harsh. Today many people cannot afford to buy fresh milk and bread every day, and homes with children need at least two loaves. We even go without tea. We now hear frightening talk about shortages of mealie meal and flour. If we have no mealie meal or bread, how will we survive? People are not only looking after extended families, they are also having to provide for the AIDS orphans. Today the people sit and talk about the AIDS orphans. How will they cope? It is not always possible to find people who will care for them, and so we see a great increase in the number of street children. Where can these children find hope? We have a Social Welfare Department that is totally overwhelmed. Its resources do not make any significant difference to the masses of the poor.

Zimbabweans are surviving mainly on mealie meal. Many have only two meals a day and a growing number can afford only one. Some companies understand the hardship and provide subsidised meals, which we appreciate. If you stood at the corner of a city street at the end of the day, Sir, you would see thousands of people trudging home on foot to save the money they would normally spend on transport for food for their families.

If you asked Zimbabweans what their first thought was when they woke up in the morning, many would say this: "Well, I am still alive; I will make it to supper." But overnight the prices of basic foods may have increased again, so the pressure grows daily. When I was a child growing up, I had never heard of blood pressure. Today high blood pressure and depression are affecting many, many people.

And a growing number of Zimbabweans are dying of AIDS. The old people have never seen anything like this before. Because they do not have AIDS, they will survive, but who will bury them? Our health system has collapsed. People with AIDS in the rural areas get no attention from the doctors. And, when they travel long distances to the hospitals, they are put on a drip and then discharged. For an AIDS patient, this is useless. Even if there is fuel and you have travelled 200km to the city to see a doctor, you still have to queue for hours at casualty. Since there is often little concern at casualty, people die regularly in the queues. In many hospitals, there is no more money for medicine. The doctors are leaving for South Africa, for Botswana and to go overseas. Our people are turning to the traditional healers for help, but they have no cure for AIDS.

The government uses the newspapers, radio and television to try to brainwash everyone, especially those who live far from the towns and cities. The people from the towns counter this by going into the rural areas and telling them the truth. They take various newspapers - the government-owned newspapers and the independent newspapers, so that the rural communities can read everything that is being written. Almost everyone in Zimbabwe can read - and we have learnt to read the bits between the lines.

In the past, people could look after their parents and families in the rural areas. They travelled regularly to see them, taking money and food. Today it is difficult to visit a country relative because you must first find money for bus fare - if there is diesel for the buses to run - and then you must find money for food. But money and fuel are not the only problems. Sometimes it is difficult to reach the rural areas because the roads have not been maintained and, after heavy rains in certain areas, only tractors can get through.

1985

At midday, the people in the factories sit outside and talk about politics. Everyone has become political. Even our children want to learn the MDC slogans. It is not good for children to live in such grinding poverty, and in constant danger. It is not good for them to see family members, friends, teachers and strangers beaten up in front of them because they do not support the government.

Last year we read reports of teachers being dragged from their classrooms by government party supporters. They were beaten and stripped naked in front of their students. Health workers were also assaulted and nurses were raped. School children were abducted.

2001

When I was a child, we used to get pocket money. Today there is none and children are lucky if their families have enough money to send them to school. Some children go to school with no food. It is hard to learn when you are hungry. In the rural areas, there is a shortage of teachers, books and stationery. Children write on scraps of paper. If they are given paper, it's like giving them gold. The government boasts about what it has done since 1980. The infrastructure is there in some places, but if you can't afford to pay school fees for your children, and you can't send them to school, what is the use of empty buildings?

Christmas has not been Christmas for the past ten years. When we were small, we could tell it was Christmas. We would have new clothes, we would visit the Park and there would be lots of food. Today it is different. And it is difficult to make the children happy. Our children need to grow up like children. The children of Zimbabwe have no childhood: they are being deprived of their youth. Many are forced to become street vendors, selling vegetables so that they can go to school or help feed their families. Their parents worry all the time, and some become violent. Because they are frustrated, they drink too much and may beat up the kids. Later they regret this and hate themselves, but the damage has been done. If ZANU PF knew that I was MDC, they would beat me up in front of my children, and this would affect them very badly.

Mr Mandela, the people of Zimbabwe are crying out aloud. They had independence, but it has been taken away from them. You have set a good example for Africa and for the rest of the world. We admire and respect you as a leader - no government gains respect by killing. We also respect the fact that you are honourable, and that you care so much for children.

We ask you to help us in our time of need. We ask you to help the people of Zimbabwe. We ask you especially to help our children. Our children deserve a future. Under this government we can offer them no future.

May God bless you, Mr Mandela

A LOYAL ZIMBABWEAN

⊠ Zimbabwe has lost more than 100 doctors and 18 000 nurses in recent years, along with pharmacists, physiotherapists and paediatricians.

THE CHIROBI STORY: INVASION INSANITY

No basis exists in which a farmer can make a rational decision about whether to proceed with his cropping intentions or not. Either way he is playing Russian Roulette...

SR Pratt, Regional Executive Officer
CFU Mashonaland East, 6 August 2000

How it all began....

At 10h00 on 27 July 2000, four vehicles carrying about thirty occupants arrived at Mr Chris Thorne's farm in the Mazowe area north of Harare. Reinforced by approximately twenty people, the invaders walked over all the lands and then regrouped at the store. Initially, they instructed that work must not stop. At 14h00, fearing for the safety of his workers, Mr Thorne instructed that all operations must cease and that the workers should return to the farm village. Shortly afterwards, ZANU PF indoctrination and intimidation of the workers leaving the area commenced, and continued for over one and a half hours.

On 28 July, the occupants of a vehicle gained access to the farm by cutting a barbed wire fence. They then drove to the shed complex where about 150 squatters had congregated. After addressing the crowd, they proceeded en mass to the eastern side of the farm. Three hours later they departed, announcing that they would return the following day with their cattle and goats to occupy the workers' homes.

At around 11h00 on 29 July, six squatters were found erecting a hut from freshly-cut brush poles on the side of the road at the junction to the homestead. A fire had been lit and was dangerously close to tall grass. Mr Thorne and a neighbour went to the hut and demanded that the fire be put out. They were greeted with hostility and withdrew. The situation was reported to the police, who went to the area to investigate.

Shortly after they left, a vehicle arrived at the camp, followed later by two more. The occupants of the latter vehicles proceeded to the workers' village and demanded that the irrigation foreman summon Mr Thorne to speak to them. Their request was refused and the two vehicles left before sunset.

⊠ During the afternoon of 30 July, about ten men arrived in a mini-bus at the store. They entered the adjacent supervisor's house, threw the family meal onto the floor and demanded to know where the supervisor was. After assaulting and harassing his wife and children, they went to the home of the store keeper, where they man-handled the teenage son of one of Mr Thorne's staff members. Eventually, after searching in vain for the supervisor, they departed.

As the year drew to a close...

⊠ On 29 December, Chris Thorne and his family arrived at Lake Kariba for a New Year's break after a difficult and tension-filled year. Before they had even unpacked, Mr Thorne's supervisor phoned to report that squatters had invaded and trashed the farm village, destroying most of the workers' possessions. He said that the terrified workers had fled to the main homestead area and were sheltering in the sheds within the security fence.

⊠ Directly the Thornes arrived back on the farm, Mr Thorne's son, Marc, went to check up on the safety of the workers, and to assess the extent of the damage. Immediately there was the sound of glass breaking as rocks were hurled at the now vacant supervisor's house about seventy-five metres away.

⊠ When Marc and a group of workers ventured out to investigate, they were ambushed by seven axe and spear-wielding invaders. Together Marc and the workers turned to run back towards the security fence, but Marc tripped and fell. He had just enough time to throw up his legs to defend himself before being struck with an axe. Fortunately the blade went behind his thigh, but the force was so great that the wooden handle smashed in two on his leg. The invader then lunged at Marc with a two-metre twist-steel spear. Marc managed to catch the shaft and they began to wrestle. Alerted by the noise, the supervisor saw his predicament and raced back to his assistance. Together they disarmed the invader, who fled with his gang of thugs.

⊠ Twenty minutes later, the invaders returned with reinforcements and began hurling rocks at the buildings and farm machinery, screaming death threats at everyone. In the meantime, Mr Thorne gathered together his family and the labourers in a sheltered part of the garden out of view of the enraged invaders.

⊠ Meanwhile the neighbours had been radioed, but had been warned by Mr Thorne not to come onto the farm as the situation was too volatile. After almost an hour, when the shouting and abuse had finally abated, two neighbours insisted on driving down to make sure that everyone was safe. They were told to use the back entrance, but were ambushed at the security fence by two mobs who hurled stones and axes at the vehicle. As the men retreated down the air strip, the mobs closed in on two sides.

⊠ Chris Thorne and Marc jumped into the farm pick-up and raced to their friends' rescue, only to be stopped by a felled tree lying around a bend in the road. Immediately another mob moved in from behind, forcing the Mr Thorne to accelerate off the road and out of trouble. They managed to drive onto the airstrip, but were too late to save the situation for their friends, who had had to abandon their vehicle and run the gauntlet. By some miracle, an axe hurled at the two farmers had passed through the cab without injuring them. The Thornes managed to retreat back inside the security fence, while the mob continued the assault but remained outside.

⊠ Eventually the police arrived and took statements but, although the perpetrators were identified at the time of writing, three attempted murder charges have not resulted in any arrests.

⊠ Marc, who trained as an agriculturalist at Gatten College in Queensland, Australia and was due to return to London on 7 January, decided to remain on the farm to help his family and their workers survive the uncertain and dangerous times.

The dreaded "Section 8" letter arrived...

⊠ At 11h15 on 7 February 2001, the dreaded official "Section 8" letter arrived at Chris Thorne's Chirobi Farm stating that the property was being taken over by President Mugabe's government. Since Mr Thorne was in Harare at the time on business, Marc had to sign for it.

⊠ Fifteen minutes after the letter had been dropped - and without any warning - 100 heavily armed squatters and ZANU PF supporters descended on the farm. Wielding axes, pangas, knobkerries, lengths of stripped electric cable and sticks, they broke through the security fence into the homestead and workshop area, scattering the workers who fled for their lives.

⊠ Marc raced to the house and, with the help of his mother and the house servants, managed to secure all the outside doors.

⊠ The invaders immediately surrounded the house and, for seven hours, shouted and screamed obscenities, demanding that the family come out since the farm was now *their* property. They then smashed the main water pipe leading from the borehole. While one group rattled and banged on doors and windows intermittently, and wrote graffiti on the walls with charcoal, other groups systematically broke open the storerooms and sheds where the labourers had been living since December, after being forcibly removed by the invaders from the farm village.

⊠ Once they had trashed or stolen all the property they could find - mainly clothing, blankets, pots and pans and food, the mob lit a fire on the slasto pathway and proceeded to cook the food. Thereafter, they ransacked the bar fridges at the pool and proceeded to drink the entire contents. Approximately ten people who were not dressed in uniform arrived in a police vehicle and proceeded to further incite the mob. (It was later confirmed that these were not bona fide police members).

⊠ An 'all stations' district radio call was sent out and, by 13h00, more than sixty neighbours from the area and as far as seventy kilometres away had assembled on the road leading to the farm. They were joined by Mr Thorne, who was on his way back from Harare. Despite the arrival of a police detail, the Acting District Administrator and senior war vets, a group of invaders stormed the cottage of Mr Thorne's 87 year-old mother, demanding beer and food. She could only offer lemonade, which further angered them. They marched her up to the main homestead, where Mr Thorne's wife, Mary Rose, let her in.

⊠ The Officer in Charge then insisted that Marc come out of the house - otherwise they would leave, he said. While Marc walked over to them, the police called for two negotiators to drive onto the farm - but in only one vehicle.

⊠ The same two farmers who had been ambushed a few weeks previously on the Thorne's farm, and had been lucky to escape with their lives on that occasion, volunteered to support Marc. Death threats were directed at all three in the presence of the police. The invaders' demands included the restoration of the water supply to the farm workers' village from where they had drawn their water. (Mr Thorne had cut it off at the request of his workers, who had been so severely harassed by the invaders that they had been forced to abandon their homes).

⊠ Eventually, at 17h00, the invaders agreed to leave, provided the "posse" dispersed. The farmers retired to an adjoining farm to regroup, leaving behind a six-man support unit.

"We have no doubt that, without the magnificent reaction of the entire valley community in support of our family, the situation would have not been resolved and evacuation would have been the order of the day," said Mr Thorne. "This was a well-organised plan of intimidation designed to coincide with the serving of the Section 8 order. The police revealed that it was the first of thirty-nine such orders to be served within the area during the next few days. In fact, several members of our group had already received the order by the time they responded to our incident."

⊠ Despite the constant intimidation and their frequent encounters with danger, Mr Thorne and his family are resolved to stay on their farm. Their decision is fully endorsed by the entire community. "Our stand is quite simple: remove the squatters so that we can farm, or pay us out and we will vacate," said Mr Thorne.

Why would the government target Chris Thorne? He is one of the most successful farmers in the country and he chairs the Mapunga Silo Syndicate of forty-seven grain-producing farms that supply a fifth of Zimbabwe's entire wheat and soya crop.

"If you support the opposition, you are a target," said Mr Thorne, "and if you are successful at what you do, you are also on the list. Defy Mugabe and your farm is taken."

In the case of Mr Thorne's Chirobi farm, the ramification of this carefully orchestrated destruction will have catastrophic consequences for the entire country.

Located in the fertile Mazowe Valley, Chirobi is pivotal within the Mapunga Silo Syndicate, the brainchild of Chris Thorne.

In 1996, Mr Thorne approached his neighbours to set up a grain consortium to achieve market advantage through economies of scale. Fifty farmers decided to come on board and approved the concept of constructing a grain silo complex to meet the escalating requirements of bakers, millers, oil expressers and seed manufacturers countrywide. Capital funding was supplied by one of Zimbabwe's first indigenous banks. Construction of the silo complex began in December 1996 and, by May 1997, it was fully operational. By the end of 2000, over Z$95 million (US$95 000) had been spent on construction in four stages, with planned development of at least another Z$50 million (US$50 000) prior to the development of a new value-adding phase.

Progress was rapid and production soared. In 1997, nine months after the inception of the project, the syndicate's annual production of mixed grains totalled 54 000 metric tonnes. Production for the year 2000 totalled 135 000 metric tonnes, generating Z$1 275 billion (US$28,3 million) in sales. This almost three-fold increase from the same producer base is rated as a significant achievement even by first world agricultural standards. In the face of the country's escalating economic decline, it was all the more remarkable.

"Our ability to perform was as a direct result of our dynamic skills as farmers and through having sufficient access to seasonal funding which enabled each farmer to do the job without financial constraint," said Mr Thorne.

Prior to the start of the land invasions in February 2000, the Mapunga Silo Syndicate group (which then comprised 47 members) employed 15 000 people and was responsible for producing 23% of Zimbabwe's entire wheat crop and 20% of the soya crop. However, as a result of the invasions, 23 out of 47 consortium members were in partial or complete shutdown by January 2001. The 23 members represented 52% of their combined production and 18 of them had borrowed Mapunga operating finance. The collapse of the Mapunga members is impacting seriously on the consortium's bank and the knock-on effect is being felt throughout the banking sector.

As a result of the severe disruption to Mapunga production, and to that of farms in other areas experiencing similar interferences, more than half of the country's wheat crop will be lost. Importation of the 50% shortfall will cost Zimbabwe in excess of Z$ 2,4 billion (US$10,5 million). The ramifications for the soya bean crop are also catastrophic for the country's collapsing economy and rapidly depleting food supplies. In addition, the consortium also produces large volumes of seed maize, cottonseed, cotton lint, bananas and horticulture, as well as tobacco, which does not fall under its jurisdiction.

"It is no coincidence that the five farm directors of Mapunga have been targeted for maximum destabilisation in this land grab," said Mr Thorne. "It indicates a heinous agenda by the orchestrators to inflict severe economic damage upon us and the nation, and has nothing whatsoever to do with needing land for the landless."

Chirobi Farm, which has been the home of Chris and Ro Thorne for the past 25 years, was set to produce approximately 2 100 metric tonnes of soya beans during summer 2000/2001, and a further 2 500 metric tonnes of wheat.

"We leased the farm for the first four years, but decided to purchase it in 1980 after Mugabe had urged white farmers to be part of the new Zimbabwe," Mr Thorne said.

On 9 March 2001, the Times of London reported on the dire consequences of the land invasions for the entire country:

The tangle of weeds and tall grass on Chris Thorne's farm in Zimbabwe has grown head high in a vivid testimony against the economics of vandalism. The gunmen who took over Chirobi Farm a year ago lectured him about how much they needed this rich red soil to grow food, but 12 months on they have not planted so much as a seed, and will not let him plant either. Farm machinery stands rusting, his workers have nothing to do, all 3 750 acres have turned to waste and Mr Thorne and his family are prisoners in their own front yard.

"I could understand if they were doing something with my farm for themselves, but the gunmen just sit watching us caged up all day and seem to delight in seeing everything go to ruin," Mr Thorne said, struggling to contain his frustration. He pointed to their veranda where the war veterans have scrawled graffiti in English to make their point. The words, in black spray paint, say "Chirobi decay". Mr Thorne, 53, shook his head: "They got that message right. This is all about destruction, not land reform...

For the moment, the veterans are content to try to starve him out. He has not earned a penny this past year, but is still paying his workforce. If he is not allowed to plant his wheat crop by next month, he will have to put his tractors and combine harvesters on sale, although there is nobody in Zimbabwe who would buy them...

Of the 47 farms in the syndicate, 23 are listed for take-over and Zimbabwe's most successful consortium is on its knees...

On 9 May 2001, The Mail & Guardian (SA) recommended that South Africa rethink its quiet diplomacy on Zimbabwe:

... The following is now clear on Zimbabwe. First, the economic meltdown cannot be prevented - it is already occurring. The country, potentially a breadbasket of southern Africa, faces a maize and wheat shortage by July; key businesses are finding it impossible to continue with the current foreign-exchange regime. With an inflation rate touching 60%, fuel and foreign-exchange shortages, last year's 23,6% fiscal deficit and more than 50% unemployment, some economists are predicting a gross domestic product shrinkage of -8% this year. The International Monetary Fund no longer provides the country with any balance of payments or other support. Foreign direct investment declined by 90% last year.

...Land redistribution is a problem in Zimbabwe, but the abuse of the issue reflects Zimbabwe's and Mugabe's perilous political state. Mugabe is clearly no longer listening to rational economic advice. Instead, his attitude and focus on maintaining his grip on power clearly illustrates the primacy of political power over economics - a recipe for disaster in a globalising world economy... The worst we can do is pretend that the situation will resolve itself. Indeed, Mugabe's track record suggests that the worst might still be coming.

In June 2001, Mr Thorne wrote the following update: "Our ordeals have been many and dramatic, and our beautiful farm has all but been destroyed in terms of the pristine and manicured way it was prior to March 2000. It is now a reverted jungle and we are effectively without the means to earn a living. However, it's a question of mindset, and we have had plenty of time to practise the art! What used to bring a twisted gut feeling is now neatly pigeonholed in the belief that one day we will have our day and be able to fix the damage.

What will not be easy to fix, however, is the destruction of the flora and fauna we have nurtured over the years. Wholesale slaughter of the animals and fish has taken place, as well as the ongoing cutting of trees for sale as firewood.

The situations we have experienced are due to the fact that we have refused to bend to lawlessness and intimidation. If we have to leave, and our suitcases have just our principles and our dignity in them, so be it. But we will rest easy knowing that we did not deal with the 'devil'."

If Zimbabwe succumbs to the predations of those who seek to destroy the very means of her advancement, those forces for but a very short time shall celebrate until they also, amidst a great hardship imposed upon every Zimbabwean, will come to understand too late that theirs was a Pyrrhic victory.

SR Pratt, Regional Executive Officer
CFU Mashonaland East

The Implications

Business Report (Independent Newspapers, South Africa), Friday, 22 June, 2001

UN puts a figure on Zimbabwe's food needs

⊠ Harare - Zimbabwe needs to import about 579 000 tons of maize, rice and wheat to compensate for expected crop deficits, a report compiled by the United Nations Food and Agriculture Organisation has said.

⊠ It said 132 000 tons of wheat and rice would have to be imported, and 447 000 tons of maize.

⊠ The government-run Grain Marketing Board (GMB) at present holds only 291 000 tons of maize in its strategic reserve instead of the 500 000 tons needed to carry Zimbabwe through to the 2002 season's harvest.

⊠ The crop deficits have raised fears of famine in Zimbabwe as the country no longer has any import cover to meet its food needs...

§⸱⟨⟩⸱§⟩⟨§⸱⟨⟩⸱§

Farming might look easy when your plough is a pencil
and you're 1 000 miles away from a cornfield.

Dwight D Eisenhower

In Mashonaland province, a crop of flowers grown for export and worth more than Z$1 million, has been wantonly destroyed.

$$\vdots \leftrightarrow \vdots \bowtie \vdots \leftrightarrow \vdots$$

Zimbabwe is Africa's second largest exporter of cut flowers. During the past ten years, the country's horticultural exports have grown at an average annual rate of over 20%, of which flowers made up US$74 million during 1999.

Roses constitute approximately 70% of the country's cut flowers. Prior to the land invasions, exports of cut flowers for the 2000/2001 season were estimated to be in the region of 24 000 tonnes, worth approximately US$86.5 million.

Magic at Mana

Foto Image Library © I. Ritchie

MAGIC AT MANA: 21 JUNE 2001

I have seen the royal lion, before sunrise, below a waning moon, crossing the grey plain on his way home from the kill, drawing a dark wake in the silvery grass...

Karen Blixen

 or the first time since 1876 a total solar eclipse would be visible in Zimbabwe, and members of our area's Wildlife and Environment Society of Zimbabwe would be gathering at Mana Pools to witness the spectacle. We left early on Wednesday 20 June, happy to get away from the stress of working on a farm beleaguered by disruptive war veterans. It was wonderful, too, for me to have a break from running a filling station, where often there was nothing to sell. Our son, home from College, completed the tripping trio.

As we drive along the highway, golden grass sways in the fresh breeze, and the blue sky doming overhead gathers into itself our soaring spirits. On the edge of the Escarpment we slow down to take in the majesty of the sweeping Zambezi floodplain below, at this time of year a fantastic panorama of lush, green forests, extending to the horizon on all sides. In scope, it is a stunning physical feature, and the colours and texture of the vegetation are also remarkable. As one turns off into the hunting concession areas and wildlife park, the bush becomes thorny and baobabs rise up like behemoths. The riverbeds are spectacular, wide and sandy, banked with huge dark green mahogany and acacia trees. Impala, monkeys, warthog and kudu forage, unperturbed by the traffic. Homo sapiens are not under the same scrutiny as other species this trip! The mopane forests are very lovely in the morning light - tall, straight trunks evenly but not densely distributed, dark against sunshine streaming through light green foliage. We emerge again into jesse bush, where enormous droppings warn us that this is primarily elephant territory. It is relaxing and enjoyable travelling slowly, looking out for game.

Mana Pools Game Reserve is unique, as motorists are permitted to leave their vehicles and walk about. For this reason, it is a favourite for both local and foreign visitors.

We report to the BBC camp. Already the day's workshop is underway, and we unfold our chairs and take our places to hear what the experts have to say. Peter Mundy, ornithologist with National Parks in Bulawayo, describes why he is on-line advising authorities in India, who are dealing with the catastrophic problem of the loss of 100 000 vultures on the Sub-continent in the last five years. Someone from NASSA says he will die a happy man after experiencing his fifteenth total eclipse, this one in our paradise of Mana.

Dr Paul Murdin from the British National Space Centre asks for volunteers to demonstrate the solar system in motion, so that we can get the idea of the magnitude of the phenomena about to astound us. If the sun is the size of an orange, he says, and ten metres away is the earth, it would be no larger than a pin head, and as for the moon... it would be no larger than a mere speck of dust. Yet, incredibly, this little speck will move between the earth and the sun at the exact distance that will allow it to cover the sun. Just imagine the odds. Know that light from the star closest to our solar system takes 4,5 years to reach us, and that distances in space are truly "astronomical". The sun termed a "dwarf star" is thousands of times larger than the earth, but out in that vast heaven, there are other stars so immense, they could occupy the distance between our sun and the earth.

The audience is spellbound. Tomorrow, as from 1.45 pm, we will don protective eyeglasses and watch the moon start to move across the face of the sun. A giant shadow will streak across the valley at 6 000 kilometres an hour. Towards 3 o'clock, the sun will be eclipsed and, at totality, we will remove the glasses and look for the ring effect, Bailey's Beads, and the radiated energy called the corona. A pearly light will envelop the land and a decided cooling will be felt.

I am absolutely enchanted by the promise of things to come. I tell my husband that I won't be observing any of the wildlife - I will be focusing my attention on the sky above for the full two hours (in spite of the forms I should be filling in at five-minute intervals). This is going to be one mighty event... is my head spinning because of the earth's rotation, or simply because my imagination is superbly energised? Until then, I'm going to be very interested in camping, fishing, game viewing and socialising. It's easy at Mana to speak in superlatives. Trees don't get much bigger anywhere. Spreading canopies of the acacias completely close out the sky above, and form natural chambers below. The dense crowns of the mahoganies, seeming to glisten all day long, make heavy shadows about themselves, and paler croton trees edge the old river course. This is like the Garden of Eden. Fat-rumped zebra gathered in a peaceful herd ignore us as we drive to the camp site, but a martial eagle bathing in a pool does object, and heaves his mighty frame into the air, to settle on a skeletal tree and shake himself dry. And, yes, the impala are abundant. No elephants yet, but we can see the odd buffalo, waterbuck and vulture. At the edge of the Zambezi, one can see a pod of hippo wallowing in the fast-flowing water, there are others on a sand bank and just hundreds of Egyptian geese, spurwing geese, a saddlebill stork and many other varieties of birdlife.

We brew tea on gas cookers and greet friends from other parts of the country - there are farmers from Rusape and a school friend of my husband's. Camping is fun when you have a big tent, the necessary gear and you keep everything simple. We are under enormous sausage trees and acacias right on the bank, and behind us is a vlei, still wet and inhabited by two crocodiles. This area is skirted with adrenaline grass, beyond which are ant-hills, large trees and a herd of waterbuck. It is just marvellous. The enthusiasts break out of camp, some to follow a group of buffalo and others to try their luck at fishing.

Night falls as early as 6 pm, and we gather round the fire to cook a communal meal and to enjoy one another's company. We all have difficulties on our farms and problems within our families. We need to share these and laugh and tease one another. It is the best therapy, and my friend Sharon loves talking even more than I do. It's great! The men discuss the selection of Zimbabwe's cricket side for the forthcoming triangular series, rugby and politics. They get on famously. Our son joins the camp further up where there are more teenagers, and has a feast of a supper. Up above, the heavens swirl with diamond-crisp bright stars and a satellite. Jack says be sure to clear everything away before settling down to sleep, as some animals can chew through a cooler box!

Observation begins before dawn - around 5.15 am. Sharon has a tripod, a notebook and other equipment at the ready. My husband gets tea brewing; I just love the luxury of drinking tea around the fire. We go back to the BBC camp for another briefing, but when we return, I am really agitated. Another party has arrived. It is 12.30 pm and all I want to do is to focus on the sun. It's too important to put off for the mundane consideration of lunch.

It starts a few minutes before they said it would, according to my watch. A nick out of the edge on the bottom right. Progress is slow. But I am patient! I hope my staff at the filling station are watching it. I got them special glasses, too, but they will see a 98% eclipse, not 100% as I will. Nothing else in nature has altered. You wouldn't know what was happening out there if it were not for the mathematicians, who, many years ago, calculated that this event would occur...and it is accurate to the last detail.

I record the encroachment in little sketches on the margin of my observation form; one orb eaten away by another, movement is from left to right, from 7.00 am to 2.00 pm on a clock. Butterflies continue to flit about in small groups, hippos aren't fazed, waterbuck are quiet. But by 2.45 pm there is a shadow on the water cast by the mountains on the Zambian side. No racing dark shadow, as yet. Further darkening of the sun... And a muted call, "Lion coming down the vlei..." I join my husband and we observe a magnificent lioness about 70 metres away, striding down the vlei, single-minded in her intention to reach a predetermined destination. She is in her prime with no visible scars. As she disappears into the grass, an enormous male lion approaches from the rear. His course is less defined - after all he is following her scent.

The waterbuck become nervous, females and young dashing away to protect themselves as best they can. He swerves aside, and is not interested. He retraces his path; perhaps human scent stirs in his nostrils. He is the epitome of power. His great mane sits stiffly around his neck, darkening to black against his chest, and it hangs down, almost to his knees. He moans softly...the indignity of intrusion during courtship... I watch no more.

The moon is almost covering the face of the sun. The special glasses come off. I see a thin, crisp white light that rings the dark patch with a dazzling diamond sparkling at 7 o'clock for a brief time. It is awesome. The purity of the radiated light is very beautiful. At full eclipse the orb of the sun is shut out, as if there is a black hole there. There is powerful radiation streaking out in a bright, white corona all around it in an area four times that of the sun. We can watch this for two minutes. I am standing in my own very dark shadow, fuzzy on one edge, in a surrealistic world. It is as if a gossamer screen has come between me and the middle distance, altering the colours with a pearly softness, muting the definition of shapes and distorting perspective.

Suddenly nature is eerily quiet, and a flock of white-fronted bee-eaters fly to roost in the mahogany tree - they think night has come. Time seems to hold its breath. Stars begin to twinkle in the darkening sky, while on the horizon all around, there are the pink and golden colours of a sunrise or sunset. Amazing. I don't take my eyes off the eclipse again. As the moon edges off the sun, I see the Bailey's Beads - small specks of scarlet light on the edge of the moon. These are visible because valleys and other distortions on the surface of the moon channel light from the sun towards us, to be refracted and reflected in a vivid red colour. The diamond ring effect is there again at 2 o'clock. It is fleeting, but simply magical. The silence has been profound, though brief.

Glasses go back on, and we watch the sun reassert itself slowly and surely. There is a tangible drop in temperature, reinforcing the feeling of eeriness. The experience has been unique, and I cling to my private thoughts as long as possible. I notice that the shadows on the side of the tent are crescent-like, exactly the shape of the exposed sun at that moment, as if proving Isaac Newton's laws on light.

Everyone is ecstatic. We go from group to group sharing ideas and observations. No one saw the racing shadow of the moon because we did not have the right elevation, but spectators on the Escarpment nearby had seen it. Sharon is completely beside herself. She trained as a radiographer and knows how important it is to be methodical and accurate when making scientific notes. The appearance of the lion blew her concentration, perhaps the video will have data she can retrieve. Paul's wife started the truck to rescue him from the lion at just the wrong moment... But...wow! Wasn't it fantastic? People gradually disperse to do what appeals to them. Some go to look for the buffalo, others gather to speculate about the lions and a number wander off to the river to fish.

Supper that night was a celebration of the wonders of God's creation. It was a truly festive time.

The lions returned in the night. Great bellowings, gruntings and other chilling noises could be heard close-by on several occasions. Pat prodded Allan in his sleep and told him to stop snoring in case one of the male lions thought he was competing in his territory and attacked the tent... At the de-briefing Dr Norman Monks identified the lion we saw as "Casanova"... Enough said!

We spent the journey home pondering the experience and listening to everyone's impressions. We called in at the filling station to collect bread and milk for supper. The staff had indeed witnessed the spectacle. Ahhhhh! Very amazing! I asked if many visitors had called in for fuel and refreshments en route to the Zambezi. Not so many, they said. The newspapers reported that 27 000 foreigners saw the eclipse in Zambia, whilst only 6 000 decided to observe it from Zimbabwe. Those precious tourist dollars had been spent elsewhere.

Blow the state of the country, I decided. Give God glory for what you have seen. For surely He will cause His face to shine on Zimbabwe and on her hard-pressed peoples...for nothing on earth lasts forever... Sharon said to me yesterday, "On bad days Jack says 'Let's sell'. I say, 'Never, ever. To hell with the war vets...it's the principle...'."

I know we are in the middle of a social and economic revolution. Zimbabwe is changing profoundly. As we stumble and fall and wipe the blood away, we inch towards a resolution. As we struggle from day to day, we must be patient, for surely that, too, is the African way. When I unpack the dirty clothes smelling of smoke and barbecued meat, I'll remember that our other two children will come home soon, bringing our family together again for a short while. I will be reminded that, even on a day when the sun sets twice, normality returns to life, and we are never without hope.

CHAOS

Turning and turning in the widening gyre
The falcon cannot hear the falconer;
Things fall apart; the centre cannot hold;
Mere anarchy is loosed upon the world,
The blood-dimmed tide is loosed, and everywhere
The ceremony of innocence is drowned;
The best lack all conviction, while the worst
Are full of passionate intensity.

From "The Second Coming" by W B Yeats

 he millennium year began quietly. The world did not come to an end after all. Computer problems did not shut down civilised society. Our freezers, stoves and televisions continued to operate, undaunted by the dire threats and warnings.

The year began quietly. January slipped into February. In February an important referendum was held. The people were called upon to accept or reject a new constitution for Zimbabwe. The proposed new constitution was rejected, a massive blow to our government. For a few days we experienced a sense of euphoria. Zimbabweans had found their voices again. Things were going to change. The times ahead were going to be challenging and exciting.

How naïve we were! Within days the first farm invasions began. Within days the lives of thousands of people on our commercial farms were indeed changed. Marauding mobs were unleashed against them in a seething surge of violence. Confusion, terror, anger and horror overtook the entire country. The world outside Zimbabwe was mesmerised by the drama of a nation unravelling. Orchestrated chaos held centre stage. It was like listening to a fighter plane, locked in a screaming dive, totally out of control.

Those of us who live in the towns and the cities watched helplessly. What could we do to help? We felt completely impotent. We had to look on, while our countrymen and women were subjected to beatings, threats and intimidation. The stress we experienced was very different, although just as real. It was the stress of wondering whether we were failing those who needed our support. We were living safely in our sheltered cocoons in the urban areas. They were exposed and vulnerable. Did they resent us? Did they wonder how we could continue living relatively normal lives, while they, every day, were faced with fresh menace?

I wondered sometimes if I could cope with the guilt and the anguish. Every time I watched a news bulletin, I would burst into tears. This made me feel even more distraught, as our farming families were behaving with such courage and restraint in the face of the most incredible provocation. Who was I to take refuge in craven, snivelling weeping in my comfortable chair in my warm lounge in front of my TV?

That April my sister sent me a book that changed my life. It was "The Artist's Way" by Julia Cameron. Julia believes in action, in confronting problems head-on and dealing with them. She advocates starting every day with writing three pages of thoughts and feelings. This catharsis helps to equip one to cope with stress and to shrug passivity aside. She teaches her readers to value themselves and to believe in themselves. I began to write "morning pages" most days. Inevitably these were mainly about the political situation in the country.

14 April 2000
Last night, while watching the international news, I wept. I cannot admire and respect the farmers enough. How they are managing to keep their cool out there while all this is happening, I just cannot imagine. We saw mobs of posturing idiots mouthing insults for the benefit of the cameras. One group was holding a farmer's arm and shoving it in the air while others brandished their fists to emphasize the slogans they were shouting. It is just so sick. The farmer seemed to be fairly calm, possibly because the news crews were there. We saw a farmer's wife who looked exhausted, but who was so brave. She said how grateful she was to their loyal and courageous farm workers. They had chased the war vets off. Even the women had taken up weapons - various types of farming implements - and had routed these paid thugs.

We feel so helpless. I wish there were something we could do to help and support them. I do hope they know how we urban people, who, so far have had it easy, feel about them. I hope their workers, who support them in the face of such horror and intimidation, realise how much we admire them. All this is like a pot simmering and simmering. Please, God, don't let it boil over. Please help these poor people, and please help us to put our country back together again. We all need each other, black and white.

17 April

Dear God, we beg you to help our farmers. They are threatened every hour of the day, and have only You to turn to for relief. Help their wives and families, all of whom are in grave danger. We beg you to guide the good, sane people of this country, and there are many of them. Thank you for the loyalty of the farm workers, themselves in great danger. If there is anything any of us can do, tell us what it is. You alone can guide us. Amen.

21 April

To watch the news, or not to watch the news, that is the question. It's difficult - we have to be informed, but the anger, depression and frustration the events of the news cause is awful. Another farm burned yesterday and many workers' homes were torched. Tobacco barns were razed to the ground. Logical? Two women were gang-raped. For a woman this is the ultimate horror.

To die or to be raped? There is an article in The Fingaz about "comfort women" of China, who were forced to "service" the Japanese soldiers during and possibly after the Second World War. The story is told by a 71 year-old woman. Can anything ever be normal again? One visualises the horror, the indignity, the very real possibility of AIDS. Can one survive this with one's mind and soul intact? What about marriage and/or a normal sex life? Is it possible? Yet we all cling tenaciously to life. We all want to live. Tomorrow the sun shines, flowers are beautiful, the rain is gentle.

To these women I say God bless and guide you. I do not know how or why such an awful fate befell you. I know that you did not deserve it. The men who did this to you do not deserve to live. Rape is a crime against humanity. It is degrading and evil, and returns men to the status of brutes. The men who are going about this "work" are brutes and thugs. You were victims. What happened to you is what all women dread most. We, the women of Zimbabwe, pray that you will find the strength to put it behind you, when you have recovered physically. We wish that we could help you.

Our lives are in turmoil. The country is tottering. Our economy is at an all-time low. I would like us all to be able to take a leap into July or August, to find that matters are resolved, things are settled, a new government is in position, no more lives have been lost, the farmers are back tending their crops and the whole land issue has been resolved. Crimes against humanity have ended, corruption has been eliminated and there is a new feeling of love and unity in people's hearts.

25 April
How can people burn tobacco barns with a whole crop of tobacco in them worth millions of dollars in foreign currency? How can they trash furniture and clothing and break apart TV sets? Why don't they just steal these things? How can they set upon their own defenceless people and injure and torture them, because they *might* be planning to vote for the opposition? What kind of people are these?

How will the people react when we finally have elections, *if* we finally have elections? Will they rise up in a body and say: "Enough. You assaulted and tried to kill us, you burned our homes and our possessions. We want you out." Or will they say nothing, and, beaten and broken, intimidated beyond hope for a better future, put their mark down for the ruling party? If they did that, could they be blamed?

26 April
Are things getting worse or better? The days all seem so strange. There is a surreal feeling about them. It is as if we live here in Zimbabwe, but not quite. In fact it's rather like the a short story by Ray Bradbury, "The Sound of Thunder". Because a butterfly was killed by a careless person, who was on a time travel safari, the whole world was changed. In some ways, only very slightly - positions of furniture in rooms had changed just a little. In other ways, drastically. The president of the US was not the man in office when the traveller left. He was not a person who would do what was best for his country. The traveller returned to the horrifying knowledge, that an act of carelessness, his, seemingly totally insignificant when it happened, had ruined the world of the present. If not ruined, then radically altered.

Similarly, we are here, but not here. It's hard to describe. It's as if that little butterfly has been trodden on. The town looks much the same. We are going through the motions at work. People are drifting back after the holidays. But all the time we are aware of things being orchestrated. Forces beyond our control, mobilised by the powers of darkness, are eroding our lives and the lives of everyone in this country. Our fate has been passed, it seems, into the hands of those who will not treat it with care and concern. They are stamping on that butterfly, grinding it into the mud until it disappears from sight.

28 April
So, Zimbabwe, what of your mystic allure and appeal now? What of your golden days, the beauty of the bush, the wide open spaces, your gracious people? What of the haunting splendour of the Eastern Districts and the majesty of the Falls? What of the silences? What of the bird calls? What of your trees and wildlife? Is this all to be a thing of the past for us, something to look back on with nostalgia, as we shiver somewhere in Europe trying to survive the winter and longing for the sun? I don't know.

10 May
Everyone is jittery again. A third farmer has been killed. The situation unnerves all of us. Yet, somehow, it is not as shocking as the deaths of the other two. The actual killing is just as vicious and brutal and premeditated. I think the difference is that violence is no longer a new phenomenon. It is happening, and we know it - the worst of it has being going on for more than a month. I don't think the ordinary "man in the street" - us - can cope with living at a fever pitch of horror and desolation indefinitely. You have to try to go back to a semblance of normality. You have to live your own little life in the most positive and effective way you can. Especially if you are trying to run a business. You cannot allow the people who work with you to become infected with and by negativity.

19 May
I am struck by how capricious the world's taste for news is and how fickle the journalists are. A fourth farmer died this week. There has been only the barest mention of the murder by the international media. Obviously, the reporters are getting used to the violence and turmoil in Zimbabwe. It is no longer a seven-day wonder, and they are now covering events elsewhere in the world - Freetown and the dreadful fire-works explosion in the Netherlands. They're leaving us to Mr Mugabe and Hitler Hunzvi. Does the world really care? Europe will return to its obsession with football and America to the good life.

15 June
This "count-down" period to the elections is truly unsettling. We all

just want to get it over with. Everyone is in such a state of limbo, it is quite eerie. It saps our strength and courage - the constant "What if?" feeling. But what must it be like on the farms?

People are so depressed and afraid. I actually felt exhausted yesterday, after trying to be positive and encouraging to everyone. It is tiring trying to be cheerful.

17 June
This time next week, it will be Election Day. A week passes quickly when you're having fun. Everyone is just so sick and tired of the tension and the uncertainty. We are all completely drained by the fear, terror and violence.

We've had no fuel for days in Bulawayo, as there has been no foreign currency to purchase it. There have been queues outside every filling station. Cars wind round block after block throughout the city centre and the suburbs. Some of the cars have drivers in them, some of them have been left overnight, securely locked, their drivers to return to them the next day.

Can you imagine anything more depressing than cars and trucks lining the streets waiting for petrol? Hunched sadly, bumper to bumper, many apparently abandoned, many whose tanks *are* actually dry and which have to be pushed from position to position, a few metres at a time? Actually, there *is* something more depressing. It is a diesel queue. This looks different, much more impotent, because, in this line, there are all manner of vehicles: massive trucks, huge, often decrepit-looking buses, commuter omnibuses, everything imaginable. Hours and hours of valuable time are wasted and tempers fray. People wait in suspense, a suspense that can last several hours. They have counted the cars and trucks in front of them. What if the supply of fuel at this filling station runs out before they reach the front of the queue?

We have lived with the situation for days in Bulawayo. It has almost surely been the same, and probably worse in Harare. And probably the same in all the smaller cities and towns.

But do you know what? Suddenly, yesterday, there was not a single queue. Not a single car waiting outside a filling station. And do you know why? Because our leader is in town this weekend to address a rally. All of a sudden there was fuel in abundance.

The rally today is known as a "Star Rally". Our local daily paper The Chronicle (which is government-run with our taxes) will tell us tomorrow how amazingly successful it was. How thousands and thousands of people attended (as they do countrywide). How they listened to the President with bated breath, sang songs of joy and prostrated themselves at his feet in gratitude for the land he is about to give them, and now for the mines, too. Lucky, lucky people. They will have farms and mines. But will they live happily ever after? Who will actually own them? Who will bring in machinery and parts to run them? Where will the money for operating costs come from? And the expertise...?

23 June
The elections start tomorrow. What can I say? Everyone is afraid. At the same time we want to get the whole thing over with. The next two days are going to be harrowing, I think. We've been told that the ruling party is putting every obstacle possible in the way of the opposition. They are making things as difficult and complicated as they possibly can. Anne says you need a degree to be a monitor. I hope the people will be able to vote without being terrified.

The newspapers are incredibly contradictory. The Fingaz is already hailing an MDC victory. The Chronicle is still talking of the President's threats and promises and of the resounding success that he expects. We, the ordinary voters, feel as if we are being buffeted by storm waters and massive hailstones. If we in the towns react like this, how do the people on the farms feel? Everyone is exhausted by the whole thing.

28 June
I couldn't face my "pages" yesterday with the whole election saga unfolding. I know that we now have a truly effective opposition, but most of the people in the country had hoped that they would have a new government. The MDC is apparently planning to challenge 20 seats. Our problem is that, at this stage, we don't understand the full implications that the different scenarios entail. I have been plunged into despair and confusion.

§·✥·§✖§·✥·§

Almost a year later we all still feel despair and confusion. Only it is worse than it was before. Farm invasions continue. It seems that every farmer one speaks to has had his farm designated. At this rate there will be no crops grown and no food to eat. The invaders and the marauders have also spilled over into the towns in a series of tidal waves designed to eliminate everything in their path. If we weren't actually witnessing this, it would be impossible to believe that such things could happen.

But they are happening. Our businesses' very existence is being threatened. Thugs, in all sorts of guises, are streaming through the doors and attempting to extort money and concessions from the already cash-strapped commercial and industrial communities. And, worst of all, a hospital, The Avenues Clinic, in Harare was invaded. War veterans forced the managing director to pay out $6,3 million to 30 dismissed employees. This was after threats and intimidation and fears that the safety of the many patients would be compromised. The employees in question had been legally dismissed in 1995.

We have received advice as to how to react to "business invasions" from an opposition member of parliament. The various chapters of The Zimbabwean Chamber of Industries are holding a series of emergency meetings. Letters to the newspapers reflect different reactions to the crisis. I shall quote from two of these.

The first, which appeared in The Daily News on 30 April 2001, is entitled "Guidelines to follow in dealing with ZANU PF bullyboys":

⊠ *Keep calm, do not lose your temper and do not overreact to their provocations, which will be deliberately designed to make you overreact.*

⊠ *Ignore their racist jokes and distortion of the truth.*

⊠ *Do not ignore their threats of assault, however, as it is well known that the police will be too afraid to protect you.*

⊠ *Warn your family and your work colleagues and employees that they will be at risk if you should escape the attention of the thugs.*

⊠ *Move yourself and your family away from home for a few nights or until it is safe to return.*

⊠ *If kidnapped, do not resist.*

⊠ *If assaulted, do your best to memorise precisely who did what.*

⊠ If your family or work colleagues or employees are assaulted whether in your presence or in your absence, protest, but do not aggravate the situation.

⊠ Decline any request to report to ZANU PF headquarters.

⊠ If subjected to long periods of swearing, abuse, ridicule, haranguing, threats and other non-physical pressures, for example at the ZANU PF auditorium keep your cool: it will come to an end sooner or later..

⊠ Finally do not lose heart. The cowards who deliberately do nothing to protect people in your position will shortly be made to realise the further harm that they are doing to our country's image and economy, and they will at last be compelled to try and control the thugs whom they have allowed to take over.

The second letter appeared in The Daily News on 3 May 2001. It is entitled "Bulawayo youths will not tolerate rogue war veterans":

"I am a young black Zimbabwean, a "born free" for that matter, who has been watching with so much pain as these so-called war veterans terrorise anyone who happens to hold different views from theirs.

This, therefore, is an open letter to all so-called war veterans.
These zealots think and strongly believe that they own this country and its people together with all the resources. They have been beating up our brothers and sisters in Bikita West and Epworth and now they are doing the same in the resort town of Victoria Falls.

The Zealots have enjoyed more than enough protection from the police, the army and even the President himself.

Mugabe is afraid that if he opposes the Zealots in any way, they will oppose his unpopular mission to remain at State House after 2002. To sober politicians like Nkosana Moyo and Simba Makoni, I say continue working for the people of Zimbabwe not ZANU PF.

However, my warning to all the so-called war veterans is: Never come to Bulawayo to perform such "cleansing ceremonies" that you have been up to in places like Bikita West, Epworth and Victoria Falls, to mention a few. The people of Bulawayo, the youths in particular, are so united and they know exactly what they want - that is - to see to it that all Zimbabweans will one day be free of the ZANU PF monster. We, the youths of Bulawayo would never let them bully us like they are doing to other Zimbabweans.

To Hitler Hunzvi and Chinotimba I say: You old men, your days are numbered and the day is coming when, together with all your puppets and cronies, you shall weep and answer for all the chaos you have unleashed upon the dictatorship-weary Zimbabweans. The protection you are enjoying won't last forever.

To The Daily News I say, all Zimbabweans are behind you and we will continue to buy your paper because the truth is what we are after. To all the partisan ZBC reporters I say the people are watching you. To all the youths in the rural communities, I say please wake up and smell the rat.

ZANU PF is using you, join other youths in urban areas to root Mugabe and his cronies out of the government and into the dustbin of history.

The situation is bizarre. It is as if we are heading towards an atomic melt-down. Confusion and chaos are the order of the day. Are we going to be left with a wasteland, an arid patch of ground where there was once a proud and beautiful country?

Is there anyone out there?

Nevah Kumalo

Nevah Kumalo

SOURCES OF ENCOURAGEMENT
IN THE FACE OF DEVASTATION

We cannot afford a complete collapse of Zimbabwe
...we've got to do whatever we can.

South African President Thabo Mbeki
August 2001 during an interview on BBC World

Farmer's Weekly is a highly-respected South African magazine which has served agriculture since 1911 and has played an integral role in the lives of Zimbabwean farmers for many years. The publication reports on agricultural activities in Zimbabwe on a regular basis.

armer's Weekly editor Chris Burgess has voiced concern that the international community's political inaction regarding Zimbabwe's government-initiated land invasions is threatening the activities of white farmers in Africa. *"Many poorly educated, landless black people on the continent perceive the ZANU PF government's actions to be an acknowledgement of the illegitimacy of white commercial farmers and are being encouraged to take the law into their own hands. It is disturbing that such a dangerous perspective is being encouraged by unscrupulous individuals or politicians for political gain,"* he said.

In his view, *"It's a familiar logic in Africa: blacks are only taking back what rightfully belongs to them when they illegally invade white-owned farms. If white farmers can be dismissed as illegitimate 'settlers', the take-overs can then be justified as an act of retribution rather than a criminal offence."*

Mr Burgess said that the situation was especially unfortunate in the light of President Thabo Mbeki's recently launched New Africa Initiative, which was widely regarded as the continent's last chance to save itself from perpetual strife and poverty. *"Africa cannot afford to estrange European and American investors, already weary of the continent's reputation as a 'basket case'. Their substantial investment in the continent, now commonly referred to as Africa's 'Marshall Plan', is intended to lay the foundation for a prosperous new Africa."*

In Parliament on 21 June 2001, President Mbeki took the unprecedented step of affirming his support for the white community in South Africa and expressing his appreciation of the role played by the country's commercial farmers:

We have the ... responsibility to ensure that no white South African feels that the emancipation of our country means for him or her, marginalisation, disempowerment, exclusion and having to live for ever under the threat of violence, dispossession and the destruction of everything he or she holds dear, including language, culture and religion...

We are also grateful to the many commercial farmers that are working together with us as we grapple with the many challenges of the transformation of our society... The government unreservedly condemns the continued attacks on and murder of farmers and, acting together with the farmers and their organisations, will continue to ensure that these attacks and murders come to an end.

(During the past ten years, 1 000 South African farmers have been killed in over 5 000 farm attacks. Fifty percent of these people have been murdered in the last three years).

The Farmer's Weekly issue of 13 July 2001 noted that, during his speech, President Mbeki had singled out four Eastern Cape farmers and six from the Free State for their contribution to black economic upliftment. The Eastern Cape's Elliot Farmers' Union Chairperson, Selby Vorster, had received a call from Mr Mbeki's office beforehand, asking whether it was in order for the President to use the farmers' names in parliament. Vorster told Farmer's Weekly that he was proud and humbled by Mr Mbeki's gesture. *"We are just normal people with our feet firmly on the ground,"* he said. *"All we are doing is helping people who are our neighbours."*

Over the years Farmer's Weekly has acknowledged the skills of Zimbabwe's commercial farmers and their own role in uplifting emergent farmers. In the issue of 8 June 2001, an article headed "Decent, Upstanding People" highlighted the publication's concern for Zimbabwe's farming community in the face of escalating violence.

The journalist wrote: *"I cannot claim to understand what the Zim farmers, farm workers and their families have been experiencing over the past few months. But I've been there often, and I've been welcomed into the homes of several characters now in the thick of it...*

They didn't set out to win medals (for their courage). They just happened to be there minding their own business when all the rules changed. A few had emigrated as late as the 1960s, but most were there simply because their parents and grandparents had constructive dreams - plus the guts and dedication to flesh some of them out... The settlers weren't all angels, but they brought more books, medicines and water pipes than guns...

They were simply attracted to a vast and beautiful land that was almost empty because few of its 700 000 inhabitants had bothered to sow at all...

Zimbabwe's population multiplied 15-fold (from 1890) because more food, shelter and medicine could suddenly be produced. The people lived longer, enjoyed a more varied diet, had better housing and got to school, too... This success owed much to the skills of a few thousand individuals who became world leaders in growing and marketing tobacco.

Nine-tenths of the supposedly 'rich and privileged' white farming families in Zimbabwe came to the country with little more than a healthy attitude... They prospered by year-round toil clearing land, tending seedbeds, nurturing the crop, picking, curing, sorting and packing leaf - often working seven days a week and through the night. And the whole time they were training other people to do the same...

Apart from the techno-talk... every issue (I receive) of Zimbabwe Tobacco has stories of beginner farmers winning prizes, tenant farmers progressing up the ladder, elderly white growers lending a hand to younger black ones and of farmers' spouses providing social services where the government has failed... Moreover, there is always a page for the ornithologists..., something about the flowers, the trees and the cricket they play and sponsor...

The 29 June 2001 issue of Farmer's Weekly describes the current situation in Zimbabwe as "bleak" and "frightening". The journalist was told by a commercial farmer that none of the farmers in his area had been allowed to plant wheat or tobacco, and that the war vets who had erected their shacks on the farms were dictating farming policy. The farmer said that the agenda of the war vets was political.

The feature continued: *An article with the headline "War vets demand $15 million for Mugabe's campaign", published in Zimbabwe's Financial Gazette of 6 June 2001 supported the farmer's analysis. The article stated, "Zimbabwe's marauding band of veterans... want $15 million from the ruling ZANU PF party to wage an aggressive campaign for President Robert Mugabe's re-election next year."*

A schoolteacher told the journalist that what was happening was very wrong. *"We need commercial farmers. Only those who can farm and who have tractors should get land,"* she said.

A security guard also had strong feelings about the farm invaders. *"How can you dig clay with your fingers?"* he asked. *"You can't. You need tractors. All they are going to do is to build their shacks on the land and then sit back and drink beer!"*

The Violence Escalates

Despite the continued hope for the future expressed by many working-class Zimbabweans, news at the time of going to publication with "Voices of Zimbabwe" early in August 2001 tells a story of escalating violence on a horrifying scale.

Vehicles belonging to Movement for Democratic Change leader, Morgan Tsvangirai and other members of the MDC were attacked in Bindura during July and there were murders and attempted murders of MDC activists in a number of other areas. Intimidation and heightened violence was orchestrated in two constituencies where by-elections were being held.

At this moment, farmers, farm workers and their families are being attacked across the country and virtually every white-owned commercial farm has been taken over without compensation and illegally. Hotels, tourist resorts, forestry plantations and various industrial properties are suffering a similar fate.

ZWNEWS of 7 August 2001 reported that, on the evening of Saturday 6 August, a group of around 60 ZANU PF militants - provided with food and ferried in on government vehicles - gathered on a farm in Nyathi in northern Matabeleland province. They camped overnight on the farm and next morning abducted 13 people from a nearby mine. They then laid an ambush for the farmer's game scouts, who were armed with shotguns, and used some of the abductees from the mine as human shields. The game scouts managed to escape, so the mob went on a rampage in the farm village, burning down three staff houses, valued at Z$500 000.

During July, an opposition report circulated in Zimbabwe noted that the government had moved to take full control of the food supplies to cut off efforts by the international community to supply the country's basic necessities. As a result, the government was committing millions of its own people to hardship and starvation.

On 8 August, 2001 it was reported in the South African media that the Zimbabwean government had fired two top state media executives, Mr Henry Muradzikwa, editor-in-chief of the national news agency, Ziana, and the editor-in-chief of the Community Newspapers Group, Mr Kuromba Munodawafa, and announced plans to merge three state media organs. The moves were seen as part of a campaign by the government to increase its grip on the media before the presidential election in March 2002.

During the same week, Mr Ralph Corbett, 76, a rancher near the Midlands town of Kwekwe, was critically injured after being assaulted, tied up with wire, hit on the head with an axe and then left for dead. He was rushed to a clinic in Harare, but died that night. The farm has been illegally occupied by war vets since last year.

ZANU PF Thugs on the Rampage in Chinhoyi

Chinhoyi is a farming town north-west of Harare on the main route to Lake Kariba. Tourists passing through often stop over to visit the famous Chinhoyi Caves, formed within the limestone hills of the area. Open to the sky, the main pool is a breathtaking sapphire blue in full sunlight, darkening perceptibly as the shadows lengthen.

Lorraine Marillier, who lives on a farm in the Chinhoyi area, is the CFU's co-ordinator responsible for AIDS counselling and home-based care. Although she has had to cope with the trauma of four family members being diagnosed with cancer during the year, and having their farm invaded and put on fast track resettlement, Lorraine continues to run a well-equipped clinic and baby welfare programme on their farm.

As the AIDS epidemic takes its toll, and the breakdown of the health delivery system in the country escalates, the pressure on clinics such as this mounts. Lorraine and her workers cope by taking one day at a time. The workers are harassed and victimised continually by the invaders, who are building three villages on the farm. In a mood of wanton vandalism, they destroyed the newly planted seedbeds. Despite this additional setback, Lorraine found the time to assist with a second

Eyes for Zimbabwe programme during which the 56 outstanding cataract operations from the area's April camp were completed.

ZWNEWS, 7 August: *(Yesterday) farmers in the Chinhoyi district received a distress call over the radio network from a local farmer who reported that his house was being attacked by a group of 40 ZANU PF thugs. The police were informed - their response was that they would send a constable on a bicycle the 24 kilometres from the police station to the farm... En route, the 11 farmers who travelled to assist the besieged farmer lost radio contact with him and began to fear the worst. On arrival at the farm, they found the farmstead surrounded and forced their way through the mob in an effort to reach the inhabitants. In the process, several of the besieging crowd - and four or five farmers - were injured, one seriously enough to be hospitalised. The besieged farmer was found barricaded inside the house, out of reach of his radio.*

The police eventually arrived and requested that the 11 farmers report to Chinhoyi police station to give statements. On arrival at the station, all the farmers were arrested. In addition, an elderly man who arrived later to bring blankets for those arrested was also detained. No ZANU PF supporters were arrested.

At 10 pm on the night of 6 August, Kerry Kay, Project Manager for the Commercial Farmers' Union's AIDS Control Programme, received a call from Lorraine Marillier informing her that Lorraine's husband and son had been arrested with the group of farmers who had gone to the assistance of the besieged farmer. Kerry drove to Chinhoyi before first light and accompanied Lorraine to the police station. In the Charge Office was a doctor, a man of 76, who had wanted to assist the farmers. He had been assaulted by a youth and had been hit with what he thought was a bicycle chain. The blow had broken his spectacles and damaged one of his eyes, causing external and internal bleeding. His son had been attacked with a stick. A teacher from the nearby school had been hit in the face by a ZANU PF supporter while she was inside the police station. She had been trying to establish if her husband and the other white farmers were safe after spending the night in the cells.

The police refused to accept reports of assault, or to provide medical report forms. As more members of ZANU PF arrived, the group realised it was safer to leave and withdrew, only to discover that tyres on a number of vehicles had been let down outside the station. They then joined a group of women at the Commercial Farmers' Union office. Shortly afterwards, they received a warning that more "rented thugs" were on the way and decided to leave town. After rescuing a stranded young woman, her small child and three dogs, they withdrew in convoy to a nearby farm.

Behind them, the thugs began rampaging through the town, beating white residents at random. A white man was stabbed at the police station, in full view of the police, and a white woman who went to the police station to change her vehicle registration document was beaten in front of the police, who did not protect her. At least seven other people were severely assaulted, six of them women.

A mother who had travelled to Chinhoyi because her young son was ill, was in the doctor's rooms when a man was rushed into the surgery with stab wounds on his arm - he had been attacked outside one of the town's larger shops. Later on, she saw a black man being hauled from a white man's car at a set of traffic lights. The thugs threatened to kill him if they ever saw him travelling with a white man again. An 87-year old white man was man-handled out of a shop and beaten severely, as were several shop owners.

Since the mother who had witnessed the above attacks - and others - did not feel it was safe to drive out of Chinhoyi, she spent the rest of the day at the school, helping to answer the hundreds of frantic parents' questions over the telephone, and waiting for evening and the staging of the end of term school play.

In a subsequent letter to a friend she wrote: *"They put on 'The Jungle Book', an excellent show, and I doubt there was a dry eye in the audience after the final song - 'The Bare Necessities'. There were many women in the audience whose husbands were languishing in jail, and the teacher who had been assaulted at the police station was the pianist - despite what she had gone through, she just soldiered on. I found it quite surreal doing something so civilised as watching a play after such a violent and shattering day. We are now home... and just pray that this madness comes to an end soon. If there were any people from Chinhoyi trying to decide whether they should leave this country, I think the events today will have made up their minds for them. We cannot even afford the air tickets at this stage for the four of us to fly to the UK!"*

While the government clearly wants to rid the country of all whites in the '70s style of the Ugandan dictator Idi Amin, the Movement for Democratic Change (MDC) has expressed grave concern regarding the flood of people - black and white - seeking opportunities in other countries. An MDC communication suggests that the movement is up to 4 000 people a week, or about 200 000 a year.

In a commentary circulated in July, an MDC member wrote, *"(Emigration is) wiping out generations of skilled and trained personnel in every field of endeavour. The benefit to the developed countries that are taking these people must be huge; the cost to us cannot be measured. Analysts are currently assessing the magnitude of the 'brain drain' and its implications for Zimbabwe.*

This is an area where we will also have to do some soul-searching. When Morgan Tsvangirai was in London, he met with a group of about 800 young (largely white) people who asked to see him. He said to them, 'We regard you all as Zimbabweans living abroad and, when you want to come home, you will be welcome. We want you to come home and we will ensure that your birthright as Zimbabweans is never lost to you.' Mr Tsvangirai was astonished at the emotional response he received to those remarks. There were many in the audience who were in tears to hear a black leader say they were recognised and wanted. Our challenge is to make sure that there is something to come back to."

Zimbabweans are also taking heart from President Mbeki's recent comments. The President of South Africa, who has been placed in an invidious position by the Mugabe regime, has nevertheless been criticised widely for his policy of quiet diplomacy on the Zimbabwean crisis. However, in a frank interview with BBC World during August, Mr Mbeki stressed that his country could not afford the complete collapse of Zimbabwe. He said it was critical for South Africa that Zimbabwe did not descend into the "meltdown" the International Monetary Fund had predicted earlier in the year, which meant quick action was needed to resolve the crisis.

At the end of August, a Commonwealth fact-finding mission will be visiting Zimbabwe and President Mbeki has said that he is committed to working with the Commonwealth team.

> *We will not submit to this injustice -*
> *not merely because it is destroying us,*
> *but because it is destroying you as well.*
>
> Mahatma Gandhi

CAN YOU HEAR THE DRUMS?

The church is silent.
The stained-glass windows glow with reassuring light.
"Come unto me all you that are heavy laden
and I will refresh you," Christ said.
"Suffer the little children to come unto Me."
I kneel at the altar rail and bow my head.

Dear Lord
My son, daughter-in-law and their three young children
are being terrorised by a violent mob
and are barricaded in their farmhouse.
Throughout the night these evil men
have chanted and beaten their drums.
They have hurled rocks upon the roof
and lit fires around the house,
so that the air is filled with acrid smoke.
They want to drive this young family out,
and while they wait, they drink, and dance,
and defecate.

The police came briefly but left,
saying they could do nothing.
While the hail of stones continues,
the children cower in their parents' arms,
and I, their grandfather,
who would gladly give my life for theirs,
am powerless.

In desperation, dear Lord, I pray for their safety.

This attack took place in the Marondera area, not far from the farm of Iain
Kay, at the same time that Mr Kay was trapped in his home, and his workers
were barricaded in a farm building.

CONCLUSION

Once there was a great forest fire,
and all the birds and animals rushed to
escape. Humming bird went to the river,
and collected a drop of water. The other
birds laughed. "What are you doing?"
They asked. She replied, "I'm doing
What I can.

Native American Story

If we lose Zimbabwe forever to anarchy and to evil, will this be the beginning of the end for the entire continent of Africa? If the blood of innocent Zimbabwean people continues to stain the earth, will not that stain spread until it covers South Africa, southern Africa as a whole and even all of the sub-Saharan region? Will our children inherit a desert from us, their parents? Will this be our legacy to the generations of the future?

We cannot allow this. We cannot embrace apathy and tolerate anarchy and brutality with a shrug of our shoulders and say, "It's not my problem." It is our problem. Whether we live in Zimbabwe, South Africa, England, America or elsewhere, what is happening here in Zimbabwe matters. It is a question of man's inhumanity to man. We are all diminished by it. No-one should have to live in fear. No-one who has been elected to a position of authority should be allowed to abuse the trust of his people. Each individual must be held accountable for his actions.

So what can we do? Well, first of all, we must understand the true nature of what is being inflicted upon our people. We have to say "No." We must vote without fear. We have to care about one another, even if we, ourselves, are not under attack now. Who knows who may be targeted next? We need to be supportive and positive. We have to work towards an understanding of one another, and ultimately, towards unity. The past must be set aside forever, as we face the future, a united and, therefore, strong nation.

The problems of the present are still with us, however. We have to deal with them wisely. The voices of anguish, pain, loss and desperation demand it.

May God bless and save Zimbabwe.

THE AUTHORS

Glyn Hunter

Born in Natal, South Africa, in 1948. Her family moved to Chegutu (then Hartley) in Zimbabwe to develop a farm from virgin bush in 1949. She, her sister Althea and brother Carl, lived on the farm from then until 1960 when the family moved to Marondera, east of Harare. She trained as a teacher in Pietermaritzburg (Natal), married and now runs her own public relations consultancy in South Africa.

Althea Farren

Sister of Glyn, and born in Natal in 1946. She returned to Pietermaritzburg for her tertiary education and taught at schools in Zimbabwe for 14 years. Now, with her husband Larry, she owns and runs a promotional business which encompasses a design studio and a screen and pad-printing factory.

Larry Farren

Born in Donegal, Ireland, in 1941, and brought up on various British Royal Air Force bases in Britain and Germany where his father was stationed, he came to Zimbabwe from Scotland in 1962 for "a few years' holiday" and to serve in the British South Africa Police. He did not get around to going home, and adopted Zimbabwean citizenship. Larry married Althea in 1970, and they have two adult children, Sean and Brian.

The authors' stories are based on their experiences in Zimbabwe over the past several decades, and on interviews and research conducted specifically for the writing of this book.

▌◆❖◆▐▐✕▐▐◆❖◆▌

I believe that, to meet the challenge of our times, human beings will have to develop a greater sense of universal responsibility. Each of us must learn to work not just for his or her own self, family or nation, but for the benefit of all mankind. Universal responsibility is the real key to human survival. It is the best foundation for world peace, the equitable use of natural resources and, through concern for future generations, the proper care of the environment.

His Holiness, the Dalai Lama

Back Cover:

NYAMINYAMI

Nyaminyami was the traditional god of the baTonga people, who lived along the banks of the Zambezi River. The rising waters of the Kariba dam, the largest man-made lake in the world at the time of its construction, displaced many of them, and they were resettled along the banks of the lake. The baTonga believed that Nyaminyami caused the flooding of the river by travelling down it every year, and that the building of the dam would separate him from his wife, who lived downstream. They considered the river god to be responsible for the many problems encountered by the dam builders, including the deaths of several construction workers in accidents, and the severe damage done by flooding while the dam was being built in 1958. Many expect that he will yet destroy Kariba.